*To the Delaware Squaw Who Married
My Revolutionary War Forebear—
and Her Name Nobody Ever Bothered
to Tell Me*

CRIMSONED PRAIRIE

The Indian Wars

CRIMSONED PRAIRIE

The Indian Wars

═════════════════════

By S. L. A. Marshall

Sketches by the author
Maps by Mark Lennox

A DA CAPO PAPERBACK

Library of Congress Cataloging in Publication Data

Marshall, S. L. A. (Samuel Lyman Atwood), 1900–1977. Crimsoned
prairie.

Reprint. Originally published: New York: Scribner, c1972.
Includes index.
1. Indians of North America—Great Plains—Wars.
I. Title.
E83.866M36   1984   ` 978   84-11404
ISBN 0-306-80226-0 (pbk.)

This Da Capo Press paperback edition of *Crimsoned Prairie* is
an unabridged republication of the first edition published in
New York in 1972. It is reprinted by arrangement with
The Scribner Book Companies, Inc.

Published by Da Capo Press, Inc.
A Subsidiary of Plenum Publishing Corporation
233 Spring Street, New York, N.Y. 10013

Manufactured in the United States of America

Contents

List of Illustrations

Maps

Line Drawings

In Explanation

REGARDING the events of which I am writing, I can no more prove that I do so wholly without prejudice and strictly as a neutral analyst than I can establish that my interpretations are superior because I moved on many fields among the actors who appear in these pages. Old, I am not that old, and these wars were not my wars.

Just possibly, however, I should stake out a small claim toward shoring up Point No.1. In the early 1920s, just prior to my escape into journalism because it promised a softer life, I was rather briefly a member of the Seventh Cavalry Regiment and rode with F Troop during extensive maneuvers in the Texas Big Bend. It was on that strenuous outing that I made a full recovery from the effects of phosgene gas inhaled near Thiaucourt due to my own carelessness. My congenial association with the Garry Owens, during which I rebounded from invalidism, might have made me a Custer protagonist had I not quickly learned that the troop commander, Captain Jack Hettinger, later killed as a brigadier during the war in the Pacific, and First Sergeant Edward Carey, my dear friend and the wisest old soldier I ever knew, took a very dim view of Yellow Hair.

F Troop had lost two officers, thirty-six men, and forty-four horses in one day due to Custer foolishness, and the souvenir menu at the Christmas feast provided a continuing reminder of the vital statistics. The Seventh was a proud outfit and never failed to whoop it up in nigh juvenile fashion when the band played "Garry Owen." But it took no pride in the Custer legend.

So it was with the two good soldiers I have named that I first fought the Battle of the Little Bighorn and through osmosis may have formed an early bias during our sitting bull sessions. My more blessed inheritance from those days is that it was my cavalry comrades who first encouraged me to write. That the best thing about the mounted service is the intelligent look on the face of the horse is therefore a sentiment to which I cannot subscribe.

On the other hand, as I have indicated in my dedication, from my mother's side I have Indian blood. That means much to our family, and our sympathies naturally incline that way. To top it off, in the early 1930s, I was adopted by the Sioux at a ceremony in the Badlands and was given the name Iron Eyes, which fits no better than most Indian names. My maternal grandfather, Lyman Beeman, was the principal of an Indian school in Indian Territory and is buried among the tribesmen.

All of this is said not to put forth credentials that establish my qualifications but rather to explain my very special interest in the Plains wars. There has been no shortage of human conflict in my century. Having generally held with the rule that a writer should stick to those wars in which he has participated up close, I have made this exception due to a belief that I have something different to say.

Rather than attempt a definitive and all-inclusive study of the conflict between red and white over the Great Plains, the Rockies, the Southwestern Desert, and the California Lava Beds, I fixed firm limits for the undertaking and thereafter held with them.

There would be no research and no writing other than on the Plains wars. In that vast enough arena, from the time of the Civil War until the last volleying in Dakota, cause and effect are clearly linked, and one insurgency ties into another. Furthermore, I decided to exclude arbitrarily some episodes, such as the Adobe Walls fight, the Beecher's Island battle, and the final, futile breakout of the Cheyenne, while concentrating on those major pieces of the struggle that are most pivotal, characteristic, or dramatic. A catchall treatment of the fighting on the Plains can become as tedious as the wending of one's way through the maze of treaties negotiated and of promises broken.

In Explanation

Many books have been written on the period. Some of the literature is warmly exciting; more of it is dull in a scholarly way, but highly informative. Taken as a whole, books about the Plains wars have one salient characteristic, that of discrepancy. That there is so little likeness in the interpretation of battles is less baffling than that there is almost no agreement on vital statistics, relative losses, or even troop numbers. The keeping of accurate records in the field has never been one of the strengths of the United States Army, and the commands that fought the Plains Indians were particularly indifferent to what should have been an essential requirement. When primary information is thus lacking, some speculation becomes inevitable, and at times there is no alternative to the making of an educated guess about what probably happened.

What persuaded me to write was the discovery that in this large library on the Plains wars there is no serious and critical examination of the characteristics of engagement. Pomp and ceremony in the frontier army went hand in hand with lackadaisical operational control. Commanders hunted the Sioux with brass bands—this supposedly to stimulate troop morale—while not bothering to get their scouts out. Hard-charging recklessness was rampant as leaders got on the scent of dangerously smiling fortune. Almost routinely, forces were wasted, communications were neglected, and supply was mismanaged, though seldom was any commander relieved for his sins. Training was in sad disrepair. It was an era of military regression wherein the fundamentals were almost forgot. To say that the people cared so little for the army that the army became indifferent to its own standards would be to shift the burden of responsibility for sloth inexcusable. An army must but try the harder to preserve tradition, up standards, and keep the trust when it is not loved —the way to solve a difficult problem hardly being to transfer one's attention to an insoluble one.

After some years of reading through the literature pretty much at random, I visited the main battlefields in Wyoming and Montana, and from going over the ground with consid-

In Explanation

erable care I learned more about cause and effect in the main actions than is to be found between the covers of books. Some tentative conclusions became hardened. Others, especially pertaining to the Nez Percé war, had to be discarded altogether.

Out of these varying experiences, I have tried in my book to highlight the essential military values, the tactical contrasts between these implacable, ill-matched sides, the shortcomings of the Plains Indian's way in warfare, and the comparisons between the afflictions of the frontier army and the problems of today's army. This is done partly in the hope of contributing something new and of value, but more so because my mind works that way.

While today's vogue is to lament the wars against the Plains Indians and all wars as a monstrous crime against nature, strictly because it is a vogue, it should be further discussed if not controverted.

In my search, Cate Marshall, my wife, secretary, driver, first reader, eyes, and conscience helped me more than all other persons together. But I must mention gratefully the assistance given me by Dr. Philip C. Hessberg of Grosse Pointe, Michigan; Kermit Edmonds of Missoula, Montana; Brigadier General Mayhew Y. Foster of Helena; Colonel Frank Meek, USAF; and Sam Gilluly, Director of the Montana Historical Society. From their knowledge I gained much, and still more from their words of encouragement. Since none is privy to my central theme, none may be charged with a war crime.

S. L. A. MARSHALL

Dherran Dhoun
Birmingham, Michigan

CRIMSONED
PRAIRIE

I

The Westward
Barrier

ABOUT the Indian wars that plagued the American West from the Mississippi to the Pacific during the quarter century that followed the surrender at Appomatox, it is commonly believed that they might have been avoided but for the avarice and aggression of the white man, coupled with the inhumanity or incompetence of his servants in Government.

While that is the slanted interpretation of the struggle that most writers in Hollywood favor, toward the end that we will become guilt-ridden, it makes of history what Lord Chesterfield called it, "a confused heap of facts."

True, Government and individuals many times grievously wronged the tribes. There is no room or reason for pride in the story of our treatment of these first Americans. They have been shamefully neglected. No other minority people has less cause to love the United States, yet they remain undeviatingly loyal to it in peace and in war. Rarely does an American Indian claim exemption from military service on any grounds.

At the same time, thoughtful reflection on the root causes of the wars in which the West was won must point to the conclusion that they were virtually unavoidable. That they were waged with excessive brutality on both sides but made accommodation more difficult, if not impossible.

The twenty-five years of open hostility and full battle did not come about simply because the tribes west of the Mississippi learned time after time that promises, pieces of paper, and trinkets could not ease or dampen valid reasons for going on the warpath.

The wars were not the poison fruit of bureaucratic negligence, nor were they strictly the evil consequence of white exploiters cheating the Plains Indian of his lawful property, though all too frequently they were given that appearance with Government giving its backing to the exploiters.

Rather, violence beset the western frontier and lasted and lasted because the fundamental interests of the two sides were so wholly irreconcilable as to leave little or no room for compromise. Due to the absence of any middle ground, there occurred intolerable grievances to white man and red. When these basic conditions are present, war or revolution becomes inevitable.

Quite familiar is the saying that the American Indian was a peace-loving, peace pipe-smoking being until the white man came. Certain of the Eastern tribes must have warranted this description, or else the early colonists would have failed of a firm lodgment on these shores. Their folkways and ideals are not, however, pertinent to this story, for indeed, they no longer symbolize the Noble Red Man.

At about the time when the cigar-store Indian began to pass from the national scene, which was more or less concurrent with the minting of the buffalo nickel with a warrior as the other side of the coin, there came about a curious displacement of one image with another. The brave who slunk through the forest afoot and engaged his enemy from behind trees was rightly the typical American primitive hero, the savage of the national tradition, he having resisted the advance of the white man for two hundred years. There was a belongingness about him, his culture like his nature having been shaped over time long before Columbus sailed west in search of the Indies. Then the paintings of Frederic Remington, R. H. Russell, and others fired the imagination, and that more tractable tribesman, the Indian who fought afoot, went into eclipse.

In our time when the American Indian is mentioned, the romantic figure that comes to mind is that of a war-bonneted brave astride a painted pony. He is a Russell or Remington figure, or Little Chief Sadman sitting at The End of the Trail.

We see the Plains Indian, one of a warrior people. Not his origin but his evolution so made him, for his agility and showmanship came late. His culture, as distinguished from that of some of the tribes east of the Father of Waters, had at its center the idea of taking what he wanted when he was strong enough to get it. While that bent made him by no means unique, above all else it gave his group its special identity.

When Columbus first sighted Watling's Island, if that *was* where the Discovery took place, there was no such force on the continent. The various tribes situated around the western prairie and venturing into the fringes of the Great Plains were fairly sedentary and lived mainly by agriculture— growing maize, beans, and squash. They hunted small game, deer and bear, and when there was no other meat, they ate dog. They had no draft animals other than dogs for pulling a travois. The wheel was still unknown in America. This lack of transport served to keep the tribes in place, noncompetitive and relatively quiet.

The chief dwellers of the Plains proper were the Crow and the Blackfeet, though the Comanche probably then were situated in Wyoming. Just beyond the tribes bordering the Great Plains, great herds of bison grazed and galloped. Except among the Crow, the meat and hide of the animal was hardly more than a marginal benefit to the Indian economy. To the brave afoot and using arrows, the hunt was both dangerous and little productive.

Some of this began to change with the arrival of the horse in America. Cortes brought ten stallions and five mares to Mexico and during the conquest more blooded stock followed. Juan de Onate introduced horse domestication to what is now the national Southwest in April 1598, when his column crossed the Rio Grande near present-day El Paso, conducting seven thousand horses, donkeys, cattle, and sheep. These notes by no means imply that the spread of the horse through America came out of that one funnel, for such was not the case. There were other early post-Discovery stables in Florida and elsewhere along the Atlantic seaboard.

Some of the stock broke away and became feral. Of the consequent breeding in the wild was produced the true mustang. Many were trapped, tamed, and trained by the Indians of the Southwest and far Northwest. The Apaches were very good at it. Also, stallions and brood mares were bartered to the Indians by Spanish brokers and breeders. The tribal horse herds grew steadily, not in numbers only but in their impact on the culture and development of red men west of the Mississippi.

By the time of the French and Indian War in the continental East, enterprising Indian horse dealers out of New Mexico and Arizona were already exploiting a bull market as far north as Wyoming and Idaho, trading horseflesh for something more to be desired. Their product was the more welcome because of the Indian's built-in adaptability. Like the Cossack, the Plains Indian had a natural way with a horse. His skill and grace were so superior that he loved to play gymnast when mounted. Giving him pleasure in a form that he had not before dreamed, it transformed him into a formidable figure.

The Westward Barrier

Here we have a freak twist in history, the white man's horse catalyzing the forming of a new frontier before the white man either tested it or understood its import.

The adoption of the horse by the Indian changed dramatically the temper and tempo of daily life throughout the West. Because of it, the Plains Indian materialized, galvanized, and became identifiable as a stalwart, though the Plains peoples still lacked unity.

Until the horse arrived, the Great Plains were virtually a vacuum, little tenanted. Then began what today is called a revolution. A major shift in the Indian population started approximately when Washington was taking his bumps with Braddock and was in full swing when occurred the Boston Tea Party.

From all around the prairie, the tribes entered upon a new way of life, based upon horsemanship and the slaughtering of the buffalo. The Dakota, a confederation of thirteen tribes better known as the Sioux, did not enter upon the Great Plains until near the end of the eighteenth century. At about the same time the Cheyenne, a stalwart people, crossed the Missouri River, migrating to the short grass country. Having been farmers, they quickly became hunters in land where the variety of game was ample and the supply seemingly inexhaustible.

Within a very few years, the Great Plains had become the meeting ground, while less so the melting pot, of about thirty different peoples, representing five quite different language stocks. The Cheyenne language, for example, stemmed from the Algonquian. The commingling eliminated many of the differences in talk and some of the differences in folkways by 1800.

Something need be said about numbers if only to indicate how ripe was the opportunity and how much of the land of magnificent distance remained unused. Nature scholars say that twenty million bison still cropped the grass of the Great

Plains in the early nineteenth century. So large were the herds, an Indian on a pony could ride all day on a straight line and not cover the herd end to end.

As for the people, about one hundred thousand Indians of the Five Civilized Tribes—Cherokee, Creek, Choctaw, Chickasaw, and Seminole—had been uprooted by Government from their Southeastern homelands in the 1830s and forcibly resettled in territory that is now Oklahoma and lower Kansas. It was pledged that the region would remain forever theirs.

That still left plenty of room in the West for the Plains Indians. The best guess is that there were about one-quarter million of them, these buffalo-hunting peoples, the larger groups being the Sioux, Cheyenne, Kiowa, Comanche, Crow, and Arapaho. There were loose alliances between some of them that shifted from time to time.

What they mainly had in common, however, was that they had lately abandoned a somewhat stable and more docile village life in favor of an existence based on pursuit of the migratory buffalo herds. From that animal came meat, clothing, housing, and bed warmth. Its chase made them nomadic. Because of the chase, the easily knocked down and transported tepee became their standard dwelling.

Wherever they roved the prairie during the hunt, displacing family and shelter, they felt they had the right to hold until time to move on again, even though the land was not theirs by title or through long and continuous possession.

The strong wrested what they pleased from the weak. There was recognized dominion only where there was power to defend. One tribe would enter into a temporary military compact with another, either to fight off encroachment by tribesmen from outside the perimeter of the Great Plains or to raid a third tribe's territory to give battle and to plunder. The essential justification for violence was martial success.

Along with their horsemanship, their means of livelihood and the freedom of the great open spaces begot in them a feeling of power less fanatic than arrogant. They did not change to warrior peoples out of any biological necessity. The urge was psychological. The mode of life seemed to demand it. True, they armed that they might eat and they became mounted that they might extend their range. But the mass possession of weapons and an advantageous mobility makes for free-wheeling and has nourished aggression in peoples much more civilized than the Plains Indians. While there are some nomadic peoples, such as the Lapps, that are reputedly gentle and nonpredatory, it is usually because no one contests their territory.

In sum, life on the Great Plains, before the white encroachment truly threatened, was far short of idyllic or even generous. The spirit of live-and-let-live wasn't there. Early records report the Pawnee killing "hundreds" of Navajo during the summer bison hunt at the turn of the seventeenth century. A decade later the Comanche, mounted and armed by the French, made unrelenting war on the Apache and Navajo. Arapaho battled with Ute. The Sioux drove westward the Crow.

Intertribal warfare developed out of the desire to dominate the richest game land, enlarge the pony herds, and loot weapons. There was also the belief that fighting served to unify the tribe and glorify the leader, and while history makes clear that this drive is not peculiar to primitives, it did not promote brotherly love among Indians. The strongest worked their will and the strongest were the Sioux. The hostility of the Oglala and Brule was extreme, and the area they ranged—between the Platte and the Yellowstone, the Upper Missouri and the Rockies—was to become the high road of westward expansion.

In the case of the Sioux Confederation, there is something in a name. The shift from Dakota to Sioux reflects how they came to be regarded by other Indians as well as by the settlers. The old name meant "ally." The new name, a shortening of the derisive Ojibway word Nadousioux, meant "snake" or "enemy." Greedy whites may be guilty of many crimes against the Indian and so may the army, but neither one nor the other may be rightly accused of making warlike the Sioux Confederation.

Within the confederation, certain tribes were particularly aggressive, among them the Teton, "Dwellers on the Prairie"; the Oglala, "To Scatter One's Own"; the Hunkpapa, or "End of the Circle"; and the Sincaju or Brule, the "Burned Thighs."

Each tribe was composed of "bands," as was true also of the Cheyenne, Arapaho, and other Plains Indians. The band was made up of firmly knit family groups that hunted together, had their own separate winter villages, and were economically and socially independent.

Each band was led by a head man and the name of the leader became the name of the band. The wisest men of the various bands formed the main tribal council and they were called "chiefs." No chief exercised arbitrary power, and within the council, decision was made by a majority rule, not binding on those who disagreed. A chief might take an opposite course—for example, withholding his band from war—without suffering vengeance or ostracism. Among warriors, that is a noteworthy tolerance.

Three generations formed the family group and each had its appointed and separate tasks. Older boys hunted small game. Women prepared the food, made the clothing, cut the lodgepoles, and dressed the buffalo skins, from which, with the assistance of the men, they constructed and raised the tepees.

War and the hunt kept the younger men busy, along with the guarding of the villages. The older girls did bead and quill work. The older males who were not physically fitted for the stresses of the chase and combat helped procure the materials for housing and clothing, and sometimes they assisted the squaws with the gardening, fashioned bows and arrows and household implements, and played politics. They were not, however, noted for their industry. The care of the very young children fell to the grandmothers.

More than from all else, the males achieved status and political importance from their deeds in war or from their feats as plunderers, either actual or what they could make others believe they had done. For extra claiming and great boasting were expected of them. The dress, the ceremonials, and other social functions mark well that the panoply of war was as bewitching to them as to the nobles of feudal times. The stimulation of the warrior spirit and the acclaiming of any daring exploit that came of it brought the pitch of excitement to the routine of village life.

At center was a coup pole. Any martial deed to which a brave laid claim, or the theft of stock from an enemy camp and other such bloodless boodling, was called a *coup*, the French word for "blow." The brave, when came the ceremony, danced around the pole "counting coup." As he proclaimed each deed, he whacked the coup pole with an ax. The bolder the deed the harder the whack. He kept whacking until he ran out of coup, which gave the show some value as a muscle builder.

In some of the tribes, each coup was rewarded with the gift of an eagle feather, the Indian equivalent of a plaque from the chairman of the board. The war bonnet was not simply a gaudy headdress. It was something to be earned plume by plume and coup by coup.

Almost as soon as the United States Army began to understand the advantages of the rifle over the musket soon after the nineteenth century opened—the War Department proceeding in slow motion to embrace the reform—the Plains Indians began reaching for the better weapon. They got the word from traders who were ready enough to hand over the hardware, also, if they had extra rifles for barter and the deal was good enough.

So in a quite small way, an arms race got going on the prairie, the Sioux preferring a weapon that would wing a

Crow at 200 yards to one which gave him relative immunity when on the run at 150 feet. There were, however, very few rifles in Indian hands west of the Mississippi until after the Civil War, though the lack did not come from any taboo or proscription. How the Plains tribes armed themselves was of little or no concern to the American public or to the Great White Father in Washington.

The Great Plains, populated only by the nomadic warrior tribes and a few white hunters, trappers, and traders, were regarded as an insurmountable barrier to the westward push of the national frontier. One of the early explorers had named the region "The Great American Desert" and the name caught on. Absurd as it now seems, that is how people east of the Mississippi came to think of it—a parched and impassible land, more fearsome in itself than were the inhabitants. All fair prospect ended where the West began.

If men in the power seats in Washington were any more enlightened than that about what the future had in store, they did not so act. The fact is, Government policy contemplated that the trans-Mississippi West would be continued as an Indian wild-game preserve in perpetuity. It was not a reasoned attempt to postpone another spectacle of humanity's ineptitude and brutality. The quiddity of the situation was that calculations for the future took no account of the perpetual unexpectedness of things. The Five Civilized Tribes had pretty well accepted the principle that trading and learning new ways to subsist were preferable to warfare. The Plains Indians were expected to follow along.

Beginning in the 1820s, a line of ten small forts was built, running from Minnesota in the north to Louisiana in the south. These lightly manned and insignificantly armed garrison points were intended to serve as a Western World "Great Wall of China." Their placement established what was officially termed the "Permanent Indian Frontier." Business, commerce, and agricultural development could expand westward up to the line of forts. But there they must stall and stop. The great beyond, thus consigned to the tribes, was considered relatively worthless in any case. For a time, the tribes regarded unblinking this dazzling prospect of a vast land to be forever theirs, with the army holding the line.

The Plains Indians were probably happier in that time than they would ever be again. The Government's fantastically unrealistic cession—this Indian gift to the Indian—was of course the answer to heart's desire. The warrior wanted nothing more than that he would be left free to roam forever on the lone and unroaded prairie, where he could slaughter buffalo and watch the deer and the antelope play. A romantic dream that he wanted to come true, it was not more idyllic than idle. There was never any such possibility. Not less than nature itself, human nature abhors a vacuum.

Yet strange as it now reads, that was how the balance rested through most of the first half of the nineteenth century. The noble red man of the West was little disturbed. He continued to live by the hunt, his temperament being totally unfitted to any other way of going.

Not until the 1840s were a few leading voices heard to cry warning that he could not be permitted to stay that way. These pessimists saw only doubt and danger ahead. They had reason. An ominous prologue to the greater tragedy to come, in that decade the Kiowa, Comanche, Cheyenne, and Wichita made war on the Five Civilized Tribes for encroaching on territory which they considered rightfully their own. An army column at first commanded by Brigadier General Henry Leavenworth, then taken over by Col. Henry Dodge when Leavenworth died of fever, took the field. When the pacification was completed, a treaty was signed with the tribes of the southern Plains. This elaborate confection of studied ambiguities was to prove wholly ineffective.

The climactic change came, however, when the myth of the nontraversable West was exploded by thousands of ox carts, mule-drawn wagons, and pioneers afoot, trekking toward the sunset over the Santa Fe and Oregon trails in the quest for gold or other sudden fortune. With that large movement of people, the spectral fear of the Great American Desert receded among the more adventurous or clearer thinking palefaces. Not simply an amusing shift in continental traffic flow, here was the beginning of a sharp and irrevocable turning in the history of the Western World. The effect on the national fortunes is comparable to, say, the Dred Scott Decision as to the bitterness and self-recrimination that would come of it. Because there was no immediate shock reaction, however, the landmark importance of the reality was little noted then and has received scant attention since. The problem being one of racial incompatability and mounting friction rather than a question of new law and its enforcement, parties to the controversy proceeded as if some new road to accommodation must await, instead of recognizing that differences were moving to a dead end. In any such situation the tendency on both sides is to pay but halfway attention to the grievances and interests of the other.

The Plains Indian simply could not adapt himself to changing circumstance, and he had too long carried his life in his hands to shudder at the thought of dying. The Big Parade to the Rockies and beyond inevitably brought to boil tribal resentment. Both of the great trails ran through the flanks of the Great Plains, and thus violated buffalo country. The migrants hunted that they might survive. To the Indian, this was his land and his game. The tribesmen resumed plundering the wagon trains and marauding white settlements. There were scalpings of wayfaring parties. The classic fight took shape between the circling warriors and the laagered wagon train, an Indian tactic, incidentally, that was not more spectacular than foolish in that it presented continuously the broadest possible target. Still, rarely was it fair contest, the main sufferers being the weaker travelers by trail.

There were other sources of friction. It was no more possible for Indians to keep their hands off of a carelessly guarded horse corral or a vulnerable herd of cattle than it was for the white man to abandon the rule that private property was sacred. The Indian knew no law against raiding. Horse stealing or the running off of someone else's beeves was to his mind an achievement, a stroke to his credit, a coup. The two scales of values were as unlike as crimson and cream and totally irreconcilable.

Government began then gradually to understand that it could not sit idly by and await the outcome of the catch-as-catch-can struggle in the West. The tribes were not less slow in getting the idea that if they did not like the price, in a little while the price would grow. Nothing is more remarkable than that these realizations were so late in dawning.

All along, the "Permanent Indian Frontier" had been not so much a chimera as a misleading mirage. To think of it as a seductive bureaucratic pretension is to believe that the national fathers were outright villains bent on duping and swindling the Indian limitlessly. No, they were only singularly blind. The population flow to the great open spaces, initially only a trickle of hunters, trappers, and traders with a disproportionate delegation of purveyors of firewater, was certain to continue and steadily expand. It is all easy to see by anyone given the gift of hindsight.

If doubt existed then, there is room and reason for none now, about the nature and magnitude of the national moral obligation to the Plains Indian and tribes farther west. His rights were being ignored. His claim was being jumped. His very existence was directly menaced. Nothing pertaining to his future had been clarified and made believable. Although not recognized as a citizen of the United States, he nonetheless belonged and was in possession of the lands that he regarded as his own.

On the other hand, Government had its peculiar problem, being beset by directly conflicting traditions. Washington could not forbid people to venture or strike out for a better way of life within their own domain. Freedom to pioneer is an American birthright. There was simply no possibility of posting an off-limits sign along a north-south line a few miles west of the Mississippi.

Therefore to protect the travelers as much as possible, the small forces of the United States Army had to be deployed deeper and deeper into the Plains Indian's homeland. The farther they moved, the more challenging became the confrontation. Then there was another thing: Because they were small forces, familiarity with the army would breed in the warrior tribes not so much contempt as an overconfidence that could well fan aggression.

Of the direct conflict of interest, however, came the wars and the numerous but mostly vain parleys that sought the end of a problem that was by its very nature insoluble. It was beyond the wisdom and justice of man to insure that the dignity of the red man of the Plains and the welfare of a young and virile nation could be equally safeguarded.

If the Plains Indian could not be left free to roam where he pleased and have his way where he went, then his right to movement had to be restricted. Yet this was no simple repetition of the centuries-old problem that arises when one people tries to dispossess another of the territory to which it claims title. The Far West was still a largely unpeopled land of magnificent distances. There remained plenty of room for the red man and for the white man.

The root of the trouble lay in the Plains Indian's rootlessness. It was freedom of movement, the privilege of ranging far and wide seasonally, that gave his life meaning and dignity. Once that freedom became threatened, his culture, his creature habits and customs, his manner of providing for his family, all of these were imperiled.

To limit him to one piece of ground that he might call his own, though it was the white man's way, must suggest to him the loss of everything that made his spirit proud. It meant living on a reservation, the very mention of which he loathed. The Indian so placed would no longer be a mounted warrior, and no longer a hunter drawing his subsistence from the migratory buffalo.

Such was the stake, the forfeit for the Plains Indian that made hostilities inevitable. There was no middle ground and little or no margin for compromise. When that is the situation, the time must come when mutual hurts and wrongs are no longer avoidable. As for the then prevailing hope among officials of the Bureau of Indian Affairs, that given time and patience the Plains tribes could be persuaded peaceably to abandon their nomadic ways for a tranquil and productive existence as farmers, that was mere wishful thinking, as the experience of the past century has well proved.

So we are speaking of wars that virtually had to be, though the notion that there is always a viable and less violent alternative is today no less popular than is the theme that the Plains Indians were without sin and were made the victims of predatory whites.

Civilization may have had a clear duty to save these people from themselves. To state it in the most obnoxious terms possible, something akin to apartheid might have been their best insurance. Civilization, however, is rarely that foresighted.

It therefore became a question of how long the Sioux, Cheyenne, and other Plains Indians could stand the mounting strain of the pressure against their manner of existence. When the limit was reached and they broke loose, men with the main responsibility for the safety and well-being of the American people saw little or no choice other than to react forcibly.

Thereafter, one wretched trial at arms or mishandled negotiation led to another, with the warfare stretching out over a greater number of years than any of the national history. Vietnam is by comparison a relatively brief period of darkness and of dismal dissension.

Individuals of goodwill in both camps continued to ask why the conflict had to be. Moving from savagery to deeper savagery, it still went to the bitter end.

By then, nothing of real value had been learned by anyone, though events had reaffirmed an ancient truth: While there are definite limits to human wisdom, there is none to human stupidity.

2

The Signs of Storm

WHILE there had been some fighting between soldiers and braves in the Far West through the first half of the nineteenth century, these were small and unrelated episodes, not only lacking the nature of a campaign, but when totaled, adding up to very little.

In fact, prior to the Civil War there was only one noteworthy clash between the army and the tribes, the dimensions of which and the follow-through, unlike the ridiculous circumstance that brought it on, might have been read as a portent of heavy trouble to come.

It is sometimes called the Mormon Cow War and its plot and point warrant that slightly contemptuous label.

In 1851, a first treaty was signed at Fort Laramie, midway along the Oregon Trail, between officials of the Indian Bureau and the chiefs of the Sioux, Northern Cheyenne, Arapaho, and Crow. By its terms, and because Government promised annuity payments and other benefits, the tribes agreed to pull away from the Oregon Trail and stay put within clearly defined areas in Dakota, Montana, and eastern Colorado—most of it well-favored hunting country.

The deal looked good on paper; one flaw in it was that the Indians didn't keep a treaty once it was signed, the people not being that controllable; another fault was that peace is always at the mercy of fools.

Just three years later, there was a great gathering of Sioux, Arapaho, and Cheyenne outside the walls of Fort Laramie, the reason being that the families had flocked there to collect their annuities, most of which they already owed to the traders. They were in a good mood and there was not a hint of hostility in the air.

Pausing briefly at the fort was a westward-bound Mormon immigrant who shortly before had abandoned a lame cow a few miles back along the road.

A right hungry Brule Sioux youth who had gone sporting about the countryside with two companions came across the abandoned animal, killed it, and dined on roast beef.

The Mormon migrant, who had thought precious little of the beast until someone brought him news of the barbecue, then quickly rated it a very valuable crittur and demanded reparations.

Hearing that the Mormon was after him and becoming frightened, the Brule boy sought protection among the tepees of the Teton Sioux and appealed for help to the Teton chief, who is called severally Conquering Bear or Bear That Scatters. By whichever name, the chief did the gentlemanly thing: He sought out the Mormon and offered to pay him $10 compensation. When that worthy replied that he would settle for nothing less than $25, the Bear backed off, protesting that he didn't have that much money and adding that no lame cow left by the trail to shift for herself could be worth $25.

At that point the relentless Mormon carried his case to Lieutenant J. L. Grattan who, though he may have known how to command a fort, gets no rating in history as a mental giant. Brashness and stupidity are not endearing qualities in a junior officer, though not a few become long-remembered only because of acts embarrassing to the army.

The Signs of Storm

After becoming tanked on whiskey, Grattan moved out with thirty men and two cannon, confronted the Teton Sioux camp, and issued an ultimatum—either pay the $25 that the Mormon demanded or surrender the cow-killing Brule boy for punishment. A more foolhardy act than this may hardly be imagined. Not only was Grattan without authority to make any such demand, he was himself breaking the law.

Vainly, Bear That Scatters protested the injustice and folly of the confrontation. As the argument became heated, the warriors behind him grew angry and made outcries. Probably Grattan, becoming frightened, lost his nerve.

Anyhow, incredibly, the lieutenant barked an order and the cannon opened fire on the mass, the opening rounds killing a number of Sioux and mortally wounding Bear That Scatters. There wasn't time for more than that.

Instead of backing away, the outraged Teton warriors fell upon Grattan and his men, beating and hacking them to death. Only one soldier broke free and made it on the run to the fort.

All of the Sioux immediately broke camp and moved away rapidly to the northeast, certain that they would be declared hostile and that retribution would be prompt and harsh.

In part of this assumption they were wrong. Though they were declared hostile soon enough, the army bided its time, waiting until the following summer. Then Colonel William Harney and thirteen hundred soldiers marched west from Fort Leavenworth to even the score.

At a place named Ash Hollow, not far from the North Platte River, Harney and his column came upon another band of Sioux under Chief Little Thunder. None of this band had had anything to do with the Mormon or his cow; none had participated in the bloodletting orgy at Fort Laramie. All were so situated that Harney's dragoons could safely attack the camp from both ends. Harney opened fire with his cannon and the band was almost annihilated. There were eighty-six Indian dead when the fight was over, and seventy women and children were made prisoner.

Harney marched on to Fort Laramie. In the interlude since the trouble there, five of the late Bear That Scatters' warriors had made a bad matter worse by seeking to avenge his death. They wantonly murdered three innocent whites who were riding in a mail wagon. Harney demanded that the five give themselves up for punishment, and under pressure from the chiefs, lest the army attack a village in retaliation, the killers came in singing a death chant. Only the intervention of an Indian agent stopped Harney from hanging them without trial. They were taken to Fort Leavenworth and there confined until Franklin Pierce shortly pardoned them. It is one of the few favorably remembered acts of a generally colorless President. Among the five was Spotted Tail, who was to become the foremost worker for peace among the Sioux. His good works made him a name on the land, the modern maps of which are printed with Spotted Tail creeks, mounts, and reserves most redundantly.

Although Harney was enormously proud of his campaign, his get-tough policy helped harden the frontier. Throwing fear into the hearts of the buffalo-hunting tribes, it changed the mood in another way. The people-to-people basis for trust that comes of informal fraternization was gone. Indians no longer rubbed elbows with soldiers to trade their trinkets for liquor and tobacco. They would go far out of their way to avoid any contact with troops. Though distance, rather than lending enchantment, whetted mutual suspicion, it lessened immediate friction. As long as the garrisons marked time in place—and four-fifths of the army was then stationed west of the Mississippi—the standoff but uneasy peace would continue.

While the situation on the Great Plains, if unstable, was generally quiescent, however, in one area the warfare stayed bitter and protracted for reasons having little to do with the thickening traffic over the main trails.

Texas had to remain an exception because Indian sentiment so made it. In that state throughout the late 1850s the Comanches under Chief Bull Hump hit the warpath and raided the white settlements. To the tribes, any arrangement with the United States perforce excluded Texas. They could be at peace with all else in the country and still feel free to raid and murder southward of Indian Territory. Texans had been so overly aggressive toward the Indian that with the coming of statehood, they were still not rated Americans.

This time the Texans didn't call on the army for help against Bull Hump's Comanches. A force of Texas Rangers, with the help of some friendly Indian scouts, retaliated by surprising and exterminating a sleeping Comanche village. That sneak-play simply fired the Comanches all the higher, and the marauding continued. Over months, there were blows and counterblows, little of it making sense, most of it victimizing noncombatants.

Either tiring of it or dissembling that he was ready to quit, Bull Hump and some of his people trekked north into Indian Territory to powwow about burying the hatchet, if anyone was prepared to listen. Either the army did not hear about Bull Hump's alleged good intentions or knowing, did not care. Four hundred soldiers of the Second Cavalry Regiment under Captain Earl Van Dorn took off to get Bull Hump. They are said to have marched one hundred miles in thirty-six hours, though this is a foundering pace and an incredible performance for ordinary remounts. In the surprise attack on Bull Hump's camp, the force killed fifty-six warriors, burned 130 lodges and captured several hundred ponies. Five cavalrymen were killed and Van Dorn was shot through by an arrow that pierced his lungs. He unfortunately survived to achieve a unique notoriety in history when as a Confederate general he was shot dead by an outraged physician upon being found in bed with the latter's wife.

None of this is written either to imply that Van Dorn was for men of his rank a rare sinner or that among Indians the Comanches were gentle and peace-loving and harshly put upon. They were anything but: They were almost as ruggedly mean and resistant as the Texans who they regarded as their main enemies rather than the soldiers.

The other volatile and highly combustible area at that time was Kansas. It was already being called "Bleeding Kansas," not because reds and whites were happily skewering one another but due to the struggle over slavery between whites in this unorganized and up-for-grabs belt of real estate. Among the troublemakers was well-sung John Brown, then unsafely above ground and possessed of a soul he could still call his own. Whether the poison of violence spilled over onto the tribes, and the fallout must be blamed for their sins, they at least did not leave the whole field of bloody action to the palefaces.

The Cheyennes struck hard against a white community. Tension had risen to the point of explosion, due to individual grievances avenged and mutually provocative incidents. Small wars and some big ones have come of this repetitive pattern throughout history. The army, acting for the country, accepted the challenge. Its small columns deployed. One of them, commanded by Colonel Edwin V. Sumner, moved against a Cheyenne village in western Kansas. Sumner was a markedly aging soldier, possibly looking too hard for one last big go. The Indians, on the other hand, were hexed by the superstition that supernatural power made them immune to any attack, a recurrent theme in the prolonged struggle for the frontier. So the warriors formed up immobile, as if prepared to take unflinchingly whatever blow the military might deliver.

Foolish as that may sound, it was topped by what followed. Sumner ordered his men to draw sabers and charge the Indian village, which they did. For the first and only time in the national history certainly, an action of record was decided by cold steel only. The troops destroyed about two hundred tepees and quite a few braves who were responding like statues. As played out, the action was not unlike an operetta written to ridicule the American military, raising the question, "Was this script necessary?"

So we turn from Sumner to Sumpter. From the Confederate batteries on the mainland, guns thundered against the weakly-held Union works of the island, blocking the harbor of Charleston, and the War Between the States was on. Almost overnight, the forts of the Far West were either left in the hands of picket-size, caretaking squads or else closed wholly and their garrisons withdrawn so that the members of the regular army could redeploy to fight and maybe die on bloodier and more celebrated battlefields—an end craved by no sensible soldier. Likewise, almost overnight, captains became generals, majors had a new blooming as possible army commanders, sergeants were pervaded by an unanticipated awareness of the possibilities of power, and for civilians as well as for the military, there ensued a different order of things that was beset by fresh and mounting anxieties as the old scale of values turned upside down.

The Plains Indians did not exactly miss what the change meant to them, though having a lesser sense of history, geography, and the meaning of nationalism than the NCO corps, with its interest in promotion and pay, they less sensed opportunity. United, aware, and well led, the Plains tribes might have turned around the national future or given it a bad case of what Mr. Lincoln called "the slows." By the end of 1861, the frontier was already stripped of military protection. Had the tribes at once moved against the thinly held white settlements, there could have ensued a slaughter grim and great. That they did not do so is hardly a fair measure of their humanitarianism.

The truth is that they barely sensed the swing of the pendulum their way. The idea of a war in which whites battled whites for authority over their hunting grounds, as well as the lost lands east of the Mississippi, was pretty much beyond Indian comprehension. So in the main, they sat out what they could not understand, and no widespread action developed.

Yet most of the Plains Indian bands were in sympathy with the Southern cause, if for no better reason than that anything else seemed preferable to a known evil. A few hit the warpath, seizing the opportunity to raid and scalp, supposedly with the blessing of a new and very remote White Father. Most were content to take advantage of a breathing space wherein they could roam and hunt without fear of being cut down. And there were wretched episodes in which Indian haters among the frontiersmen banded together to maraud the villages, killing indiscriminately or settling old scores, knowing that the nation and the scant law enforcers were too preoccupied to pay much attention.

Gold had been struck in Colorado and there was another mad rush across the Plains by fortune seekers toward the settlement next to the Rockies that became the city of Denver. The chiefs of the Southern Cheyenne and their ally the Southern Arapaho would have sidestepped this onrush. In 1861 some of them had signed a treaty, agreeing to shift their people to an area south of the Arkansas River in eastern Colorado. The majority of the braves, however, would have none of this deal. For three years their dissident bands continued to raid, murder, and pillage, hitting the outlying settlements and harassing the wagon trains. Their unchecked depredations stored up for the hostiles a large reservoir of hate among the whites in rough and rowdy Denver.

The big blow fell in quite another quarter in 1862. There was an uprising of Santee Sioux in Minnesota, not far from an undergarrisoned army post named Fort Ridgely. It came where trouble was least expected. The Santee Sioux, depending largely on a government annuity even though they still hunted the buffalo, seemed to be taking to civilization. Some of them had become farmers and were sending their children to school and attending the mission churches.

Like most such explosions, this tribal revolt came of a small incident as trivial and irrelevant as the butchering of the Mormon farmer's lame cow, and still more grotesque in its violence.

Twenty young braves were returning from an unsuccessful hunting trip. One of them came across the well-filled nest of a hen that had strayed from the coop and made her deposits alongside a public road. The brave picked up the eggs. Another Indian warned him that he was stealing the property of a white farmer. There were taunts back and forth, leading to an argument about whether young warriors should be afraid of whites or loath to kill them.

Of the twenty, four set forth to prove their manhood. Coming to a home where several white families had gathered for Sunday services, they murdered three men and two women. Then they hustled back to the reservation and boasted of their deed to Chief Little Crow. There followed a great tribal council. Little Crow and several other chiefs spoke for peace. Some of Little Crow's words were later handed down, "The white men are like locusts. They fly so thick that the whole sky is like a snowstorm. We are only little herds of buffalo left scattered." In the end the vote was for war, the council reasoning that since the tribe would be punished for the crime of four men, the Santee had best strike first. Little Crow agreed to lead the hostiles, reluctantly, so it is said.

At dawn next day the full-armed war party fell on white families dwelling near the agency, killing twenty-three men and capturing ten women. There followed looting of the buildings, which diversion enabled other whites to escape across the Minnesota River via the ferry. Other war parties fanned out and ravaged the countryside for thirty miles around, burning houses and fields, gang-raping the women, slaughtering children, and scalping the males in an orgy of merciless destruction. The first day's death toll ran high into the hundreds.

When the first fugitives reached Fort Ridgely in midmorning, the commander rushed a detachment of forty-seven men to the ferry slip. There they were promptly ambushed. The survivors fled into a thicket, and less than half the force got away alive. One Indian was killed at the ambush site, the only brave to die on the first day.

Fighting and raiding continued through the second day, and on the third day Little Crow invested the fort at the head of eight hundred warriors. Through three days of siege, the garrison stood its ground, and at last the Santee, having lost a hundred braves, pulled away to sack and ravage the settlement of New Ulm, already swollen with refugees. What had started as a massacre had by this time become full-scale war. The nine hundred settlers in New Ulm fought back, and there was combat house-to-house and man-to-man. Much of New Ulm became ashes. But the center of the village was turned into a citadel where resistance steadily stiffened until Little Crow gave over the fight and withdrew his warriors.

In the meantime the Minnesota government was frantically raising militia, the command of which was given to Henry Sibley, a fur trader and former governor of the state, who knew much about Indians and practically nothing about the conduct of war. Due to that extraordinary handicap, the newly-made colonel was understandably slow about shaping up his forces and taking the field. Some of the dragooned militiamen were recruits awaiting forwarding to the Union Army.

While the mustering proceeded, the Santee continued their raiding of the settlements. After several minor clashes between the hostiles and state forces, the war that had begun on August 17 with the theft of a few hen's eggs ended on September 22 in a pitched battle between sixteen hundred militiamen and Little Crow's main force. Roundly beaten, the

Indians quit the field and scattered in an effort to save themselves.

Sibley was utterly relentless in his follow-through. From there on, all Indians looked the same to him. Scouring the countryside, he summarily arrested about two thousand tribesmen, not more than one-fourth of whom could have belonged to the war party, the majority being peaceful Sioux.

Within one month, just under four hundred of the prime suspects had been run through the form of a trial. The average hearing lasted less than ten minutes. By the end, 306 braves had been sentenced to hang for murder, rape, or engaging in a battle. Thereon Henry Whipple, an Episcopal bishop, appealed to the White House to restrain Sibley's monstrous intemperance, and Mr. Lincoln ruled that since the Santee had indeed gone to war, Indians could not be hanged simply for fighting.

The thirty-six that had been found guilty of statutory crime were hanged together at Mankato, the traps all being sprung at one time. As for Little Crow, he first fled to Dakota, then got away to Canada. One year later, however, he made the mistake of recrossing the border. Still hostile, he staged one last raid within sight of St. Paul and killed about thirty people. A day or so later, he was shot from ambush while picking blackberries near Hutchinson, Minnesota.

If in the beginning, as legend says, he was no cockalorum but a reluctant war leader, his subsequent mad career gave the white community cause to be thankful that there were few such.

The month-long war was not more unjustifiable and frightful than devastating to red and white alike. A region embracing twenty-three counties in southwestern Minnesota was left practically stripped of population, and years passed before it was resettled.

The Sioux were literally wiped off the face of Minnesota.

The reservation was abolished. Some few of the Indians who had personally and provably befriended or shielded the whites in their hour of peril were permitted to remain. The others—the innocent along with the guilty—were packed off to a reservation in northeastern Nebraska. Their several hundreds of descendants still dwell there, for the most part holding with Christianity and living by farming. With few exceptions, they know little or nothing of the circumstances causing their expulsion from Minnesota. Their white contemporaries whose forebears were victims of the conflict are hardly better informed. A strange cloud of reticence and equivocal silence surrounds the subject, as if there were an unconscious effort to wipe the Little Crow War from memory.

One of the least known of the Indian conflicts, it nonetheless marked another divide. Until the Santee uprising, there was present at least the prospect of conciliation, however illusory. Further embittering both sides, the very nature of the war blocked the last approach to accommodation on the prairie. Goodwill had run out.

One tribe of the Dakota had proved to be not only treacherous but barbarous in the extreme. It would not be forgotten by the whites of the frontier. The Indians were no less served warning that when crossed, Government and its security forces would retaliate beyond reasonable limits, exiling or exterminating a great body of people, if that were deemed the expedient course.

There had never been any reason for Indians to believe that the reaction would be otherwise, though the Sioux were among the late ones in getting the word.

3

Massacre and War

THE newcomer to early Denver did not have to be an Indian hater to settle there, though it was a qualification that made him more congenial to the society. Public outrage over the recurrent raiding against the wagon trains and the outlying ranches was the more intense because the community could do so little about it in an organized way, Colorado not even having a territorial government.

Besides, at the foot of the Rockies, the Arapaho exemplified how the well-disposed Indian should behave. Their camps played friendly and promised to stay that way, so long as there was no white interference with their right to continue war against their traditional enemies, the Utes.

The frustrated bands from elsewhere that moved across the plains of eastern Colorado had as much reason for resentment as any camp of gold seekers to their west. What had lately been a bountiful hunting ground was fast becoming a plucked prairie wiped clean of game. The Oregon Trail traced through it on the north, as did the Santa Fe Trail on the south. Although the mass move toward Cherry Creek and the rush to the digs on Clear Creek kicked up relatively little gold, the wide trail that it beat through the center of the region so drove off the herds that no bison were to be found within two hundred miles of the mainline east to west. The traffic devitalized the very heart of the Cheyenne domain. Some of the raiding into the wagon trains of the migrants was done by starving Indians seeking only to survive. They stripped the wagons of the food stocks and let the people go.

The seeds of war were planted in 1864 with the arrival in Colorado of John Evans, who was to be its territorial governor. He was something less than God's gift to a troubled and complex situation. The kindling incident was the report of a rancher that some Indians had raided his place and had driven off his cattle, an act that while felonious is hardly a declaration of belligerence. Evans reacted promptly. With the rancher whose name was Ripley serving as their guide, forty part-time soldiers under a lieutenant took off to track down the stolen stock. The column came upon some Indians pushing along a pack of ponies. The Indians had stopped; they came forward offering to shake hands. Ripley claimed that the horseflesh belonged to him. The Indians replied this was untrue. Some of the soldiers moved to grapple with the Indians, as if to strip them of firearms, which is not the way of wisdom.

Bullets and arrows flew. Five soldiers were killed and one was wounded. The braves galloped off unscathed.

Absurd as it now sounds, the incident was reported as an unprovoked attack by Indians, and it was enough to convince Governor Evans that round and about him the tribes were hostile.

Another punitive column commanded by a major was sent forth when Evans got the report that the Cheyenne had raided a ranch area on the South Platte River and had driven off all of the settlers. True or not, the expedition found no displaced settlers, abandoned ranches, or hostile Cheyenne. The major continued on, however, until his soldiers came upon an unalerted Cheyenne village. The place is called Cedar Canyon. There they overran a Cheyenne band not known to have offended in any way, burned all of the lodges, and killed twenty-six Indians, while wounding thirty others.

The troops in these quite senseless and provocative forays were not federally trained soldiers but Colorado militiamen serving only a few days under arms. In command over this ignorant army was Colonel John Chivington, one of the least appetizing figures in the history of the western frontier. A man of ponderable bulk, standing well over six feet, Chivington was an ex-preacher and missionary turned avenger, a change of cloth not likely to be attended by moderation. To give him his due, he might have won a crown had he not become teamed with the weakling, Evans.

Next, a company under a lieutenant was launched from Colorado to raid the Cheyenne in western Kansas, which could be called a whale of a march order. The Indians there were said to have made off with cattle belonging to a contractor selling beef to Government. After looting and burning two villages, from which the Cheyenne fled on noting his approach, the lieutenant beat back to Denver to replenish his supplies. Then marching east again, he found a large camp of Cheyenne on the Arkansas River. Chief Lean Bear, one of the head men, rode forth to powwow with the lieutenant. Two of Lean Bear's retainers approached the soldiers with their hands raised. They were immediately shot down. The braves came swarming from the camp, firing their weapons. Before getting away as best they could, the Coloradoans had three dead and four wounded. The damage done by the day went far beyond that. Anger became all, and the reasons for it, muddled and distorted, seemed to be as nothing except in one hard-tried quarter.

All of the militiamen might have been slaughtered or maimed during the getaway but for the intervention of Chief Black Kettle. The head man of the Cheyenne rode up in time to restrain his warriors and stop pursuit until the soldiers were lost in distance. If Black Kettle did not want peace with the palefaces, his actions on that day are beyond explaining.

The routed lieutenant returned to Denver to claim a great victory over hostile Indians. The pretension was not abnormal; any junior officer in such a position would likely have done the same. When he turned west, the death of his soldiers began to assume an increasing unimportance, and well before reaching Denver, his fright and anger had given way to a detached view of his own interests. On the road back, however, and quite by accident, he had accomplished one good deed. On the trail he encountered William Bent, a celebrated half-breed trader of the Old West and a close friend of Black Kettle's people. Bent's wife, Magpie, was a Cheyenne, and she had given him five children. To Bent, the lieutenant boasted how he had fought and killed a body of Cheyenne, though his soldiers had merely murdered two Indians in cold blood.

Bent, holding his temper and probably not believing one word of what he heard, decided to investigate. Black Kettle gave him his story of the action, said that the Cheyenne were seething because of the attack, could not understand why whites could commit such an atrocity, and were talking about hitting the warpath.

Seemingly convinced that Black Kettle, rather than the lieutenant, spoke truth, Bent went to Chivington, to talk and to warn. It was wasted breath. Chivington, who must have craved above all else the reputation of a military hero, answered Bent that the Cheyenne were already making war and that no choice remained but for him to keep on killing Indians.

Directly rebuffed, while still not believing what he heard, Bent did not at that point give up his one-man crusade. As at any time in any place, within the frontier society there were persons who talked loudly of peace while doing nothing for it, as there were others who, never boasting of their good works, strove quietly to bring men together. Bent was thus bent. The differences between the ex-preacher and the squaw man were irreconcilable, and their separate characters rather than their bloodlines and personal interests so made them. Bent continued his good try.

By taking the appearance of things as their reality, Evans continued to make a worse mess of it. More and more alarmed at what he had helped start, the governor in June published a proclamation, calling on the several tribes to assemble and move to the protection of the military bases in the Denver region. By so doing, he said, they would prove that they were friendly and it would keep them from being "killed by mistake." Since compliance would mean the forfeiture of their hunting season, they were promised food and other help if they would show goodwill.

A few stray Indians closed on the fold; the mass, if they ever received the invitation, ignored it. The breed trader, Bent, still playing the lone missionary, arranged for negotiations at Fort Larned between the Cheyenne chiefs and the military. Through ill fortune, at the convening hour a band of Kiowa under Chief Satanta drew up close to the fort to stage a scalp dance. Although until then Satanta had never fought the white man, or so he said (he had battled Texans, but he put them in a different category), Satanta was to become a thorn in the flesh of the United States through years to come.

His estrangement began when, during the scalp dance, he and a kinsman quit the dancers and together they approached the fort's main gate. The sentry first challenged, then tried to warn him off. When Satanta kept coming, the luckless soldier fired his carbine. Satanta responded by putting two arrows through the sentry. That brief exchange stirred an uproar in the fort, and during the tumult, the band of Kiowa ran off with all of the post horses. The unhorsed troopers could not pursue, a finishing touch that made Satanta's coup practically perfect. The raid also succeeded in scuttling Bent's conference.

Too soon thereafter, a band of Arapaho under Chief Left Hand appeared before Fort Larned to parley and demonstrate a friendliness toward whites that boded ill for Utes. Made skittish by the earlier misfortune, a trigger-happy soldier doing guard duty fired at the Indians with a cannon. Although he missed them, that round washed out Left Hand's store of goodwill and the band galloped off, as who wouldn't?

Scene after scene, through these opera bouffe exchanges, the two sides pulled farther apart. It was as if the hoodoo mocked Bent's every effort.

Yet as violence grew among the tribesmen, with Evans declaring open season on all mobile Indians and white reprisals mounting apace, Bent would not stop. Evans was by this time so panicky that he was beseeching Washington to send federal troops. His gory reports pictured the Colorado plain as a welter of blood, which was far from true. The Civil War being at flood stage, Mr. Lincoln had to refuse to divert forces to quell these small bickerings. Still, the War Department authorized Evans to recruit a new regiment of militia that would serve for one hundred days. It was designated the Third Colorado Cavalry.

Then at last Bent gained an ally, Major E. W. Wynkoop, one of the few moderates on the scene, a soldier truly dedicated to peace. Taking with him 130 riflemen and a battery of artillery for insurance, Wynkoop moved from his command post at Fort Lyon to Smoky Hill, a site far to the northeast of Denver, where Black Kettle and other tribal chiefs had gathered for a powwow. Not only were the seven hundred tribesmen gathered there noticeably restive, their position was compromised by the fact that they were holding four white children captive.

Still, with Black Kettle leading the talk for the tribesmen, Wynkoop accomplished the two things that should have counted. He persuaded the chiefs to yield the four hostages and then go to Denver for talks with Governor Evans.

Toward the end of September, Black Kettle, White Antelope, and seven other chiefs arrived at the conference seat,

Fort Weld, just outside of Denver. A first and final confrontation, the day of damage opened on a note sweet and low.

"All we ask is peace with the whites," said Black Kettle.

Governor Evans did not dance to the overture. First reminding the chiefs that in the spring he had invited the chiefs to move their bands to the protective custody of the forts, he added that he had no new proposal to make. Then he warned them that the Civil War would soon be over and that the whole army would be turned west to suppress the tribes. Here was negotiation with a bludgeon.

The real situation further unfolded when Chivington spoke, belligerently and unbending. Once over the edge, this chest-beater was not to be stopped. His message of goodwill was that when men resist, whether they be red or white, it was his duty to fight them until they laid down their arms. The fun was over, so let the battle begin.

Incredibly, some of the chiefs, especially Black Kettle and White Antelope, took this bullying unblinking and left the conference believing that they could get along with Evans and Chivington. Once they brought their people to the fort, the fighting would end, the families would be safe, and food for all would be forthcoming. In their ready acceptance of total dependency, there could have been wishfulness or the pressure of plain necessity, there being extra reason for them to yield temporarily. When the snows pile deep and the grass goes, Indian ponies get thin and too weak for the warpath. Winter was just around the corner.

So there came about a movement of the bands to the ground just outside of Fort Lyon, where the Indians anticipated being under the guardianship of their newfound friend, Edward Wynkoop, through the hard months ahead.

Had it been left to Wynkoop, there would be one less black page in the national history. He was a strong man with a lustrous record. A Philadelphian and son of wealth, he had headed for the Rockies while in his twenties because he loved adventure. One of the founders of the settlement on Cherry

Creek, it was Wynkoop who named it Denver. When war came, he joined the Union Army and led a cavalry charge at Glorieta, sometimes called the "Gettysburg of the West."

But the Indian faith in Wynkoop proved to be a vain hope. The steady and highly regarded soldier-pioneer was too true to be good in the eyes of Evans and Chivington. His peace initiatives had offended them. They saw his influence and presence as a threat to their positions. They had pressed Washington for authority to raise a regiment that the white settlers might be spared a holocaust. Now that the Indians were turning peaceful, the regiment would be marking time until mustering-out day, and their case would be proved hollow.

Wanting war for peculiarly personal reasons, the top conspirators had to get rid of the obstacle. So they requested army higher authority to relieve Wynkoop, and the army shamefully complied.

The Indians might have smelled danger when Major Scott J. Anthony arrived at Fort Lyon to take over. This shoddy soldier moved in simply to conspire to a mass murder. There is no other possible reading of his subsequent actions.

Anthony's first move was to order the Indians to pick up their tepees and relocate at considerable distance from the fort. Here was a direct breach of faith that bespoke an intended treachery, though the chiefs failed to read it that way.

The reassembly of the submissive took place along Sand Creek, an almost dry watercourse about forty miles from Fort Lyon. At that site arose a new village of more than a hundred lodges, sheltering two hundred warriors and more than five hundred women and children. Anthony's pretext for ordering the displacement was that he was short of rations to sustain the Indians and at the new location they could resume hunting. The motive? What really counted was that at the new location they no longer had sanctuary under the terms that Governor Evans had laid down, not being within the shadow of the fort.

The one-hundred-day service of the Third Colorado Cavalry was within twenty-four hours of expiring. There had been no red violence through the autumn. Wynkoop meanwhile had been ordered back to Fort Leavenworth, where he was kept on the hook by Major General Samuel R. Curtis, who had so summarily relieved him.

On the night of November 23, after a forced march through deep snow, Chivington arrived at Fort Lyon leading a mounted column of 750 men, mainly members of the Third Cavalry.

Then began a conference between birds of a feather. Chivington told Anthony that he intended to march on and wipe out the Sand Creek encampment; he hoped that some of Anthony's regulars would join the surprise attack.

Anthony was all in favor of the operation. His failure to object surprised and angered his officers. Several of them protested vehemently that under the agreement made by Wynkoop they were honor-bound to protect the Indians. With Anthony seconding him, Chivington bullied and abused them into silence.

At 9:00 P.M. the same night, with time running out for the Third Colorado Cavalry, the column moved out on its terrible mission. Anthony had committed all of the regulars except a small caretaking force.

Even before the start, they were behaving like men gone a little mad. Chivington had given them their orders in these words, "I want you to kill and scalp all, big and little; nits make lice." None of his listeners protested what they heard, and when the time came, most of the militiamen would obey to the letter. They were not soldiers but butchers.

One more damnable entry is a measure of the vice in Chivington. He had compelled Robert Bent, one of the sons of William Bent, to come along with him as a guide. Encamped at Sand Creek, soon to be massacred where they slept, were three of the daughters of William Bent.

Several up-early squaws saw the column descending the bluffs just as dawn broke, and they ran through the lodges crying warning. Still, the village did not spring to arms, for there had yet been no firing or any sign that the force intended to attack.

Then as Black Kettle ran from his tepee to raise a white flag and the national emblem on a lodge pole while shouting words of reassurance to the people, cannon and rifle fire tipped and riddled the lodges, setting some afire.

White Antelope at age seventy must have been resigned to death, spectacular or not. As the militiamen and soldiers advanced firing, he calmly folded his arms and went into his death chant, "Nothing lives long except the earth and the mountains." At the last word, a bullet got him through the heart.

So began a full day given over to blood-lust, orgiastic mutilation, rapine, and destruction—with Chivington and Anthony looking on and approving. The horrifying scenes of that prolonged slaughter, as described in detail in many books, must shock and sicken any sensitive reader. They are not for this writing.

Only one gallant military figure stands clear. Captain Silas S. Soule, a regular, commanded one of Anthony's companies. Having already protested Chivington's order, Soule ordered his men not to fire or participate in any way, and they obeyed him. Soon thereafter, he would be murdered on a street in Denver. Young Bent, the breed scout, though wounded by a bullet through the hip, moved about the field, trying to help people and making written notes of everything he witnessed. That Chivington let him live was an oversight.

Some few of the braves fought back until killed. Although they struck down a few of their enemies, theirs was a pitifully weak resistance. When Black Kettle tried to make a stand, some of his warriors swept him up, mounted him on a pony, and led him off. On the ride out, he passed the body of his wife, hit by seven bullets. Mistaking her for dead, he carried on. She miraculously recovered and later rejoined him.

The exact count of dead is not known. Robert Bent, who stayed at the shambles after the military had cleared away, put it at 163, of which 110 were women and children. Of forty-six Arapaho, only four survived. Out of 137 Cheyenne that fell, twenty-eight were men, the others women and children.

Chivington speeded a battle report to Denver fresh from the bloody field; "Attacked a Cheyenne village of from nine hundred to a thousand warriors . . . Killed between four and five hundred . . . All did nobly."

The French word for it is *panache*, a natural gift for making or faking a good military show.

Upon their return, the fire-eater and his raiders demonstrated around Denver, waving their trophies, more than one hundred drying scalps. They were acclaimed as conquering heroes, which was what they had sought mainly. One local paper said editorially, "Colorado soldiers have once again covered themselves with glory," which was disputed by another paper, it being against policy to agree with a rival.

That was how it went for a short while. Chivington and Anthony went riding again, hoping this time to exterminate another band of Arapaho reported in camp on the Arkansas. But the news of Sand Creek had traveled very fast, and Chief Little Raven had taken off with his people for other parts.

Wynkoop was restored to duty, relieving Anthony, who wasn't made to pay for his derelictions. By that time, bit by bit, the truth had begun to surface that Sand Creek had been no battle but a monstrous atrocity without a wisp of provocation. People sensed that Chivington and his mob had accomplished nothing except to inflame the frontier all around. The survivors of Sand Creek had rendezvoused at Smoky Hill. An enraged council gathered around them and sent off war pipes to the Sioux and other Plains tribes. Although it was winter and by their custom not the season for fighting, the Indians arose as one. More ambushing of wagon trains and raiding of settlements followed.

Once the public got the reality, Evans and his Lord High

Executioner became politically discredited; Chivington had speeded the denouement by trying to bluster his way through. But the cost to them regrettably was little more than that. The hundred-day home guardsmen had their pay held up for a time, but were mustered out before they could be brought to account for the mass murder.

The Civil War bloodbath had dulled the public sensibility and there was no real cry for justice to Indian-killers. So Sand Creek was indecently buried and stayed mostly forgotten until more than a century later, when My Lai caused historians to cast about for a comparable outrage.

During the following October, the Civil War having ended, the United States tried to make amends to Black Kettle, Little Raven, and the offended peoples. A great council was held in Kansas and of the powwowing a new treaty was signed. The nation acknowledged war guilt for the "gross and wanton damage" done by Chivington, Anthony, et al. at Sand Creek and agreed to pay indemnity to the widows and orphans victimized by the massacre.

As for what this gesture contributed to promoting an era of good feeling, it was money down the drain. Most of the hostile and semi-hostile bands never heard of it. There was no way to spread the word, and moreover yesterday's act of goodwill rarely buys more than twenty-four hours of gratitude. The damage lasted. The bounty did not. A few rare spirits such as Wynkoop, Bent, and possibly even Black Kettle continued to work for peace along the frontier. As a whole, the Plains Indians could neither forget nor forgive Sand Creek. It was an attitude not peculiar to those tribes nor to their time and place.

The ending of the Civil War brought a pivotal turn to the wars on the western Plains, widening the area of turbulence and giving a fight-to-the-finish pitch to the conflict between Americans, red and white. The sharp change might be taken as proof that more of the Plains tribesmen than not opted not to seize the opening made theirs by the absence of regular army to prey on the new settlers when they were relatively defenseless.

Though of that point in their favor much has been made —the argument being that when the settlements were vulnerable they did not lay on—the idea doesn't quite wash.

The war had slowed and thinned the tide of migration to the Far West. Except in areas like Colorado and the Mexican border country from the Rio Grande westward, the lines of fundamental self-interest did not cross and clash sufficiently to convulse the region. Other than in Oklahoma, the tribes for the most part stayed mobile and were spirited enough to resist, or temporize with, enforced concentration on a reservation. That their freedom to roam widely was little hampered is dramatized in practically every trial-at-arms of the time.

The same bands led by the same chiefs are to be found operating in Colorado, Kansas, Indian Territory, and Texas. The settlers settled, or at least tried, and the Plains Indians remained virtually as footloose as before the white man came. Of that freedom from confinement, they continued to think of themselves as the rightful possessors of the lands they traveled.

Bison were still plentiful except where the slowed-down wheels of white migration cut and kept a beaten path. That they did not make continuous war was less because the Plains Indians ignored the threat to their future than that they were too little unified to think about how to resist it effectively. The hunt had to be pursued that they might live. Their day-to-day preoccupation with the requirements of tribal existence thus kept them relatively tranquil.

Still, the Plains Indians must have been perplexed and of mixed counsel on how to react to the Civil War. Except in Texas, they were too far removed from the battlefields to appreciate its dimensions or forsee what its ending would mean to them. If their attitude was streaked with naïveté, it is still understandable. Remote from the thudding of the guns, they for the first and only time were dealing with agents or missions speaking for two quite different Great White Fathers. It was enough to make a Sioux or Crow wonder if he was afflicted with double vision.

There is hardly a more ludicrous passage in the story of the Indian or of the Confederacy than the scene in which the wooing ended. The two generals had already met at Appomattox and agreed to stop the bloodletting forthwith. Then came the penultimate. The largest tribal convention on record met to get the good news about how Jefferson Davis planned to bring lasting peace to the Plains.

For months, a Creek brave with the gift of tongues, which he needed to get around his own name, had been moving among the western tribes, waving credentials from the Richmond Government. Due to this supersalesman, Tukabatchemiko, on May 1, 1865, some twenty thousand Indians collected on the banks of the Washita River to hear the message. There were delegations from the Osage, Pawnee, Kickapoo, Washita, Kiowa, Comanche, Cheyenne, Arapaho, Navajo, Sioux, and Apache.

They listened to spokesmen for the fugitive President pledge a treaty of eternal friendship with the tribes provided they quit marauding and acted brotherly. Nothing being said about confining red men to reservations, the chiefs were happy enough to sign the paper.

The commissioners were not leg-pulling or conning the Indians into betting on a dead horse. They honestly did not know that the war was over. The chiefs stayed unaware that the Southern Great White Father was already a relic. They went back to their cliff dwellings and wickiups satisfied with a good day's work and possibly feeling a trifle committed. That for some while they continued in ignorance may have helped the peace of the frontier a little bit for a little time.

Massacre and War

There was a small calm before the storm. Then the main trails to the Golden West began to fill, and the overflowing brought grievances that prickled and rearoused the tribes. Raiding and plundering were resumed. Migrants, settlers, and territorial administrators again besought Washington to send protection. What remained of the standing army after demobilization had pared it to the size of a constabulary, other than the garrisons deemed necessary to police the Erring Sisters, was highly available to be shipped west for a go at the Indians.

Size considered, that army was the meanest army that the country has ever put afield. Formed out of Blue and Gray veterans, wtth a large leavening of newly-arrived immigrants, chiefly Germans and Irish, it was battle-seasoned in many parts and its average file had signed on because the excitement of war was to his liking, and he wanted more of it.

The higher commanders were generals and colonels who had moved to the top in a hard school. Having learned to kill their white brethren without compunction, they would have little mercy on Indians. They had fought one war to unify the country and they were still committed to that line.

On one main count, however, most of them fell far short. They knew little or nothing about the way of the Indian in warfare. Like the American in Vietnam just one century later, they would make many blunders and pay too high a price for lessons learned the hard way.

It was also a rowdy army, far more so than the AEF of 1918. A large portion of its enlisted people were habitual drunks and few of the officers shunned the bottle. Payday invariably became a mass spree, phasing into a forty-eight-hour hiatus. Living conditions were little supervised or inspected and quarters were cramped, austere, and ill-ventilated. The food issued to troops and the general supply were abominably cheap. In fact, the army was worse served than at any time since the Revolution. Its weapons, drawn from Civil War stocks, were already out-moded before the start of campaigning.

The weekly issue to the company unit consisted of salt pork, dry beans, green coffee beans, brown sugar, soap, and an amount of wheat flour, depending on how many men qualified for the ration. The flour was often wormy or moldy; the soap was the cheapest that could be found on the market. Some kind of fresh meat was issued twice each week, and in that respect the Indian-fighting army did better than Pershing's AEF—the company messes of which got none. If the troops of the Indian-fighting army craved fresh fruits or vegetables, they had either to grow them or steal them. And they did both.

This army went long-haired, moustached, and bearded to war, most of the men and some of the officers. Rather than being uniformed by a strict quartermaster, it let individuals wear pretty much what they pleased, within limits appropriate to the mission. The bounds in each unit were set by the commander at the time.

But if the purpose of this permissiveness was to uplift the spirit of the average soldier, it certainly fell short of the object. That it was anything but a happy and contented army is indicated by a desertion rate that started abnormally high and so stayed. If a soldier saw a better line of main chance anywhere in his travels, he usually bugged out. Desertion figures during the Vietnam years do not begin to compare.

Many of the recruits gave false names upon enlisting, either because of a spotty record that they chose to conceal or because their families and friends regarded regular army service as socially beyond the pale. Almost as promptly as the Civil War ended, civilians had ceased being friendly to soldiers. A later wartime generation of Americans did not even wait that long.

Army pay was $13 a month for the private. That may

sound like a pittance, although fifty years later, or just prior to World War I, the private's pay was only $15.

Many items were passed over in the recruit's stipulated uniform issue, and he had either to buy them on half-pay or do without. Once he got on full pay, he stayed in debt most of the time, either to the unit's slickest gambler or to the sergeant-banker who loaned money to soldiers at usurious rates, about 20 percent per month, and always stood by to collect when pay call sounded. Proper commissioned officers ignored his operations.

In 1860 the regular army had numbered sixteen thousand. At high tide in the Civil War, there were twenty-six thousand on its rolls. After 1866 its line strength or combat elements were comprised of 630 companies of infantry, cavalry, and artillery, the average unit mustering seventy men. Thus the total of the fighting force should have been about 43,100. But the Congress had authorized a paper strength of 54,302 while increasing the cavalry by four regiments, changes that say clearly enough that the main military policy of the country was aimed at the menace on the western frontier. Of the new cavalry regiments, the Ninth and Tenth were black, the first such ever recruited by the army, and the Seventh was to win more public attention in Indian-fighting than all other horse outfits, still leaving open the question whether seven is a lucky number.

Though the army looked strong enough as the Congress had set it up, volunteering dragged and the effective strength for all arms hovered around thirty-eight thousand, which was far less than the number of rifle-armed tribesmen. Within the next ten years, there would be more than two hundred engagements fought between Indians and soldiers, the army operating clumsily, yet rarely losing a decision. In many minor clashes its people were ambushed, slaughtered, and tortured, and they in turn fought back savagely and killed wantonly. Most of the company commanders were ten to fifteen years older than today's youthful captains. Military promotion was slow, and despite the push to populate the West, good-paying jobs in civilian life were few. Strong captains are the backbone of any army and in this respect the Indian-fighting army was fortunate.

At its top was General-in-Chief U. S. Grant with General W. T. Sherman as his Chief of Staff. General Phil Sheridan would soon be in command in the West. Success had not mellowed any of the three outstanding leaders of the old Union Army. All were so laden with dignity, honors, and administrative burdens that they could not give primary attention to the problem of pacifying the Plains. Rarely were they close at hand when pivotal decisions had to be made by their subordinates in the field. Mainly because of their attitude and policy-making, the warring with the Plains tribes became steadily more brutalized and was pushed to the point of extermination. Whether a more conciliatory approach would have tranquilized and prospered the West must still be doubted. There was little possibility of reconciling the minimal desires of the tribes with the vital interests of the expanding nation.

The highest drama invariably attended those battles in which the army was defeated, as in the first campaign which was about to begin.

When Colonel Henry B. Carrington led a seven hundred-man strong battalion of the Eighteenth Infantry Regiment into Fort Laramie in June 1866, that post was already uncomfortably overcrowded. A federal commission, none of whose members rated fame enduring, was seated there trying to persuade the big wheels of the Sioux tribes into conceding an unopposed right-of-way over a new trail that cut directly through virgin country. A more bountiful hunting country was not to be found in the Far West. Meadows of tall grass gave it an especial beauty. The snow-fed white water streams abounded with trout and the foothill slopes were fir and aspen clad, with forests of Lodgepole pine and Ponderosa.

Called the Bozeman Trail, the new route, a spur of the Oregon Trail, hooked northwest around the mountains of Dakota Territory and of southern Montana Territory, with one leg of the trail paralleling the Yellowstone River. The new route could be used throughout the year if the Indians permitted. The way had been blazed several years before by John M. Bozeman and John M. Jacobs, prospectors seeking a more traffickable path into the recently opened gold digs at Bannack, Helena, and Virginia City. The quest almost cost Bozeman his life. He had been stopped, stripped naked by the Sioux, and then turned loose before he could complete his exploration.

The freighting parties that followed in Bozeman's path, trying for the gold camps, were treated less gently by the warriors, and Washington was besought to provide military protection for the fortune seekers. With the Civil War on, the military could do little. The army did, however, send forth a general who arranged to make annuity payments to certain Indian bands if they would grant thoroughfare. But he had made his contract with the wrong people; the chiefs who really counted still held out.

Once the Civil War ended, the government was ready enough to help, irrespective of the affront to the tribes. But having only seen halfway through the problem in the first place, the army then far underestimated what force levels would be needed, and thereafter proceeded as if unaware that there is no profit in kicking at the blade of an ax.

The inevitability of the struggle is epitomized in a few hours of parleying at the edge of the wilderness. In one dramatic incident at Fort Laramie, we see the army entertaining hopes unduly high, the hostile chiefs recoiling in outrage, protesting that they have been betrayed. The events of a single afternoon reveal how and why the conflict of interest between red and white became head-on and nearly absolute.

So long as political authority was determined to use the army to break resistance wherever it threatened the security

47

of the migrating white, there could be no peace along the frontier, if the tribes were no less determined to stand their ground.

Several of the semi-hostile chiefs and their bands had been at the fort since March, drawn there early, less by the prospect of negotiations than by a government food handout. Even so, out of the frequent contacts, some of the key figures, especially Chief Red Cloud, had become increasingly friendly. The formal talks had begun routinely with the commissioners pleading for a binding conciliation and the chiefs listening hard, as if believing that every word was spoken in good faith. Now and then one would rise to discuss a point or grunt agreement.

Along came Colonel Carrington, followed at some distance by his dust-laden and footsore soldiers. They entered upon the scene at the worst possible moment. Whether this fateful timing was by accident or by design, their arrival rocked the assembly. Word of what the Eighteenth Regiment's men had been sent forth to do had been unintentionally leaked to the Indians. Either it is so, or the unhappy chance that brought Carrington into the area just as the chiefs had agreed to sign the treaty was mistakenly used by the commissioners as additional pressure.

The tactical blunder aside, the truth would have surfaced soon enough in any case. The troops had been marched west to build and garrison a line of forts, having the object of safeguarding traffic over the Bozeman Trail. Their presence spoke for itself.

To the council of chiefs, the happening looked not less like a challenge than a deliberate double cross. While professing to court the goodwill of the tribes, the agents of Government were at the same time preparing to seize and hold what was wanted. The hand so badly overplayed was certain to be called.

Red Cloud, the Oglala, pointing to Carrington's insignia,

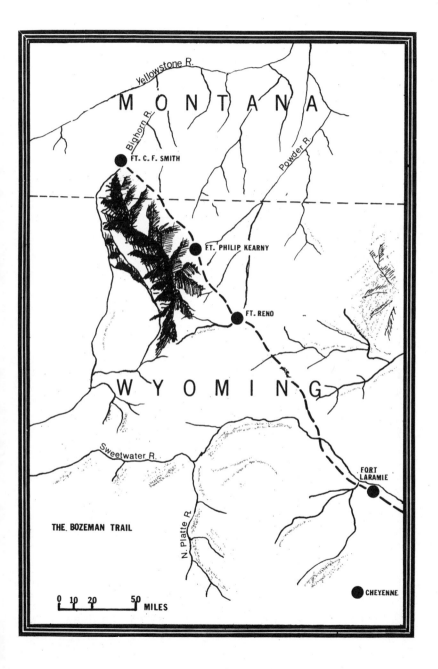

MONTANA

Yellowstone R.

Bighorn R.

Powder R.

FT. C. F. SMITH

FT. PHILIP KEARNY

FT. RENO

WYOMING

Sweetwater R.

FORT
LARAMIE

THE BOZEMAN TRAIL

N. Platte R.

CHEYENNE

0 10 20   50 MILES

shouted in reproof, "So here is the Eagle come to steal a path through the Indian's land!"

Chief Man-Afraid-of-His-Horses, another Oglala and a much more taciturn Indian, all along had been opposed to signing any treaty, unlike Red Cloud.

Chief Spotted Tail of the Brule was willing to continue talking terms. Spotted Tail, during his year in custody at Fort Leavenworth, had become convinced that the white man's power was boundless and had returned to his people a thoroughly discouraged Indian.

Still, it was Red Cloud who held the spotlight mainly. He was as handsome a leader as the Plains Indians ever raised. His portrait fits becomingly the role he played in history, which can be said of relatively few men. For it was his destiny to become the only war leader among the tribes to defeat the forces of the United States over a prolonged campaign and compel them in the end to back off and sign a treaty on his terms, though he fell far short of being a military genius.

The legend goes that he made his exit dramatically at Fort Laramie, lofting his rifle and shouting, "In this and the Great Spirit, I trust for the right!" Then he sprang from the platform to exit under the shelter of pine bows, struck his tepees, and went on the warpath. Man-Afraid-of-His-Horses and a few other chiefs followed along. As theater, it was unbeatable.

Still, the commissioners did not take the threat very seriously. Of Red Cloud as a warrior, they had little or no measure. Their report to Washington noted optimistically that the chiefs who stayed to sign the treaty represented seven-eighths of the Oglala and Brule.

Colonel Carrington, a competent professional soldier, was largely a blameless victim of these unpropitious circumstances. He had his orders. With the troops and 226 wagons conveying the machines, fittings, and supply essential to the building of the Bozeman Trail forts, he continued on his journey across the Plains. In the ambulances rode a number of the army families.

At some risk to himself, General W. T. Sherman, protected by only a few retainers, had earlier reconnoitered the Bozeman Trail and had personally decided that the journey and the mission would be safe enough for women and children. To supply their needs, there were milk cows and poultry moving with the expedition, while one herd of a thousand beef cattle brought up the rear. This small fortune in livestock in itself affords eloquent proof that Carrington anticipated no serious trouble, since the cattle would have to be grazed and guarded outside the forts.

Chilling as might have been the conclusion of that fateful parley, the column moved on with its people in high spirits, cheered by march music from the Eighteenth Regiment's band. The travelers had rested for several days at Laramie. Red Cloud had disappeared from sight and he was accordingly out of mind.

Both Red Cloud and his antagonist-to-be, Carrington, lived well into the twentieth century. They are not remote silhouettes on a far skyline. Their personalities and characters continue to fascinate moderns. More has probably been written of these two men than of any soldier and brave that came to head-to-head encounter in the struggle for the West, with the possible exception of Custer and Crazy Horse.

In one particular only, they are markedly alike. Having more than an average talent for military operations, neither gloried in war. It was for both a painful business.

The portrait of Carrington made familiar by Michael Straight's moving novel is that of a middle-aging, quiet soldier, a scientist and a scholar, a seeker after final truths. He did not like the duty he was doing, and on the other hand, he could not shirk it. If he did not fear the dangers of combat, he loathed its suffering.

Having raised and trained the Eighteenth Infantry Regiment, he had not fought at its head during the Civil War, becoming diverted to the rearing of other regiments and other nonbattle assignments, which often means death to a career. No hard-charging fighter, Carrington was a first-rate builder of human organization as of the works that give it sustenance, security, and a future. Today he would be classified as a logistician.

The character study of Carrington is convincing. Yet Straight raises the question of whether Sherman truly trusted Carrington; if not, it is ironic that he entrusted him with a command that put his own credit at stake. Two men could not be less alike. Sherman had the look of an angry cockerel and delivered himself that way. He was dour, overdemanding, and unrelenting. Ice water ran in his veins. The personification of professionalism, he saw all things in terms of black and white, and he mistakenly believed that every soldier should be as hard as himself.

Carrington was gentle. For a soldier, much too gentle.

Five more days on the trail and the column arrived at Fort Reno, a run-down post not far from the headwaters of the Powder River and one hundred miles from Laramie via the Bozeman Trail. Two companies of badly demoralized militiamen had been manning it and they were overjoyed to be relieved. The very evening the regulars hit Reno, a band of Sioux raided the post and ran off some of the horses, a first signal that the expedition was being followed.

Carrington pared off one rifle company to overhaul and garrison the fort. Then after resting for a fortnight, the main body resumed the march, pushing uptrail another sixty-four miles, guided by the renowned Mountain Man, Jim Bridger.

On a grassy shelf not far from the fork where Little Piney Creek mets the Big Piney, Carrington found what he had been seeking. There the column pulled up and went into tent camp in mid-July.

Even today the site of Fort Kearny, just off the expressway between Buffalo and Sheridan, Wyoming, fascinates. It

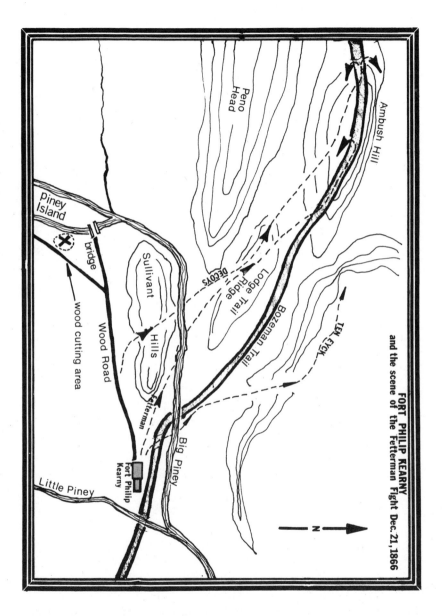

FORT PHILIP KEARNY
and the scene of the Fetterman Fight Dec. 21, 1866

Peno Head

Ambush Hill

Piney Island

bridge

Sullivant

Hills

DECOYS

Lodge Trail Ridge

Bozeman Trail

TEN EYCK

wood cutting area

Wood Road

Fetterman

Big Piney

Little Piney

Fort Philip Kearny

N

bespeaks that an infantry colonel had a shrewder appreciation of ground than most military engineers. No doubt the crossing of the Little Piney by the Bozeman Trail determined the general location, though that was rather incidental.

What caught Carrington's eye was the commanding placement of a subridge, standing about thirty feet above the flats to the east, west, and north. Agreeably even-surfaced for the most part, this feature is about three hundred yards long and seventy-five yards across. To the east, the subridge slopes out very gradually. From its crown, observation is unimpaired in all directions, the fields of fire are long and evenly sloped, with no dead space whatever. The closest natural cover was the line of cottonwoods along the Little Piney about six hundred yards to the east. For hostiles to approach the ground from any direction unobserved was next to impossible, though then as now the rise was surrounded by hayfields that billowed gently under a slight breeze.

With one exception, it was the ideal setting for a fort. The distance that had to be traveled to get useful timber was almost prohibitive, should there be continuing hostilities. The nearest stands of pine were about five miles away in a wholly different compartment of terrain, beyond an upland plateau, or meadow, next to the foot of the towering Bighorns. The track thereto spiraled up a twisting gulch that was densely overgrown with brush and stunted trees. Within that relatively short distance, one moved from prairie to mountain. For Carrington, that would be the critical testing area of operations. Without timber, Kearny could not be built or maintained.

The start was promisingly smooth. A logging and sawmill operation milling the plateau timber got underway unharassed. The building of the palisaded post was quickly begun. It was an ambitious project, almost thirty buildings including a bandstand, these to be fitted within an enclosed area approximately treble the size of a football field.

Fort Kearny, as it had come to be by mid-August,

looked stout enough to stand off a hostile force of almost any size. Hardly had it been raised and barricaded, however, when the Sioux staged their first night raid, running off about two hundred mules and horses, while shooting down five soldiers when the army pursued. During the thirty-day reprieve, the garrison had grown a little bit careless.

Thereafter, blow followed blow and incident piled upon incident. Whenever the Sioux saw a chance to hit and run, on the trails, against parties moving to and from the lumbering operation, or near the fort when cattle drovers or horse tenders relaxed vigilance, they killed and plundered. It was all-out war according to the peculiar pattern of the Plains Indian. Heavy toll was taken of the wagon trains that overhopefully had followed the army up the Bozeman Trail.

Although the incursions should have cried warning, Carrington held to his plan, whether because he underrated the incidents or felt that Washington would not tolerate weakness. In August two companies of the Eighteenth Regiment were detached and sent seventy miles deeper into hostile country. Their mission was to build and garrison the post that became known as Fort C. F. Smith, named after the general who took a long time dying at Shiloh. The attempt to shield the Bozeman Trail was thereby extended into Montana.

As a military enterprise, it made little sense. Over such distances as Carrington continued to pare down his main body, the several garrisons could not be mutually supporting. Should the Indians besiege any one of them while maneuvering in main strength along the flanks of the trail, the others would be as powerless to help as to safeguard migrants between one post and another. The forts intrinsically did not threaten the tribes; the challenge was real enough, but in practical effect, Carrington's operation merely immobilized that much military strength along the frontier. When soldiers take to cover, they yield to the other side the advantage of movement.

Here was simply an interesting example of professional overenterprise prior to the onrush of winter and before the extent of the danger had been truly measured. There was only one argument in favor of it. Beyond Fort C. F. Smith the trail ran on for 280 miles to Virginia City. All of that territory, however, was "Crow country," and the Crows not only tried to get along with the palefaces but fairly fawned on the army. It was reckoned that if the Laramie-to-Smith stretch of the Bozeman Trail could be made fairly safe for travel, the job would be almost done. The calculation was not unlike that of the report of a frontier jury, "Five of the bullets fired at the deceased had no effect, but the first one shot him dead."

By the time the first snows fell, all three forts—Reno, Kearny, Smith—were fairly snug. The constructions were almost complete, but not so the wood-cutting to keep the mess stoves and the barracks' hearths fueled. Tons of hay out of a countryside where hay more meets the eye than rocks and people, had been scythed and stored for the horses, mules, and cows. What had been done toward sustaining life for Plymouth Rocks and other poultry is not recorded.

With marked regularity the Sioux, who had never ceased watching from the nearby and almost barren ridges to the north, nor ceased lurking in the vales beyond, hit the wood-cutting parties and terrorized the harvesters during the haying season.

Before the onset of winter, the large herd of cattle had been cut to less than one hundred head. This vital statistic marks less the appetite of the garrison for prime ribs than the success of the Indians marauding off-base where cattle grazed. They killed and they scalped now and then as they ran off stock at every opportunity.

The load imposed on Carrington by his avowed enemies should have been more than enough for one man, though he was oddly accursed. As November opened, there arrived at

Kearny a company of cavalry, and with it, as a conspicuous attachment, came one captain of infantry, William J. Fetterman.

A member of the Eighteenth Regiment during the Civil War, he had served with outstanding gallantry and had been brevetted to light colonel. At times he had commanded.

Here should have come a jewel, a right bower on which Carrington might lean in emergency. It didn't work out that way.

Fetterman was bitten by what today is sometimes called the combat-hero syndrome. A hot-head and braggart, so certain of his muscle that it went to his mind, he not only had a contempt for Indians but loathed Carrington because he had not fought the war with his own regiment, whereas he, Fetterman, had been a steady battler up front.

Fetterman frequently boasted that he could take eighty soldiers and cut his way through the whole Sioux nation. It was always eighty and not seventy-nine or eighty-one, and the figure became quotable.

From the hour of Fetterman's arrival, the unity of the Kearny garrison began to fray. Until then, the crowd was seemingly devoted to the commander. Fetterman's ridiculing of Carrington for what he termed timidity won the ear of the malcontents of the command (there are always some), and they became his converts.

Carrington, having earlier overstretched his command, on second thought concluded that in view of the thinning out of forces, the poor condition of many of the firearms, the shortage of ammunition, and the aggressiveness of the Indians, the guardians of the Bozeman Trail had best go on the defensive to last out the winter.

It was perhaps the wisest decision he ever made, and his estimate of situation is beyond fault.

But then there was Fetterman, who was not only brazenly intimating that his commander was a coward but was asserting that with a few bold forays the troops could lift the siege.

For it had come to that: Fort Kearny was isolated. Since no one enjoys the condition, Fetterman grabbed by the ear every wishful thinker who believed that deliverance could be just around the corner. The lure of offensive action, ever tantalizing to most generals, is the largest booby trap in the path of soldiers.

To dwell on Fetterman for a moment longer, if unpleasant, may be pertinent. He was the very caricature of the army caste. Personifying militarism through his blustering foolhardiness, he obviously believed that shooting one's way out is the only practical solution. So thinking, his kind of soldier transforms war, which is ever a grave and terrible thing, into a mockery. Making black of white, defying authority, putting his personal interests above those of the people, Fetterman set forth to reaffirm a truth to which the centuries had provided few exceptions—that the losing of a war is most often the consequence of monumental blundering.

On the other hand, for whatever might go wrong at Fort Kearny, the army was bound to hold Carrington responsible. And in the strictest sense, the army would be right in so doing. There was a flaw in Carrington. He could have stopped the nonsense by placing Fetterman under arrest, charging him with insubordination or "conduct unbecoming." Either Carrington was afraid that putting down a popular fire-eater would further divide the garrison, or his hand was restrained by an untimely gentlemanliness.

At the time Fetterman began to buck Carrington, five tribes of Sioux were already arrayed in hostile camps along the Tongue River, which drains to the north above Fort Kearny. There they had been joined by bands of Arapaho and Cheyenne, said to be still thirsting to avenge Sand Creek. According to the Crow scouts, with some backing from the Mountain Man, Jim Bridger, not less than four thousand warriors were concentrated within a one-hour pony ride of the fort.

Whether the Indians could even count in four figures is unimportant. It was definitely the largest confrontation by Plains Indians until that hour, and there were far too many to be overrun or stampeded by eighty soldiers.

4

The March of the Wood Soldiers

╒╕╒╕╒╕╒╕╒╕╒╕╒╕╒╕╒╕

FORT Kearny's Achilles' heel was the wood supply operation that had to be kept going daily through the early weeks
of winter if there was to be fuel for warmth, bath water, and
the kitchens.

Here was the one weakness in the otherwise ideal location
of the post. Kearny had to be placed on relatively flat and
clear ground, close to an abundant water supply. But so lo-
cating it meant accepting the risk that the garrison could be
denied access to the nearest timberland in the foothills of the
Bighorns. The haul from cutting ground to post took at least
one hour in good weather. With winter fast closing, the garrison became increasingly dependent on that lifeline, priority
in wood-cutting operation until then having been given to
construction. There were too many things to be done and
too little time.

The Bozeman Trail passed within a stone's throw of the
community, running north of it across the same marge of

prairie, and from there angling northwestward. The road to the timber ran approximately west, then turned sharply south when it entered upon the high ground beyond sight from the fort. In the angle between the Bozeman Trail and the wood road, rose two smooth-sloped and rather barren ridge lines, the first of many such. The nearest one, named the Sullivant Hills in honor of Mrs. Carrington's family, overlooked the utility road and in fact dominated it from just off the reservation to the point where it turned and climbed. Beyond the Sullivant Hills within the triangle, rose the Lodge Trail Ridge, and though its closest slopes were only two miles away, it was normally rated off-limits for skirmish parties maneuvering to protect the wood train, the distance making it too dangerous.

Due to the pressing need for fuel, there could be no such easy avoidance of the close-by menace of the Sullivant Hills. While the ridge line was mostly barren with little or no rock and tree cover, the Indian mounted parties didn't need concealment, for the smooth slopes could be taken at a gallop in a straight run from the crest line to the utility road. Thus the raiders could swoop down on the wood wagons before a reaction force could clear the gate of the fort.

That is what they started doing in early December almost daily. Some hard actions were fought and a number of officers and men were killed or wounded. Yet the hostiles seemed to be less interested in going for an all-out kill against the wood parties, which were relatively small, than in practicing ambushing tactics with the use of human decoys to see how far they could draw forth a reaction body out of Kearny. It became a game in which the grand object must have been to determine how to lure the garrison into overextension, though Indians also got killed playing it.

Carrington's men were at first quite baffled by this business. So were other Americans when they came up against the same game—the use of human decoys—in Vietnam exactly one century later. They were certain they were witnessing something new under the sun. Yet the ruses used by the Sioux in the fighting under Red Cloud were identical with the stratagems employed by the Viet Cong to trap an overconfident platoon or company, time and again.

At the same time, the Sioux were overlooking a more obvious and decisive tactic. By concentrating war parties in strength on the wooded slopes of the approach to the pine land, they could have forced Carrington to fight all-out or to abandon Kearny.

During the feeling-out period as the two sides sparred lethally, each seeking a weakness in the other that might lead to larger undertakings, the exchanges built upward over the wood-hauling operation along the flat ground, with never an attempt to block access to the pine land in the foothills. It was all touch-and-go fighting rather than a studied pressure aimed literally to freeze out the garrison. When the wood wagons under attack called for help, a relief party left the barricade to counterattack, the decoys sought to draw the reaction force northward away from the utility road and into the Sullivant Hills, and occasionally succeeded. The bloodier incidents came of this venturing.

Both Carrington and Fetterman were getting pieces of the action. Fetterman, while fighting, was seeing no reason to change his mind that boldness only would beat the Sioux. Their persistent hit-and-run tactics further persuaded him. Carrington, on the fringes of several of the skirmishes, was thinking mainly of how to provide better protection for the all-important wood-hauling operation. Denied fuel, the dependent-encumbered garrison would be finished.

Carrington at last came up with a solution. The wood train would travel under a large cavalry escort. A lookout post would be mounted and outguarded daily on high ground overlooking the first ridge line. When a war party was observed heading toward the fort, the outpost would do the alerting and the escort party would get the signal. The forty or so wagons would form in a double, outward-facing oval, the escort soldiers to fire from within the protection of this enclosure. Carrington drilled the wagoners and guards in the making of this quick shift so that no time would be lost in its execution as the attack came on.

Far from being original tactics, although they are so described by some historians of the frontier, Carrington had done what comes naturally to the soldier with an instinct for making the best of a bad situation. His system duplicated the improvisations of John Zizka, the Hussite leader who fought a war against German nobles and their pikemen at the beginning of the fifteenth century. Zizka, who had been employed by the Belgian cities, adopted a rampart of wagons as the pivot of his tactics. The fortified wagon laager, called the "Wagenburg," became his contribution to tactics in a time when any explosion-propelled missile had a very short range. His armed men fired from within the protection of the barrier and his idea worked for quite a while. Still, it is highly unlikely that either Carrington or the westward-moving pioneers had ever heard of John Zizka when they too adopted the wagon laager.

Far from being impressed with Carrington's defensive creation even after it had been tried and proved sound, Fetterman viewed it as just another sign of weak, defensive thinking by his superior. In the company of a confederate, Captain F. H. Brown, the regimental quartermaster, Fetterman therefore moved to a showdown with Carrington. In their talk, he proposed a wild-eyed scheme by which he and Brown, leading a hundred troopers, would sally forth to wipe out all of the Sioux and other tribal lodges along the Tongue River. Face to face with a junior who he knew was undercutting him, Carrington must have felt tempted to laugh the proposal to scorn. Still, he held his temper and told the two to think it over and return with something more realistic.

So the face-up fizzled, where there might better have been fuss and fireworks. For the issue stayed unchanged; the garrison knew all about it and hence pride was still on parade.

Fetterman had to play the gallant plunger unto the end, and Carrington could not ignore that in the eyes of many of his soldiers, Fetterman was rapidly becoming a *beau sabreur*, the embodiment of the spirit unafraid. Carrington, while knowing that he was being cursed, could not bring himself either to discipline Fetterman or deny him the chance to play hero when the hour came that heroes were needed.

There being no real contest of wills, there was never a confrontation. The events of December 21 brought this unseemly rivalry to its almost inevitable climax.

The Indians struck hard against the wood train when it rolled forth to gather yule logs and crop foliage for Christmas wreaths. Carrington at once rallied a support force under the command of the steady cavalry leader, Captain James Powell. Before Powell was given time to measure the hostile pressure, Fetterman pressed Carrington to give him a hand in the game, and Carrington, his position assailed above all else by his own perplexity, yielded.

Fetterman was authorized to lead forth a mixed column of infantry and cavalry to reinforce Powell and complete the rescue of the wood train.

Even so, Carrington's limiting order to Fetterman was clear and unmistakable. There must be no headlong pursuit; yet allowance had to be made for the moral and tactical advantage that might be gained by a short pursuit.

Carrington said, "Relieve the wood train. Under no circumstances pursue the enemy beyond Lodge Trail Ridge."

In setting that boundary, Carrington was still giving the reinforcing column extraordinary latitude. It could range upwards of four miles beyond the palisade, which for infantry traversing hills is more than one hour's march. That would take it well beyond ready-support distance from the fort.

Carrington was so doubtful of Fetterman, and so concerned that the order not be misunderstood, that he followed him to the gate, where he repeated the stricture, and then passed it along to two of Fetterman's junior officers.

Until this point, Carrington's only fault was that out of

gentleness he had tolerated a brash and disloyal subordinate. It was a different matter when he then placed him in a position where lives were dependent on his judgment. Honor required no such concession. The extreme trials of the trail and of the defense had been Carrington's mainly for eight months, and he was an older man. Fetterman, through part of this time, had been coasting on his battle laurels. His position had as little virtue as that of the young bull challenging the herd sire. Defying authority, he had in no sense acted responsibly. Yet Carrington's own fortune would be riding on what Fetterman did with his life from here on out. The decision was a shocking command failure.

The wood-cutting party—about eighty men—had gone forth at 10:00 A.M. Just one hour later had come the alert.

There is no doubt that the tribes had set up for the big kill on this day. They had come on with a larger war party than ever before and a long line of mounted flankers serving as decoys. Yet at first, there had been no oblique maneuvering. The change necessarily called for a larger than usual reaction force and it should have prompted an extra measure of caution. Yet the signs were not read that way by Carrington.

Fetterman's rifle company had forty-eight enlisted men. To that contingent, Lieutenant George W. Grummond joined twenty-seven cavalrymen, making the total seventy-five. Captain Brown, Fetterman's henchman, rode up on a borrowed charger, saying that he would like a chance to kill another Indian before departing Fort Kearny. The armorer of the Eighteenth Regiment, Private Maddeon, showed up, rifle in hand, and volunteered to join the party. He was welcome and no one stood by to tell him nay. Then at the last minute, two civilian employes, James Wheatley and Isaac Fisher, begged to go. War veterans and sharpshooters both, they packed sixteen-round Henry rifles, which made them better armed than the troops that were still carrying Springfield muskets.

By these unbelievable flukes, Fetterman came up with his

magic number—the eighty men that he had said were all he needed to overrun and finish the whole Sioux nation. When the noses were counted, it might have been read as an omen, good or bad. Instead, it simply became the least credible line in a scenario already overloaded with fantasy.

Being senior to Captain Powell by date of commission, Fetterman demanded of Carrington that he be given command of all troops maneuvering outside of the stockade, and once again the colonel weakly let him have his way. He did not have to yield. There is no such absolute prerogative in the army. Had there been such, Fetterman would have commanded automatically. Further, Carrington himself could have retained command.

Fetterman's column got away from the gate before Grummond's cavalry was ready. Instead of leading it to the beleaguered wagon party, Fetterman struck off for the far side of the Sullivant Hills, with the seeming object of getting on the Sioux line of retreat and thereby hastening the Indian withdrawal. With foot soldiers against mounted men, that was such an extra-high hope as to be a direct violation of Carrington's order to relieve the wagon train. Carrington this while had been preoccupied with a small hostile party that had forayed to within easy howitzer-range of the fort, and had paid no attention to Fetterman. He was helping to adjust the fire of the guns. Grummond and the cavalry had galloped on to overtake the infantry.

After the disappearance of these troops within the first hour, Carrington's concern swung back in their direction with the realization that the committed units were without surgical help. He sent forth the assistant post doctor, C. M. Hines, with a half-squad escort, on a mounted mission to join the force afield. By noon, Hines, an amazing enterpriser for one of his calling, came galloping back to report that he had reconnoitered as far as the crest of Lodge Trail Ridge, could find no sign of the Fetterman force, and that the valley of the Little Bighorn beyond swarmed with armed and mounted warriors. Here was a feat deserving of the Medal of Honor, although Dr. Hines, one of the legitimate heroes of the day, did not get it.

By the time of his return, the attack on the wood wagons had ended in a withdrawal by the Indians. That information, coupled with what Hines reported, must have signified to Carrington that somewhere among the ridges to northward the bag had opened, a large part of his garrison had charged in, and then the bag had closed on a body of troops fighting blind. If he did not reach this dismal conclusion, having heard nothing from the Fetterman force, at least his reaction reflects that this was his assumption.

At once he ordered Captain Tenedor Ten Eyck to take his fifty-four-man company out on a great curving sweep to the northward that would carry them past the Bozeman Trail and well beyond where Fetterman had been authorized to go. It had to be a decision based upon intuitive grasp of the desperation of the situation. By this move, the already depleted garrison became so critically thinned down that the fort defense was without hope if the tribes were arrayed to come on against it in main strength.

As it worked out, Red Cloud and the Indian tacticians had not thought that far through their problem. They were clever in staging a relatively simple deception, but like most primitives could not plan on a grand scale. Or maybe it was instinctive with them that when they brought off a smash victory, they had to celebrate and ceremonialize. Fort Kearny was wide open through that afternoon and they did not come on. To that extent, Carrington's gamble paid off, though on second thought he had sent another forty soldiers to beef up Ten Eyck's party.

Ten Eyck, who was no man's fool, marched his column almost due north, crossing the Bozeman Trail well to the east of the line that Fetterman's force had taken. He then led it up the outer slope of the easternmost ridge, which gave him a good line of retreat. That placed him at least three miles to

the east of where Fetterman had probably met doom, and he
needed all that distance to be sure of conserving his force.

As his men moved upward to the scarp, they could hear
some sounds of shooting to the west, though the sounds died
before they surmounted the crest. There, looking down into
the valley, Ten Eyck could see hundreds of Indians dancing
about. They in turn saw the company standing clear on the
ridge line and they taunted the soldiers to come down and
fight. Ten Eyck would have none of that.

The mass of Indians gradually thinned out as many of them
took the trail to the westward. Straining their eyes, the soldiers thought they saw prone white figures lying around the
edges of the trail and guessed that they were the bodies of
Fetterman's men. Yet there remained at least two thousand warriors in between. At dusk, the last band of Indians having
cleared away, Ten Eyck cautiously moved down the ridge
and led his men to the battlefield.

Fetterman's and Grummond's men were all dead; most of
the bodies had been stripped, scalped, and mutilated. Ten
Eyck had forty-nine of the bodies loaded into the wagons
he had brought along up the Bozeman Trail, and most of the
forms were already so grotesquely transfixed by death and
the extreme cold that it was difficult to handle them. Dark
closed and ended the search. That the Ten Eyck column got
back undamaged is another mark of Indian inconsistency
rather than mercy. But Ten Eyck had done quite a job.

Fetterman and Brown, the two senior officers, had met
death by shooting themselves. That is known because of the
nature of the wounds. Obedient to orders, Captain Powell
had brought his company back after reaching the top of
Lodge Trail Ridge; he had saved his men from Fetterman's
frenzied clutch by the simple expedient of lagging behind.
The other eighty soldiers, led by Grummond's cavalry right
on the heels of the decoys, had gone whooping on to their

doom. But Powell had lost sight of them before they reached the Bozeman Trail.

About how the trap was sprung, men may only speculate, according to the mute evidence to be found on the field, along with what was said much later by some of the Indians who fought that day.

The Bozeman Trail itself was used as the cul-de-sac. When the decoys suddenly separated, their ponies darting to right and left of the trail, that became the signal. Thousands of warriors who had lain concealed in the tall grass on either side of the trail sprang up, confronting the soldiers from all around; and then they came on, using their weapons in an ever-tightening attack. Although only a fraction was fire-armed, at that short range the arrow was as deadly as the bullet. Grummond had charged on ahead of Fetterman's infantry; his troopers were separately surrounded and killed, Grummond being the first to die. The signs read that the two civilians, Wheatley and Fisher, had fought back more powerfully than anyone else, piling up braves around about them with their quick-firing Henry rifles. When the battlefield was at last policed, more than sixty frozen pools of blood were found around their bodies. The Indians had riddled Fisher's body with 105 arrows.

From the start, it was still a futile resistance, one that could only end in massacre, and in which no quarter was to be expected. The fight must have gone just as the Indians planned it and could not have lasted more than half an hour. The eighty bodies were strung out over several hundred yards of trail space.

As Carrington well realized, the loss and shock to the garrison made the situation at Fort Kearny desperate, if not hopeless, should Red Cloud and the other chiefs determine on an extermination campaign and lay siege with all forces. He directed that the women and children would repair to the powder magazine in the event of an attack. Should the fight be lost at the final barricade, he himself would blow the magazine. Yet if Carrington seemed to behave like a man badly frightened, other acts show that he was remarkably self-possessed.

Late that same grim night, before he had seen the field or recovered the last of the bodies, Carrington wrote out his battle report and an anxious request for reinforcement. A civilian scout, John (Portugee) Phillips, volunteered to carry it to Fort Laramie, 236 miles away, though the weather had turned bitter cold and a blizzard was bearing down on the Bighorns. Carrington gave Phillips his own thoroughbred charger, though he thought he was sending horse and rider to their deaths; that presentiment proved to be only half right. Before Phillips was well started, the temperature was sub-zero and still falling. Four nights later at Fort Laramie, it was 25° below. That was when Phillips arrived, his fingers, ears, and cheeks frozen, his buffalo-hide clothing caked with ice.

He staggered into the BOQ, where the Christmas ball was going, gasped out the terrible news from Fort Kearny, handed Carrington's written message to the commander, Colonel Palmer, and collapsed on the floor.

No other feat of courage and endurance by man and mount begins to match this one. The thoroughbred died the following day and Phillips spent months in the hospital. A cavalry mount at walk-trot can do about thirty miles in one day. Phillips had doubled that. Either the thoroughbred had been at extended canter part of the time, which would have risked foundering, or Phillips had not quitted the saddle except to relieve himself or feed the animal.

Next morning, Carrington's message to Brigadier General Philip Cooke at Omaha was put on the wire at Fort Laramie, "Give me two companies of cavalry at least forthwith or four companies of infantry. Promptness will save the line but our killed show that remissness will result in mutilation and butchery beyond precedent. Promptness is the vital thing."

The March of the Wood Soldiers

Yet there need not have been this pressure, and the extreme agonies of Phillips had been largely wasted. The Indians did not renew the attack, and though Carrington did not yet know it, all of the lodges were gone from along the Tongue River.

The tribes had had their victory, the army had paid dear for the commission's trickery at Fort Laramie in the spring, and further, the fury of the elements and the scarcity of food made it impossible for the chiefs to hold together the assembly any longer.

There was a mass burial at Fort Kearny on Christmas Day. A more mournful time and scene for such a service is not to be imagined. It filled the cup to overflowing. In the five months since the fort had been laid out, Carrington had lost 145 men, killed trying vainly to safeguard the Bozeman Trail.

Of what had happened, or might be happening, to the reinforced company at Fort C. F. Smith, Carrington had no notion. Conceivably, it no longer existed. That post was wholly shut off from the world and no news came through, then or later in the winter.

Although he was as yet unaware, however, Carrington's trials in the region were almost over. Immediately upon getting the message requesting help, General Cooke had wired his reply to Fort Laramie, "Colonel Carrington is hereby relieved. Colonel Henry Wessels is hereby appointed. Four companies of the Eighteenth Infantry and two companies of the Second Cavalry will proceed to Fort Kearny as soon as weather permits. Colonel Carrington will return at once to Fort Sedgwick."

The speed with which Cooke reacted bespeaks that he was looking for a scapegoat. Had he relieved Carrington out of a belief that he had lost his nerve, Cooke would hardly have reinforced with more troops than Carrington requested.

With sixty soldiers for an escort and all of the dependents

going along in wagons, Carrington marched east over the trail in early January. His resentment of Cooke burned deep, especially because the timing of the action implied that he was responsible for Fetterman's folly. Historians usually wax indignant that he was treated so shabbily. Yet he was far from blameless. Not only had he withheld from any real attempt to control Fetterman, he had in fact capitulated to him in an hour of extreme danger. Knowing that Fetterman was both reckless and disobedient, he had entrusted him with several hundred lives, counting the wagon party and Powell's company. As a commander, Carrington was all bug and no lightning.

General Cooke, who had been fighting Indians for more than thirty years, had grown old and sour. General Sherman, who had estimated that Fort Kearny would be quite safe for women and children, being in no position to reprimand himself for his miscalculation, soon took the occasion to sack Cooke. His departure made Carrington partisans feel a mite better without in any degree easing the problem along the Bozeman Trail.

On first hearing of the fatal charge that wiped out Fetterman's column, General Sherman, true to his nature, again used the word "extermination," said that it was time for the army to go after the Sioux "vindictively," and spelled it out as meaning that ten Indian lives should be taken for every soldier killed.

By way of contrast, while there was a loud to-do in the Congress and in other official quarters, press and public were not stunned and did not bay for vengeance. Not only had the nation become sated on bloodshed and violence during the Civil War, there was a widespread discontent with the government's Indian policy, arising less from sympathy for the tribes than from the feeling that by their rivalry, separate approaches, and crossed purposes, the War Department and the Indian Bureau of the Interior Department were largely to blame for the inflammation of the frontier. While there was some truth in this plaint, it was by no means the whole truth. It was clear enough, however, that the political parties intensified the heat by making the subject a partisan issue.

Even while General U. S. Grant was still the No. 1 soldier of the nation, with Sherman serving as his Chief of Staff, the army that he had led to victory was already suffering a sharp decline in public favor because of the unwanted war in the West. The common soldier who had lately saved the nation had that quickly ceased to be a popular hero. In fact, he became nigh an object of scorn. A change in the national mood not unlike that which occurred exactly one century later, it was not better reasoned or any more logical.

5

Marching Through Indians

౼౼౼౼౼౼౼౼౼౼

WHILE sensing the radical change in the public emotion, General Sherman was no more disposed to buck it than to back away from his overextended operation in Montana Territory. It was time to straddle, time to take a softer tone while keeping in mind the object, however difficult.

Sherman had committed himself to the winning of the West. That small operational setbacks would occur was part of the game. Having made up his mind as to what the nation should be seeking, he did not deviate because a plan of his own making went awry. The burden of such resolution is not infrequently made a grim trial to subordinates.

Lieutenant Colonel Henry W. Wessels, who had taken over the command from Carrington, must have sighed with relief when the reinforcing companies arrived at Kearny via the trail. Too quickly he learned that their arrival had compounded his problems. There were that many more bodies to feed and the cupboard was bare. Within the military, logistics should never be the enemy of logic.

Although no Sioux warriors had come against Fort Kearny in the interim, the events of December had left a permanent chill on its garrison. Staying immobile and buttoned up, the people ran out of fire logs long before the winter was through.

Such was the trickle of supply coming over the trail from Fort Reno that clothing gave out and food became rationed pitilessly. The remaining animals, hayless and grainless, starved and died. Bootless soldiers ate horsemeat and likely gave no thanks.

Due to the scant and unbalanced diet, the troops were hit by scurvy and the nonduty figures grew larger day by day. Morale, like the weather, stayed just a few degrees above zero.

With the onset of the first spring thaws, the Sioux reappeared and resumed their harassing attacks against the fort. It was small stuff and strictly pestilential, aimed at intimidating rather than alarming.

Even so, a column of these hard-pressed men from Kearny, nursing their miseries, went over the trail to see if anything or anyone was left at Fort C. F. Smith, which had been unheard from since the onset of winter. It cannot be said in fairness that the whole nation was anxiety-ridden about the fate of troops at C. F. Smith. The whole nation never becomes that much concerned about anything.

To their delight, or more probably to their disgust, the rescuers from Fort Kearny found the garrison at C. F. Smith not only unhurt but in prime health. Soldiers, like other people in adversity, do not like to learn that while getting all the sweat, they have been persuaded to worry about the wrong things.

The mess sergeant at Fort Smith was a genius of sorts. By purchase at the mines, he had put away large stores of cabbages, potatoes, and other vegetables designed by nature for the balanced diet that would ward off scurvy. This wizard knew how to make sauerkraut with corned beef and to prepare other antiscorbutic dishes. Although few mess sergeants are pinned with medals, the deservingness of this one is beyond question.

Throughout the tail end of winter and the months of spring, Forts Kearny, Reno, and Smith stayed virtually besieged. The Sioux and the Cheyenne kept the Bozeman Trail blocked, raiding or ambushing any parties that tried to move thereon, while at the same time pestering the army garrisons. The strong points were much too far apart to be mutually supporting. Self-evidently, Sherman's plan did not suit the situation. The next question was whether the hostiles were sufficiently war-wise to exact the proportionate payment for his mistaken judgment.

The tribes were set on hitting the Bozeman installations another main blow, but among the chiefs there was divided counsel about where and how to do it. Neither side would yield, and in the end both had their way through a splitting of forces.

A force of about five hundred warriors, mainly Cheyenne, attacked Fort Smith on August 1. Three miles northeast of the post proper, in a ripe meadow, a haying detail of six civilian employees guarded by nineteen soldiers was earning its pay when this horde came whooping on. At hand was a corral of heavy logs where the mules stayed penned while the haying was done. The twenty-five men ran for the cover of this breastwork and opened fire. In one other thing, fortune favored these heroes. One week earlier, some Springfield rifles, redesigned to make them breechloading, had arrived at Smith. In the hands of the hayers and the soldiers, that new weapon became a countersurprise.

For two hours, the Cheyenne pressed the attack, using their full bag of tricks: circling, setting the grass afire, riding up at an angle while clinging to the far side of the pony—they called it "squaw riding"—and firing under the neck, and charging straight on in a body. Toward the end, they dismounted and tried to wiggle forward as skirmishers. Nothing worked; the corral defense stayed solid. By the end, dead and bleeding Indians had ruined not a little of the hay, with a loss to the defense of three men killed and three wounded, to say nothing of the losses among the mules.

Lieutenant Colonel L. P. Bradley, who commanded at Fort Smith, could hear the sounds of this fight. Urged by his juniors to send a relief column, he refused, closed the gate of the fort, and ordered his men to stand by and defend the barricade. For so doing, he was scorned by some of his people, and later, by many writers. Yet he suspected that the attack on the corral was only an opening gambit toward drawing out a larger force that would be ambushed, and he was no doubt right about it. The Indians acted as if they were conducting a sideshow; by staying on and risking more, they could have exhausted the defenders' ammunition. When it became obvious that the garrison would not stir, they drew off. It all supports the idea that their aim was for bigger game.

Exactly this same ruse was used many times, with occasional success, one hundred years later by the enemy in Vietnam. Sometimes it worked. The Ia Drang Valley, Dong Tre, and Toumorong are among the places where it was tried.

The action, thereafter known as the Hayfield Fight, which titling did not require much imagination, was a small and satisfying success, much needed by the soldiers strung out along the Bozeman Trail.

Exactly one day later Red Cloud, in person, and more than a thousand warriors moving under him, struck at Kearny. The target was the familiar ground, the woodcutting area six miles to the west of the post. The defenders were the woodcutters and their rifle-armed protectors. The scenario differs from the play in the hay field only in the details of the mise-en-scène.

But in command at the spot was the superior soldier, Captain Powell, the one leader who had kept his head and obeyed orders on the day that Fetterman would have destroyed his company also.

There had been dropped at the logging ground about

77

fourteen wagon boxes so that the vehicles might haul more and larger timber. The boxes had been formed in an oval for defense. The thin wood panels were protection against arrows, and while not stopping bullets, would deflect them. It may seem a small point. Such is the nature of the military rifleman, however, that he feels tenfold safer if he is firing from behind a small sapling than if he is exposed nakedly in the open. Because of that added sense of security, instead of surrendering to fear and cowering uselessly, he will make good use of his weapon.

Although Powell might not have thought this idea through, he did everything right. There were thirty-two men with him. They jumped to within the protection of the wagon boxes as the Sioux came on. It is reported that he said to them, "Men, here they come. Take your places and shoot to kill!" No eloquence there, in fact nothing but stilted and imprecise phrases, which suggests that the words were dreamed up later.

The wood-chopping detachment was beautifully set to do just what Powell had ordered. In fact, it was better off than if it had been occupying earthworks. Flattened out within the wagon boxes, each fighter could hear and feel the ready support at his rear and on either side, a condition that stimulates action and keeps down panic. Furthermore, within the protection of the boxes, the defenders could regroup at will to that quarter from which the main threat came at any stage of the fight. Within the oval were already disposed cases of ammunition, bags of grain, cordwood, yokes, and other harness that could be used for revetment.

Undetected earlier, the Sioux in numbers uncountable had come charging down from the ridges to the north about two hours after dawn, at the time when Powell and his people were about to close on the wagon box field, and another escort party, covering a log train full-loaded, was ambling back to the fort. Instead of staying concentrated, the Sioux split and went after both detachments—thereby reaching for too much and losing most of the initial advantage of surprise. Hard embattled, the wagon train made it to the fort, and its fight alerted the garrison. In the attack at the logging ground, the Sioux ran off the mule herd, while Powell, though rushed and harassed, got his people deployed within the wagon boxes without loss.

The opening assault was the familiar ride-around by a circle of ponies, perhaps five hundred of them. The Indians, clinging to the far side of their mounts, were hardly to be seen, and their aim was highly erratic. The main sacrifice was that of good horseflesh.

It proved to be a stupid maneuver, though it was based upon a reasonable expectation. The warriors had reckoned that after a first volleying by muzzleloaders worked from behind the boxes, there would then be a cessation of fire during reloading. In that break, they would charge and overrun the boxes. The pause never came. The defenders were armed with the same remodeled, breechloading Springfields that had saved the haying party at Fort Smith the day before.

It was this one weapon that made all of the mounted Sioux draw off, their plan aborted, their early confidence shaken. More than that, having won the first round, and finding the Springfield good, the defenders were proportionately heartened, though one officer and two enlisted men had been killed. Not the circling warriors but snipers, firing within easy range of the boxes from the lip of a rear bank, had taken this toll.

Red Cloud had been watching the assault from a safe distance. When the mounted attack failed, he called a council of war. The decision was made to try again with the warriors moving as foot skirmishers. The assault would be mounted out of the defiladed ground where the banks had protected the snipers.

The horde came on in a wedge-shaped mass so tightly bunched that its leaders, while working their weapons, masked the weapons of those that followed. This was not skirmishing; presenting the broadest kind of target, it threw away every advantage of ground to be had by hundreds of men crawling in an ever-widening circle and wiggling forward on their bellies.

By shifting all of his people to one side of the oval, Powell could so mass fire against that human tide as to make every bullet count. The slaughter of the attackers, moreover, required little marksmanship. The field was quite level and barren of boulders or brush. Even so, the wagon box ring was almost overwhelmed. When at last the mass of Sioux broke and ran, there were dead Indians within five feet of the barricade.

They did not try again and they had not tried very wisely in either attempt. During those minutes when the dismounted horde pressed forward, a large mounted band waited immobile beside Red Cloud. Had that cavalry been loosed against the other side of the wagon box oval at the high tide of the infantry assault, Powell and his small detachment would probably have been overrun.

Yet Red Cloud looked on and made no move. The outcome indicated that while the most formidable tactician among the Plains Indians chieftains had a sharp talent for ambushing, he could not comprehend how to move against a stoutly held defensive position. In fact, the necessary balance between offensive action and defensive security in the conduct of war as a principle wholly eluded the Indian imagination.

Somewhere around noon, a relief column from the fort, with a howitzer in tow, got through to Powell. Seeing this piece of ordnance, the Sioux who had lingered longest dashed for the hills and were soon out of range.

In the action that not unnaturally came to be known as the Wagon Box Fight, Powell lost three men killed and two wounded. The siege had gone almost five hours, with two periods of intense pressure. Upwards of fifteen hundred warriors had been repulsed by a handful of soldiers and loggers. About one-tenth of the attackers had been killed, it was

MASTER OF THE BATTLEFIELD—CHIEF JOSEPH.

Too gentle for command—
Colonel Carrington.

Like an angry cockerel—
W. T. Sherman.

AN INFLATED REPUTATION—
CHIEF RED CLOUD.

SCENE OF THE WAGON BOX FIGHT. The monument is within a few feet of where Powell made his stand. In the background are the Big Horns.

U. S. Army

U. S. Signal Corps, National Archives

THE MIGHTY HUNTER—
GENERAL CROOK.

THE INDISPENSABLE MAN—
GEORGE A. CUSTER.

BAD MEDICINE FOR WHITES—
CHIEF SATANTA.

THE CUSTER 1874 EXPEDITION IN THE BLACK HILLS.

BATTLE OF LITTLE BIG HORN.
The romanticized scene by the artist, Fuchs.

LUCKIER THAN CUSTER—
JOHN GIBBON.

THE CAREFUL OPERATOR—
NELSON A. MILES.

No great claimer—Chief Gall.

SCOUT CURLY WHO SPREAD THE NEWS.

THE MEDICINE SHOW MAN—SITTING BULL.

SOME OF CROOK'S SOLDIERS
RESTING AFTER SLIM BUTTES.

THE PINE RIDGE AGENCY CAMP IN 1890.

THE CUT BANKS at the northeast corner of the Bear's Paw Battlefield, Snake Creek here being at its widest. In midfield it is trenched more deeply.

CAUGHT NODDING AT BIG HOLE—
CHIEF LOOKING GLASS.

MEMBERS OF BIG FOOT'S BAND of Hunkpapa Sioux shortly before Wounded Knee.

THE BEAR'S PAW BATTLE as imagined by a contemporary artist working for *Harper's Weekly*. The ridge lines are not this rough and no soldier would have dared to fire while standing on the sky line.

THE FIELD OF WOUNDED KNEE.

roughly reckoned, there being no official body count in those days.

If the blow was not enough to alter the balance of power along the Bozeman Trail, it at least had for the army that fresh, sweet smell of success, evening the score for the Fetterman thing and causing morale to soar.

Nothing more important, however, was to come of that. The political wind was again shifting.

In the summer of 1867 the Congress passed a well-intentioned resolution, calling for peacemaking with the tribes and pledging an effort to settle the Indian problem with justice to all.

While today that reads like a piece of pie in the sky, on July 20 President Johnson approved an act toward this end, appointing a high-level, seven-man commission to get on with the task. The bill required that three general officers be named to the body of peacemakers, striking a balance with three civilian big wheels. Lieutenant General Sherman and Brigadiers A. H. Terry and W. S. Harney were initially named. Then a third brigadier, C. C. Augur, was added so that the military would never be outvoted.

Why Andrew Johnson so acted, history makes perfectly clear. He was unreservedly committed to the building of the transcontinental railroad. If Government could not insure a tranquil right-of-way through truce negotiations with the hostile tribes, then the army must continue to fight forward of the advancing rail lines.

Though Sherman at times doubted that the grand object could be achieved during his lifetime, he saw eye-to-eye with Johnson as to the endeavor. In fact, Sherman had talked to the rail chiefs well before this time and they had won him over. He was prepared to make guarding of the railheads the army's No. 1 priority, and if that venture meant crushing the tribes and eliminating the buffalo, so be it.

Soon after the Hayfield and Wagon Box fights, the commission headed west. Much of its traveling through hostile country was done on the riverboat, *St. John's*. In mid-September, it began calling on the belligerent chiefs to repair and negotiate. For all of two months, the results were not only sterile but affronting. The chiefs boycotted the meetings, sending messages that they were too busy to powwow, a hardly unintentional slight to the seven dignitaries. Well beyond biting his lip, Harney became so riled that he asked Sherman how many troops it would take to smash the tribes in the Powder River country once and for all.

Harney got no better comfort when the commissioners sounded out the commanders of the Bozeman Trail garrisons. They could give him no such estimate, and while they did not despair of lasting through the winter, their garrisons, they said, were no more capable of keeping the Bozeman Trail open than before.

Sherman then realized that the game was up. His plan for opening up Montana Territory had been tried only to fail. Continuing the fight on that line would bring no peace, and in his new role he still had an obligation: Though Red Cloud had won his war, the war wasn't everything. The Union Pacific had notified the army that unless more protection was provided, construction would have to be suspended. So first things had to be put first.

One officer from the Fort Kearny garrison had already talked to a gathering of chiefs about what terms they would make if the Bozeman forts were abandoned. For the field army, this was a form of insurance. Knowing that peace was in the air, the tribes would be less aggressive through the winter.

So it happened, and in the following spring the Peace Commission returned to Fort Laramie to sign a treaty with the several tribes of Sioux and the Arapaho. By its terms the tribes agreed to take as a reservation that half of the present South Dakota that lies to the west of the Missouri River. The signed paper further pledged to cede them as a permanent and exclusive hunting ground the wilderness country beyond the North Platte and Republican rivers "so long as the buffalo range there in numbers" to make the chase worthwhile. While that sounded like a generous concession, it implied that once the herds were gone, the tribes were doomed to the reservation. And in fact, Generals Sherman and Sheridan saw this as the critical line of attack: Kill off the bison, and the Plains Indians would have no hold on the old way of life.

Chief Red Cloud did not appear for the signing and he would not agree to respect the treaty as long as any soldiers remained in the Bozeman Trail forts. That he was skeptical of the worth of all such papers was a measure of his wisdom. Furthermore, as many of the tribesmen held with him as held with the chiefs who had made the treaty.

The army at last gave up on the forts by an order signed on May 19, directing their evacuation. By midsummer the garrisons were gone.

The buildings and barriers were ablaze almost before the troops were beyond the horizon, not because a stay-behind detachment had fired them, but because the tribes were waiting to dance around the torched timbers. There remained to mark the site only ashes and the cemeteries.

With the landscape returned to its former primal look, or nearly so, and the Bozeman Trail closed, Red Cloud came to Fort Laramie to sign a treaty that would close out the war. His only such appearance, he probably wished to savor the full flavor of a military victory that was not more complete than transient.

By the treaty, he pledged that he would never make war again. The Government, for its part, promised that the Bighorn country would be regarded as unceded Indian land, forbidden ground to white settlers, an exclusive hunting ground for the tribes that had fought to save it.

Red Cloud kept his promise never to make war again. Not only did he bury the hatchet for good, he was given to writing letters to the editor in praise of himself as a man of peace.

Nothing said of him, however, is intended to imply that he was a gentle soul. Far from it. Once when warring on the Utes, Red Cloud saw that a brave, trying to cross the stream on a wounded horse was about to drown. He jumped his pony into the stream, pulled the Ute ashore, and scalped him. On another occasion, he killed an Indian stripling just before running off the horse herd he was tending.

Because of Red Cloud's abstention from war, other Indians accused him of going soft and being a runaway when once again hostilities arose over possession of the same countryside for which he had fought. That did him scant justice. Earlier than most, he had sensed the futility of the struggle; there was too much strength, too much grasping power in the white man to be resisted. He advised the tribes to note well the white man's example and follow it.

This is what he said, "You must begin anew and put away the wisdom of your fathers. You must lay up food and forget the hungry. When your house is built, your storeroom filled, then look around for a neighbor whom you can take advantage of and seize all he has."

While these may not be the most contemptuous words ever spoken of the American way of life, they are worth nominating for the prize. If there were not something in them, they would not have been handed down. They were uttered by a chief whose character was generally respected throughout the frontier a full century before the national conscience became stricken over how the land had been misused, its resources overexploited, its waters and atmosphere polluted, its shorelines greased with crude oil. Red Cloud may not have been the personification of the Noble Red Man. But he possessed some wisdom, and his portrait has appeared on more dust jackets and calendars than any Indian in history.

Two years after the event at Fort Laramie, President Grant and the Congress, in effect, washed out the treaty provisions and the tentative approach to conciliation that had come of Red Cloud's war. The change in policy was not abrupt and absolute, and it had the merit of doing away with past pretensions. Thereafter, none of the tribes was to be treated as sovereign or to be acknowledged as the rightful and titular possessor of a homeland within the national boundary.

The treaty system was renounced. The new law prohibited any future treaty-making with Indian tribes. They would be dealt with as wards of the government. That was how it had been done in practice all along, but at last it was out in the open. Although the term was not in use at the time, the Indian had been voted a second-class citizen.

As for what it contributed to the well-being of the tribes and the tranquility of the frontier, the new order of things was neither better nor worse than what had preceded. More wars were inevitable, the conflict of interest being unalterable. The Western settler wanted stability and security; the Plains Indian still fought for the right to range where he pleased. There was no common ground, no prospect of compromise.

All that followed virtually had to be, although historians are loath to acknowledge that perfect and final solutions of life's larger problems are seldom, if ever, possible.

To put the policy, problem, and military programing of that time in the clearest perspective, however, it must be reemphasized that making the trails more secure by clearing away the hostiles or protecting and tranquilizing the frontier were not in themselves the primary interest of the Peace Commission or the main mission of the field army.

General Sherman's own writings say plainly enough that the governing consideration was the safeguarding and advancement of private enterprise. The railroad was certainly not a national property. Speaking of the discussions of the seven men as they toured the West aboard the *St. John's*,

Sherman wrote, "We all agreed that the nomad Indian had to be removed from the vicinity of the two great railroads then in rapid construction, and be localized on one or other of the two great reservations south of Kansas and north of Nebraska."

The Iron Horse had begun its invasion of Plains Indian country in 1865 as the Civil War ended. Thereafter the White House attached such importance to the continent-spanning rail project that whatever stood in its way had to be swept aside. Although Sherman went along enthusiastically, his real motive is called into question by his own language. He had highly favored the construction of the two rail lines thrusting westward toward the Rockies because these parallel roads would "prove fatal to the game and consequently fatal to them [the Indians]." This is spoken like a ruthless warrior who viewed the railroads as an exterminating machine rather than a humanitarian regretting that the march of progress necessitated the displacement of the tribes.

The reasoning which caused Sherman and the military to bed down with the railroad builders, while eminently non-conservationist if not barbarous, was at the same time politically astute. Everyone was biting on the same bullet, and the army was in fact a little slower than the American public to warm to the new love affair with the railroaders.

It was a peculiar age. To the average American, the most glamorous and exciting adventure of the time was the thrust to span the nation coast to coast with iron rails. The linking of East and West had captured the national imagination in a way that the far more critical problem of reuniting North and South could not.

The constructors, the lifters of ties, and the drivers of spikes, had become the greater heroes of the decade. The survey parties and the thin screen of soldiers detailed to protect them, though many were veterans of the Civil War, were pretty much the Forgotten Men.

Yet the hardship, danger, and sacrifice were mainly theirs.

There weren't enough soldiers to provide adequate protection. Their worst enemy was not the mountain massif or an untoward twisting in the river channel. They were hit time and again by Sioux, Cheyenne, and Arapaho on the warpath, and the marauders, who vanished with surprising suddenness, left behind a litter of dead surveyors and soldiers, with a few wounded now and then who lived to tell how it had happened. The raiders did not dare to attack the main track-laying crews. They were too heavily guarded. Not having enough troops to cover all points sufficiently, the army fixed undue risk on the pathfinders.

The advance of the rails toward link-up was followed with enwrapped attention by the American people, while the fighting off the flanks by the field army was regarded casually as an almost unrelated and not particularly important sideshow. The popular songs of the day had as their themes railroad building, while ignoring the bloody struggle to secure the frontier. Wrote Joaquin Miller, the Bard of the Sierras, "There is more poetry in the rush of a single railroad train across the continent than in all the gory story of burning Troy." Bret Harte was not far behind. When Harte, the greatest of American parodists, started a new magazine, the device he chose for its cover to symbolize progress was a railroad track.

Still more extraordinary was the underreaction of the Plains tribes to the steam-powered encroachment. The railway track and the system thrusting it forward were their main adversary, and not simply because it doomed the bison along the frontier. The chief appeal to the big-time investors promoting the construction was that they would multiply their fortunes by grabbing Indian lands along the right-of-way. That, more than the prospect of traffic to be carried, made the speculation attractive. Yet the Indian responded to the advance of the Iron Horse as if bewitched, benumbed, and bewildered.

At the time that Union Pacific construction terminated

temporarily around the forks of the Platte River, there occurred one violent incident significant above all others. A band of Cheyenne, brooding over its miseries, and blaming them on the white invasion, launched an attack of the railroad.

The operation was begun with a crudely rigged derailment, a log tied rail to rail. The first conveyance to come down the track was a handcar. It hit the log, bounced high in the air, and as it overturned, the five members of the maintenance crew ran for dear life. Run down by the Cheyenne who were waiting in ambush, they were scalped.

Using the implements on the handcar, the Indians next lifted the spikes on one section of rail, pulled up the ties, and heating the rail, bent it. Along came a freight. The locomotive ditched as it hit the gap, and the cars piled up. The one crew member not killed in the wreck was tomahawked. The cargo was plundered. What the Cheyenne could not carry away on their ponies was littered over the prairie. So ended a day of high adventure, from which the Indians learned nothing.

A startling success, the raid stands out only for the reason that it was so wholly exceptional and was not thereafter followed up. The Indian mind was incapable of understanding the principle that warfare, when properly conducted, is primarily an attack on lines of communication. The wisest battle leaders among the tribes thought of war as a contest, with the sole object the overcoming of living things, the killing and capture of people, the running off of horse herds and mule trains. Because of this blind spot, the vulnerable railways, tracking through the heart of Indian country, were given a grant of immunity when protection over the route was beyond possibility. The Indians were lacking in that kind of judgment, deplored by Justice Brandeis, that leads a man to step in front of a locomotive.

At the time the Peace Commission made its Western tour, Union Pacific construction had reached Cheyenne at the eastern edge of the Rockies, well on its way to the juncture with Central Pacific construction coming from the Pacific Coast, which meeting would be celebrated by the driving of the golden spike at Promontory Point, Utah, on May 10, 1869, while an army band played. The Kansas Pacific line out of Kansas City was three-fourths of the distance to Denver. Northern Pacific construction out of Duluth was barely underway, and the survey parties were moving into the Plains.

While the consequence to the old life of the Great Plains was not yet final and fatal, forces inherent in the march of civilization already portended its extinction, and the worst had happened within the brief span of five years.

The great trails of migration invariably follow water courses where possible, these being the lines of least resistance, lowest cost, and speediest settlement. So the Santa Fe Trail from central Kansas had traced west as far as Fort Lyon, Colorado, along the north bank of the Arkansas River. From Kansas City, the path taken by gold seekers and settlers Colorado-bound held to the valley of the Smoky Hill River most of the way to Denver. Out of Omaha, the Oregon Trail migration trekked almost due west along the valley of the Platte River.

As run the trails, the rails usually follow, the surveyors seeking the easiest and least costly gradient. On its way west, the Kansas Pacific held to the course of the Smoky Hill; the Union Pacific followed the Platte on the opposite shore from the Oregon Trail.

Sherman said it very well. The building of the railroads, twenty years after the trails were first beaten, "settled the fate of the buffalo and the Indian forever." That the fast-dwindling herds and other game were frightened away from the once relatively tranquil grazing in the well-watered valleys was the least of it. Along with the construction crews moved a hungry and adequately strong escort of soldiers for protection. To help feed the camp, professional hunters ranged outward from the guarded railhead, slaughtering bison, deer, and other game, often killing far more than was needed to keep the kitchen cars supplied.

By the time the two railroads had linked up in the line that connected Denver with Cheyenne, however, though the bison herds north and south were critically thinned out, they still counted in the millions. It was the invasion of the Plains by an army of professional buffalo hunters, who killed for what the hides would bring, that doomed the bison. This took place in the early seventies, an onslaught coming of the perfecting of a new method of curing the hide that made it excellent leather, long wearing and pliable. The hide-hunters killed wantonly, with no regard for the animal and little for their own economic future. A skilled hand at this business of extermination would kill one hundred head in a day and continue at that rate for several months.

True enough, to begin, as the West opened up, the slaughter of buffalo had what might crudely be called the sporting touch. By 1868 the Kansas Pacific was selling excursion tickets to all comers wishing to join the big hunt on the prairie. It was possible for a time to shoot into the herds from a moving train.

The great westward push of the professional buffalo hunter, however, did not get underway until 1871, when the inventor of the new process, a Vermont wood-cutting contractor, ordered one hundred hides for $3.50 each. The slaughter went on at such a rate that in three years the market was glutted, and the prime hide of a bull was worth only $1. In 1873, not by casual estimate but by Government count of the hide processing, more than four million buffalo were killed. The prairie fairly stunk with rotting flesh. In ruining their market, the hunters all but exterminated the herds. Government had made no real attempt to curb this monstrous folly. It was still holding with the theory that with the buffalo gone, the Plains Indians would have to become more tractable.

Other aspects of the Great Invasion were still more threatening. The farm frontier pretty much followed the railroad frontier, though at respectful distance. Under the Homestead Act that had been passed in 1862, any landless family could stake out a claim on a quarter section and ultimately get title to it. In Texas, where the Homestead Act didn't apply, the ever-extending dominion of the cattle barons had the same practical effect. The Indian was simply crowded out.

Every ten to twelve miles along the major trails, there would be a stockaded ranch or a small community with a facility called "the pilgrim station" to take care of wayfaring parties. Communications overhead made even more phenomenal progress. By the end of 1861, a telegraph line, following roughly the valley of the Platte River, had become linked at Denver with a wire from Salt Lake City. The Plains Indians were so little comprehending of what this advance was doing to them that they made no real effort to break it up.

If in that particular their thinking was more than a little confused, it was yet more so in their failure to understand that violent resistance had no payoff.

Hostilities were to continue along the western frontier for another fifteen years. And all of it was futile. The tribes were simply fighting to retain the vestiges of a way of life, the substance of which had already been denied them.

Though possibly pride, anger, and tradition so compelled them, there was no other object to be served, really. They had lost the game in both senses of the word. By continuing to resist, they would have to settle for much less in the end, due to the rancor and bitterness generated by prolonged conflict.

As vain as it is to lament that no smoother path toward conciliation, settlement, and conservation was sought and found, it is not so to regret the shameful attitude in high places that circumscribed and thwarted any such search.

When in 1870 the Commissioner of Indian Affairs counseled the Congress on how to view the problem, it was with these words, "When treating with savage men as with savage beasts, no question of national honor can arise. Whether to fight, to run away, or to employ a ruse, is simply a question of expediency."

That is to say that anything goes, and first of all, the abandonment of every civilized standard.

6

Chiefs Against Generals

╠╬╠╬╠╬╠╬╠╬╠╬╠╬╠╬╠╬╠

So strong ran the anti-military sentiment when General Grant moved into the White House that under the nose of the soldier-President the Congress cut the army from forty-five to twenty-five infantry regiments.

Many serving officers were mustered out and made jobless. Making use of an act of Congress passed in 1834, with Grant's approval it was arranged that eighty-eight of these surplus hands would be transferred to the field service of the Indian Bureau, displacing civilian appointees, while retaining their commissions.

Bridling at this usurping of its patronage prerogatives, the Congress promptly passed an act declaring that any officer who so moved must first vacate his commission. Grant's motive was both logical and laudable. In any war zone, from that day to the present, the army finds it more satisfactory to work side by side with civil servants who are ex-military. They are usually more cooperative and courageous than the average civil servant without such experience.

Grant promptly hit back. Calling in the politicians who had crossed him, he said, "Gentlemen, you have defeated my plan for Indian management, but you will not succeed in your purpose, for I will divide these appointments up among the religious churches, with which you dare not contend."

He had read their tempers aright; the congressional leaders backed away, rather than buck the new list. As things worked out, it proved to be not one of the more enlightened actions taken by a provoked President. The first names on the list were those of Quakers. Although other denominations followed, it came to be known as Grant's Quaker policy.

One of the products of Grant's turning to religion was Agent Lawrie Tatum, a Quaker by faith. History speaks well of him, an honest man, wholly fair in his dealings with the Indian and the army, though inclined to be overly trustful. In July 1869 Tatum was sent to Fort Cobb in Indian Territory, where he was to serve as good shepherd over the Kiowas and Comanches. As ferocious as any of the Plains tribes, and less dependable than most in their dealings, the Kiowas and Comanches had been given the word that they would have to concentrate at recently built Fort Sill. Winning their acquiescence was Tatum's prime responsibility.

One of his charges was Chief Satanta of the Kiowa, last heard from when he killed a sentry and ran off the horse herd at Fort Larned, Kansas. By this time, aged fifty or so, Satanta, despite the legend that he sought the friendship of the white man, was about as mean and as crafty an Indian as the West ever grew. After his raid on Fort Larned, for example, he had sent a message to the post quartermaster, saying that the stock from the army remount was of inferior quality and that he hoped the army would do better before he hit again.

Dissembling, Satanta moved his band to the fields outside Fort Sill in response to Tatum's directive. This is wide open and quite flat countryside, given to high winds and quick changes in temperature. The soil is easily tillable, and once the Kiowas had come to Fort Sill, Tatum undertook to turn

the warriors into practical farmers, with Satanta seemingly
blessing the conversion.

Not exactly a deception, the Kiowa response was a pretty
clever attempt to operate in both directions at one time by
Satanta, abetted by Chiefs Satank, Big Tree, and others. The
farmer-Indians continued to break the earth's crust, plant
seeds or sprouts, and pose as if awaiting a harvest. Under the
chiefs, the Kiowa warriors kept raiding into Texas mainly, as
if killing, maiming, and capturing were the only truly worthy aims of tribal life.

Tatum was taken in wholly, and the army did not immediately get the scope of such a two-sided tribal campaign, in
part because it too greatly depended on Tatum's judgment,
the more so because the army command tended to underrate
the guile of red men like Satanta and Satank. (The names
mean White Bear and Sitting Bear.)

To resolve any difficult problem, there must be a working
measure of good faith and understanding on both sides. In
this case there was none. The army left it to Tatum and made
no attempt to fault him. Tatum in turn believed that when a
chief such as Satanta gave his word, he must be telling the
truth. So he kept insisting to the army that the reports to the
effect that Fort Sill was being used as a sanctuary by the raiding hostiles were false. There was no doubt about the hit-
and-run killing and looting across the border in northern
Texas, but someone else had to be doing it. Tatum was no
doubt sincere and more than a little innocent.

Success in this lethal game of deception made the Kiowa
and Comanche increasingly bold. So notorious became the
unchecked depredations and the mystery of where the guilt
lay that General Sherman in 1871 went West personally to
investigate. By an almost unbelievable accident of time and
place, he became the central figure in the sequel.

From New Orleans, the Chief of Staff proceeded into
Texas by road, riding in an army ambulance, with an escort
of some fifteen cavalrymen. On a bright May morning, this

small cavalcade came posting along the dirt road just to the east of Fort Richardson in north Texas. So doing, it passed unknowing and unharmed, a large band of Kiowa concealed in a thicket of scrub oak and bois d'arc, lying in wait for the sole object of ambushing whites.

The plan had been laid the night before. One chief of the ambushing Kiowa, Mamanti, or Skywalker, was also esteemed as a medicine man. During the council, an owl had hooted. Mamanti interpreted the bird call in this way, "Tomorrow two parties of Texans will come this way. First will be a small party. But it will not be attacked. The medicine forbids. Later another party will come. This one may be attacked. Success will come of it."

So Sherman and his small party, having been saved by the hoot of an owl, rolled on along to Fort Richardson, none the wiser.

Three hours later, a convoy of ten mule-drawn wagons loaded with corn and fodder for the army came even with the wood-patch ambush, and the hundred Kiowa warriors struck. Twelve mule skinners were killed; five jumped from the wagons, made for the copse, and stayed hidden until the Indians cleared away. The band made off with the forty-one mules, carrying along three dead warriors lost in the brief skirmish.

That night, a wounded teamster made it to Fort Richardson and told his story. He had walked the seventeen miles. Sherman listened. Then he said to the post commander, Colonel Ranald S. Mackenzie, "Pursue with one hundred and fifty cavalrymen; they are to take thirty rations and stay in the field until the raiders are caught."

The chase proved to be a dry run, heavy rains having washed out all of the signs. Sherman had continued on in his ambulance to Fort Sill, four days' ride to the north, where soon after his arrival, Mackenzie appeared to report his failure.

Coincidentally, Satanta, Satank, several other chiefs, and a large band of Kiowa rode into the reservation next the fort, a circumstance that was in itself suspicious, though the Indians had returned because this was the day on which they drew their government-issued stores.

Sherman had already told Tatum about the attack on the mule train, and at last the Quaker agent was ready to concede that he had probably been wrong all along.

Satanta and the other Kiowa chiefs were brought into the agency building, where Tatum faced them and made the accusation. It was a chilling indictment. Some of the teamsters' bodies had been found by Mackenzie's troops mutilated and charred, and bound to the wagon wheels, mute proof that the victims had been burned alive.

Satanta must have realized that the double game had ended. He arose and said, "Yes, I led the raid. I have heard that you have been selling a large part of our annuity goods to the Texans. Some years ago we were taken by the hair and pulled close to the Texans. When Custer was here several years ago, he arrested me and kept me in confinement several days. Arresting Indians is no good now and is never to be repeated."

He then named his collaborators in the leading of the raid, Satank, Eagle Heart, Big Tree, Mamanti, and the rest.

Tatum told them that the Big Chief of the army was at Fort Sill and needed to hear the story. Sending word to Sherman of what he had learned, he also alerted Colonel B. H. Grierson, commander of the Tenth Cavalry whose black soldiers garrisoned Fort Sill. Figuring this was the hour for a getaway, Eagle Heart, Mamanti, and others of the band jumped on their ponies and fled the scene.

The meeting between Satanta, Satank, Big Tree, and Sherman took place on the veranda of Grierson's quarters. No attempt had been made to disarm the Indians, so the risk run by the Chief of Staff was extraordinary.

Incredibly bold, Satanta repeated the story of what he had done, filling in some of the gruesome details. Then again he spoke his defiance.

97

Without blinking an eye, Sherman told him that along with his accomplices, he would be arrested and tried for murder.

"I'd rather be dead," said Satanta, and throwing back his blanket, came up with a revolver.

Sherman gave a signal.

The shutters of the veranda were thrown open. In each window was a group of black soldiers, standing there like so many firing squads, their rifles pointed so as to cover every Kiowa. The blowing of a bugle brought more cavalrymen boiling out of the stables to cover the house from the front.

Manacled head and foot, and under guard by Mackenzie's cavalry, Satanta, Satank, and Big Tree were loaded in wagons, and the train was put on the road to Jacksboro, Texas, the town nearest Fort Richardson.

For Satank, the ride was soon over. In his sixty years, he had proved only that he was a bad Indian. He even looked the part. One eye drooped balefully, and unlike other chiefs, he wore a scraggly moustache, the ends of which looped down toward his chin. To match these physical details, his uncontrolled temper and mysticism made many of the Kiowa fear and hate him.

But he was not going to pay for his meanness on the gallows.

Before the train had cleared Fort Sill, he said, speaking in Comanche, the common language of the Plains, "I am a chief and I am old. Tell my people that I died beside the road."

But only a Caddo Indian chief, with the unlikely name of George Washington, who was riding alongside, heard and understood him. The driver and the military guard paid no attention.

Satank launched into a death chant.

"O Sun, you remain forever, but we Ko-eet-senko must die."

The line he repeated over and over, with only Caddo George paying him any heed, and as a point of honor George would not tell the soldiers.

Pointing to a tree less than a furlong ahead and next the road, Satank said to the other chief, "See the tree? I will be dead before we reach it."

Then he slipped the handcuffs over his skinny hands, pulled a knife from under his blanket, and went for the guard next the driver. Slashing at the soldier, he wrenched away his carbine, and raised it to fire. Before he could pull the trigger, he was shot dead by the guards who were covering Satanta and Big Tree from the wagon on ahead.

They returned to the post with his body to deliver it to the tribe. That quickly, however, all of the Kiowa, including the gardeners, had fled from Sill. So Satank had to be buried in the military cemetery, and for the same reason, Chief George Washington was unable to pass along to the tribe Satanta's parting words of wisdom, "Tell the Kiowa to bring back those mules and don't raid any more. Do as the agent tells them."

In Jacksboro, after a scrupulously fair trial, Satanta and Big Tree were found guilty and sentenced to be hanged, a verdict that seems reasonable enough.

Immediately there was an outcry over the country from the reform element, which held with the view that such was the oppression against the tribes that almost any act of counterviolence, however atrocious, could not be considered a crime. The fate of Satanta and Big Tree, though they were in themselves intrinsically insignificant and quite villainous, became a cause célèbre.

Direct pressure was brought to bear on General Grant and he appealed to Texas Governor Davis to pardon the chiefs. There was little justification for it; the Kiowa had not taken their chances and waged open warfare but had fought covertly. That was the Texas view of it. Put in the middle, the governor made that same kind of decision, commuting both sentences to life imprisonment.

Two years later, Satanta and Big Tree were released on parole. Whether from soft-heartedness or naïveté, officials in the Indian Bureau helped bring this about. The Kiowa and

Comanche were still marauding. The argument was put forward that going easy on the chiefs might make the tribes more conciliatory, which even today reads like wishful thinking.

General Sherman was so outraged over the release that, forgetting his manners, he wrote the governor of Texas a letter that seethed with impropriety. It ended with the expressed hope that if the parolees took any more scalps, Davis's would be the first. Since this pair had come within an owl hoot of taking Sherman's hair, his indignation was probably more personal than professional.

Too soon, Davis was being blasted from all sides. Dashing the high hopes of the Indian Bureau, the Kiowa resumed raiding, burning, and scalping. Getting in full cry, the Texas press not unnaturally placed the blame on the two parolees. Satanta and Big Tree swore they were innocent as lambs. A Quaker school teacher who moved among the Kiowa also avowed that while some of the raids were taking place, Big Tree was confined to his tepee with some mysterious malady, and Satanta was ranging far and wide hunting the buffalo.

Never again caught red-handed or in a confessing mood, Satanta and Big Tree managed to stay out of prison for one year, which is the best that may be said for them. Since they would not stay committed to a reservation, they were certain to be the prime suspects, according to the old adage, "Give a dog a bad name."

There are only two main possibilities.

Either they were guiltless as they claimed, or during two years of thinking it over while behind bars, they had learned how to play the double game without detection.

As to the answer, nobody knows.

At last becoming bored with them, the Government decided to put them away for good if given the slightest excuse.

The two chiefs had been assigned to a reservation, where they did occasionally report to the agent, in between prowls. Then one day they showed up at another reservation, saying that they liked it better and wished to stay.

For this bit of nose-thumbing, they were treated like common criminals. Picked up, they were returned to prison for violating parole.

Satanta stood it for four years, growing ever more bitter and protesting that in his last year of freedom he had been a good Indian.

In 1878 the fierce old warrior jumped from an upper story window of the prison, landed on his head, and so killed himself.

Big Tree was ultimately paroled and died free, or as free as a reservation Indian may be. First a son, then a grandson of Satanta named James Auchiah, a prominent Oklahoma artist, spent years trying to persuade Texas prison authorities to yield the old chief's remains. Not until 1963 did Auchiah win his battle. Satanta's bones were removed to Fort Sill, and with Kiowa ceremony, reburied in the post cemetery next the grave of Satank.

7

Custer and the
Great Design

᠎᠎᠎᠎᠎᠎᠎᠎᠎᠎

GEORGE Armstrong Custer is a unique figure in the lineup of
front-rank American military heroes. His fame endures not so
much because of what he did with his life but because of the
manner of his spectacular death. It is a distinction not unlike
that of the Boy on the Burning Deck.

This by no means is to say that his career was otherwise
undistinguished. The stars in his crown burned bright and
early. He was the youngest brigadier ever in the United
States Army and the younger major general in the Civil War.
Yet these rarefied heights, while important, did not make him
memorable. Today's average American, if tested, would be
hard put to name the youngest brigadier in World War I or
the junior among the many who won four stars in the several
wars that followed. Who today recalls that General Billy
Mitchell was the youngest second lieutenant in the conflict
with Spain?

Custer and the Great Design

Yet Custer stays a name in the land even among juveniles who know no more of him than the caricature they viewed in *Little Big Man*.

Many commanders well senior to Custer led their soldiers more skillfully and with clearer insight of the enemy than he in the wars against the Western Indians. Some few were all-around tacticians, deft in their handling of the combined arms, whereas Custer was essentially a horse soldier. Save by historians, the names of his contemporaries in the field are all but forgotten.

When those wars are mentioned, it is the figure with the long and flowing yellow locks and the tawny moustache, the wearer of garish field costumes self-designed, that comes immediately to mind. Custer dominates the scene and period as no other; despite that, his time span was relatively brief and his performance less than brilliant.

Custer was an indifferent student at West Point, not only numbered among the goats, but also an habitual prankster and a thorn in the flesh to the authorities. He rose swiftly when war came, this dashing and nervy leader of cavalry who believed that war was no place for a gentleman unless he sat a horse.

In the postwar years, when cut back to lieutenant colonel, he proved to be both erratic and intractable, a source of worry to his military superiors, so impulsive that his actions several times shocked and embarrassed the President. He was anything but a disciplined soldier, really. The wonder is that he was not bounced out of the army.

Habitually, he was overly demanding of troops and pushed them far beyond reasonable limits.

On one occasion he ordered twelve soldiers shot out of hand for desertion, at a time when desertion was such a common offense that the Secretary of War cynically commented that it might be the best way of populating the West.

Another time he deserted his own post of duty, and without proper authority, took an escort of soldiers with him on a long march because he was worried about Mrs. Custer, after getting word that she was ill at a distant station.

For these and other offenses all covered by charges, he was tried by court-martial and found guilty. The sentence was that he would be suspended from his rank and command and receive no pay for one year, which was like a slap on the wrist.

Then, too, he was a nepotist. Relatives swarmed with him to the field, some on government payroll as civilians. Still more peculiarly, when campaigning, he insisted on being accompanied by a pack of hounds, all of which shared his tent, and some his bed. Custer was a teetotaler, but he went to the dogs in his own way.

The court-martial was hung on him in the late summer of 1867. It followed what is loosely called a campaign in western Kansas, during which Custer's Seventh Cavalry, acting under the orders of Major General Winfield S. Hancock, engaged in several long-range sparring contests with the Cheyenne, and vainly sought a showdown with the band under Chief Black Kettle, that already overtried warrior.

Not even a touch-and-go operation, it was all run and no hit. During the hot season, the cavalry remounts simply couldn't overtake the well-fed and lightly loaded Indian ponies. Horses that finish last do not score either in sport or war, which fact of life the army was a bit slow to learn. The best that may be said of Custer his first time out against Indians is that he tried hard and got nowhere.

He had accomplished nothing in that tour toward assisting historians in clearing up the overriding mystery of his life— why high authority rated him as the superior Indian-fighter.

On the other hand, much that had happened around and about him in that same period underscored the army's need of commanders who were capable of coping efficiently with the Plains Indian on the warpath, even as it spelled out that for Government, there could be no graceful or halfway solution of the besetting problem.

Custer and the Great Design

A season that for the army ended in a gloom out of nigh total frustration, at the same time had realistically projected the nature of the contest and the shape of things to come.

For General Hancock as for Custer, the showing for the summer had been fully dismal—weeks of campaigning and only four dead Indians to show for it. While the Department of the Missouri could claim hardly any larger body count than that by the end of the year, the score reading eleven Indians killed and one wounded, it definitely was not for lack of provocation.

According to the official statistics, 147 whites had been killed and fifty-seven wounded, including forty-one that had been scalped. Fourteen white women had been raped by Indians and 426 women and children had been carried off into captivity. Of horses, mules, and cows stolen by red raiders, 627 head had been reported to headquarters. Twenty-four ranches or settlements had been hit and destroyed, eleven stage coaches attacked and four wagon trains wiped out.

Studying his office statistics, Sheridan, on taking over from Hancock, could reasonably conclude that the enemy was an elusive sort, though hardly aflow with the milk of human kindness. Here was a tide of depredation not to be stemmed by a counterdisplay of good manners, offers to negotiate, or a resigned acceptance of the possibility that the violence proved only that some Indians, like some whites, were criminals. The trouble was too widespread and persistent. Halfway measures were tried: The problem remained. Its nature is seldom acknowledged by historians who attack the army's action as ruthless in the extreme. If there was to be any room, any security, for other Americans in a vast expanse of the national domain, force had to be met with force. The chiefs could promise, but they lacked the control to make the promise good. So saying is not intended to imply other than that in the average case they lacked the goodwill, also.

In late 1868, or as quickly as it might be done gracefully and without public criticism, the army recalled Custer from the family home in Monroe, Michigan. His sitting-out year had been no real hardship. His wife adored him, so did his neighbors, and as a national idol, he drew many distinguished visitors to the town and continued to hold court.

Jumping from the bench to the saddle, Custer was directed by General Phil Sheridan to get the Seventh Cavalry Regiment ready as fast as possible to march against hostile Comanches and Kiowas in the Wichita Mountains.

The Seventh was far less well prepared to take the field than was Custer to give it a rough shaking-down and a rude reminder that war in the West was no tea party. No quarter was the right term for it.

His order to the regiment read that any brave not killed in battle was to be hanged. All women and children were to be made war prisoners. All ponies were to be slaughtered and all tepees were to be burned during the winter campaign.

This was Sheridan's doing. Sheridan held with but one solution to the Indian problem—extermination—and Custer was his quite pliable instrument. This may explain why Custer was so speedily recalled from purgatory. Birds of a feather do flock together just as misery loves company because nothing else makes misery tolerable. Custer's were no doubt the most brutal orders ever published to American troops, though more wretched atrocities from word-of-mouth orders have occurred in our time. The reflection makes the performance no more palatable.

On the second time around, Custer was much more successful, which is another way of saying that the hapless enemy was less mobile, less suspecting, and less expectant.

Reveille sounded for the Seventh Cavalry Regiment at 3:00 A.M. on November 23, the ungodliest of hours, an awakening that shouldn't have to happen to a dog and is absolutely forbidden in relatively sane households.

Loonier still, once the horse soldiers had downed their breakfast of cornmeal mush with corn syrup and hot coffee, the regiment stepped off in the dark to the tune of their regimental theme song, "Garry Owen," played by the regimental band. This is an Irish jig number that seems to mesmerize be-whiskered colonels without touching the privates. In the view of other cavalrymen, the Seventh might have been easy to live with, but for "Garry Owen."

Custer had a passion for the music. Getting with the band was no less imperative than getting up before the crack of dawn. The column moved out and with it went the bandsmen, not as musicians converted to fighters, but as a pack of tootlers.

Bizarre as it now sounds, when exactly six days later the Seventh Regiment charged pell-mell and without warning, parley, or reconnaissance into an Indian village on the banks of the Washita River, the buglers sounded the charge and the band again played "Garry Owen." This was Custer's way of gentling war: It made killing more rhythmic.

The luckless target was a collection of Cheyenne under Chief Black Kettle. Against Custer's eight hundred men, the camp had no chance, though some of the braves fought back. Even Black Kettle's luck ran out at last, and that much-tried and sometimes reasonable chief who had survived the Sand Creek massacre was among the more than one hundred Indians slain.

All of the lodges were burned and nearly nine hundred ponies were slaughtered.

On the army side at the camp site, Captain Lewis M. Hamilton, grandson of Alexander Hamilton, was killed, and a score or so of enlisted men were wounded.

When some of the tribesmen broke through the closing circle of cavalrymen to make their escape, they were followed out by Major Joel Elliott and nineteen troopers. Elliott had commanded the regiment prior to Custer's return. In the backwash of the fight, he and his group became surrounded by Cheyenne thirsting for their blood.

The noise of this fight as the Indians closed in could be heard back where the regiment was mopping up the camp. Although urged to do so, Custer did not see fit to rush reinforcement to Elliott's rescue. The reason for the refusal was never explained. Some days later, Elliott and his soldiers were found, mutilated in death, their bodies stripped. It scandalized the regiment. Some of the officers muttered that it was all Custer's fault. The charge was probably unfair.

From thereon, to Custer's high personal credit, and although he was not being restrained by higher authority, he put his campaign on a new and exemplary course. Risking his life several times, he rode with a single orderly into other nearby Indian villages, offering friendship and urging the tribesmen to submit and make their way to the reservation as soon as the grass turned green. That many of them became persuaded marks this as his great hour on the frontier. Soon thereafter, the Seventh Cavalry became scattered into company units, which were deployed into the Deep South to put down the Ku Klux Klan. Custer for a brief while faded from the Indian-fighting scene.

Though this is not the complete story, we see him once again leading the reassembled regiment, heading this time into the Black Hills of South Dakota in the summer of 1874.

All of the western half of that territory—a munificent gift—had been ceded to the Sioux and the Cheyenne as a homeland. Hardly a reservation in the accepted meaning of that word, it was a wonderfully scenic, well-watered, and game-filled countryside and also included the Black Hills, which were already old before the Alps and the Rockies were formed and when the Himalayas were a stagnant marsh.

The cavalry's invasion of this territory was certain to offend the tribes, although in that hour, fortunately, most of the Indians were attending the big annual powwow in the Powder River country.

There was, however, a legitimate object for the expedition. For years an unconfirmed rumor had circulated around the nation that there was gold in the Black Hills. After the signing of the 1868 treaty that made western Dakota Indian country, the rumor reverberated so loudly that the trickle of prospectors and traders into the area became a fairly steady stream.

Worrying about this highly volatile problem and unable to stem the encroachment on the tribal preserves, someone in Government had an inspiration: Why not send a military-scientific expedition into the Black Hills to prove once and for all that there was no gold to be found?

Custer, who was commanding at Fort Lincoln, on hearing of the scheme not only volunteered to lead the expedition but pressed hard for the assignment.

Sheridan was at first reluctant to name him, worrying that he might act irresponsibly, but in the end gave his approval.

When the ten troops of cavalry, about one hundred covered wagons, and a large company of Indian scouts marched out while the Seventh's band played "Garry Owen," they were followed along by a platoon of mineralogists and prospectors. There was also a group of news correspondents, although Custer had been specifically instructed by Sheridan not to include the press.

This time, Custer accomplished his mission in reverse. The expedition established beyond doubt that gold was to be found at French Creek in the Black Hills, and the discovery was acclaimed with the blasting of many trumpets. The whole nation got the news as if from one broadcast. Thus the experiment worked out not unlike the story of the bushman who was given a new boomerang and went crazy trying to throw the old one away.

Not unnaturally there swiftly followed a white stampede to the heart of the new Sioux-Cheyenne homeland, and almost as quickly, the opening up of much richer gold prospects.

Though the army and the Indian Bureau may have felt slightly duty-bound to protect the Indians against this trespass and denial of basic rights, together they were incapable of resisting a tide so strong, and only a few feeble motions were made in that direction. For example, there was a negative ending to a proposal that the government pay the Indians for mineral rights in the Black Hills, while not excluding the area from the Great Sioux Reservation. After vainly fencing through the first summer with the motley horde lusting for lucre, love, and loot in the Hills, Sheridan gave up the fight as futile, and by mid-1875 there were at least 25,000 people mining, storekeeping, and brawling in Deadwood Gulch alone.

Thereupon some of the warriors went hostile and resumed marauding the settlements and scalping innocent wayfarers. Their depredations afforded an excuse for the gold seekers and adventurers to strike back at any Indian within reach, though of the white invasion had come the initial red grievance.

Chief Red Cloud on the whole took the irruption rather mildly, saying, "I do not like General Custer and all of his soldiers going into the Black Hills, as that is the country of the Oglala Sioux." What Red Cloud said out loud, however, was seldom at one with what he thought.

To recapitulate, during ten years the Sioux and the Cheyenne uprisings had come almost full circle, the tribes having fought in Montana, Colorado, Wyoming, Kansas, Minnesota, and Dakota. Much of this warring over a vast countryside had engaged the same bands. Though each war had been a relatively small affair, the impact of a threat as ubiquitous as that which they imposed was anything but local.

The problem being national, the direct cause of the next round was Government's exasperation over the revolving menace to the peace and population of the Great Plains. When patience died, the hope of finding a soft solution was put aside. On December 3, 1875, Government published an order, directing all Sioux and Cheyenne to fold back into the Dakota reserve by January 31, 1876. The bands who remained outside would be treated as hostiles.

Due to winter conditions and the lack of communications,

compliance with this ultimatum was virtually impossible. That fact—the outlawing of the Sioux and the Cheyenne in cold blood—the authors of the order well understood. Of course it was unfair to the Indians. The practical effect could only be to declare an open season on the two tribal groups.

By the time the hour for submission by the Sioux and Cheyenne had come and gone without visible result, it seemed unlikely that Custer would get in on any of the hunting. Having earlier affronted the Secretary of War, William W. Belknap, Custer went East to testify before the Congress that the civilian head of the army was a small-time grafter and that the President's brother, Orvil Grant, was a cheap chiseler who had pocketed $1,000 illegally.

Although Custer was right on both counts, his testimony was all based on hearsay, unsupported by any item of material proof. President Grant, fed up with him at last, directed the army to shunt him to the sidelines, which should have ended his military career. Still, the imbroglio must have found W. T. Sherman in Custer's corner. Sherman had been directly responsible for Belknap's being named Secretary and Belknap had responded by treating him like dirt.

The plan by which the army proposed to enforce the order of December 3 was already at that time in full bloom, and Custer had been cast for the starring role. So the production was about to become *Hamlet* without the Dane.

Provided they followed tradition, the bands of Sioux and Cheyenne who were still at large were expected to stage their annual get-together during early summer in the Powder River country of southern Montana. The affair was called the Teton Council. The squaws, papooses, and braves would all be there and the powwowing would last so long as there was food for man and beast.

Thus it was arranged that from three directions the army would move on the assembly and bag it. One army column under Brigadier General George Crook would move on it from the southeast. A body of cavalry under Colonel John

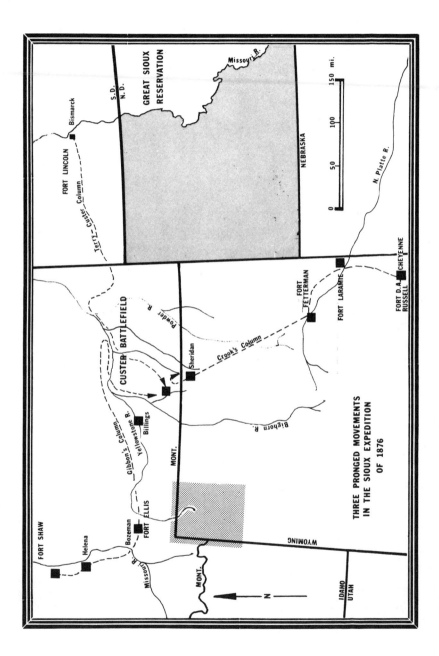

THREE PRONGED MOVEMENTS
IN THE SIOUX EXPEDITION
OF 1876

Gibbon, a campaigner as leathery as a fresh boot, would march east from Fort Ellis, Montana. The third and main force under General Alfred Terry would advance west from Bismarck, a town made of a temporary stop in the western push of the railroad.

Of all the forces in the programed convergence, Custer and the Seventh Cavalry, who were to march under Terry, were rated as the stellar battle element, though the reason why evades serious explanation. It is a measure less of the regiment's excellence than of the army's general weakness.

To speak truly, it was not a very bright plan, the synchronization of such a movement over great distances being next to impossible.

For reasons not to be found in his record as a commander on the Indian frontier, Custer was still considered "The Indispensable Man." He had flair and color, or what the modern war correspondent calls "sexiness," and the notion persisted that he was Lady Luck's darling. This is sometimes enough to win preferment for the mediocre.

After President Grant ordered him shelved, his military superiors still came to Custer's rescue at the risk of incurring White House displeasure. Terry, a highly congenial man who had been an attorney prior to the Civil War and then turned professional soldier, probably backed him for compassionate reasons. Or it may have been Custer's fatal charm.

Custer himself wired Grant, appealing to him as one military comrade to another. Surprisingly, the President, who knew that Custer had political ambitions, softened under these supplications and restored him to good standing.

Custer had by then returned to the West, where he stood booted and spurred, ready to spring to the saddle when the bugle blew.

With that mount-up, the well-known Custer luck began to run out.

Marching at a reasonable gait to spare the horses, the column under Terry made its way to the mouth of the Powder

River—"a mile wide and a foot deep" the troops said of it —where the Powder joins the Yellowstone. The Yellowstone valley is broad, the embankment of the river is level and smooth, almost a bridal path for cavalry. The column load was lightened by the flat-bottomed river boat, *Far West*, which brought Terry up the Yellowstone, served as his command post, and floated most of the expedition's supply. Terry was fighting as comfortable a war as possible.

Abroad the *Far West*, Terry held his final command conference. There he directed Custer not to fight a main engagement with the Indians until the other two columns had come up to within strike distance of the hostile encampment. There is an odd aberration here: Terry signally failed to provide for the coordination of the general movement and he thereby put the burden on Custer. Yet having given the order or direction orally, he then repeated it in writing and handed it to Custer, who pocketed it.

No one saw fit to ask, "Now how is this to be done?" Custer did, however, remark to some of his people that once the Seventh was turned loose, he would do as he pleased. He would not be restrained by Terry, although Terry had saved him.

We see Custer and the nine hundred men of the regiment when on the morning of June 22, they mounted up in readiness to ride into hostile country. The pack mules were loaded with the reserve ammunition and enough field rations to last fifteen days, mainly hard bread, coffee, sugar, and bacon. They also carried a large supply of salt in case the troops had to live on horse meat. Each soldier had one hundred rounds of carbine ammunition, twenty-four rounds for his revolver, and the two weapons, a canteen and a light pack. In a slung bag next his saddle were twelve pounds of oats for his horse.

With that much weight and the long trail ahead, there was reason enough to waste no energy on pomp and circumstance. At noon that day, however, the regiment passed in review before Terry and Custer. From the musics came a last great blaring of trumpets. The silence would be on after the parade was done.

When Custer mounted up following the ceremony, preparatory to riding to the front of the column, Terry shouted, "God bless you!"

The parting words of Colonel John Gibbon sounded a wholly different note. He sang out, "Now, Custer, don't be greedy. You wait for us."

Custer called back, "I won't," which might have meant anything. But there was no doubt about what Gibbon meant. Knowing Custer, he expected him to jump the gun. Coming from Gibbon, however, the words did ring a bit hollow. Although he has never been given sufficient credit, he was another death-or-glory boy.

The regiment had hardly moved beyond the first rise enroute to the upper waters of the Rosebud when the troops realized that there had come an end to all moderation. The momentum of the march tells its own sad story and is the best measure of Custer's intentions. A prelude to catastrophe, it invited nothing other than that. The right word for it is *brutish*. Everything about the drama was becoming more than a little bit unreal.

Custer was setting a pace that if continued much longer must certainly founder the expedition. On June 23, the regiment marched thirty-five miles, all of it in flat, fairly smooth going, but still in burning weather. On the twenty-fourth, from 5:00 A.M. to 8:00 P.M. the Seventh held to the saddle, covering forty-five miles.

There followed a three-hour break, sometimes termed a *bivouac*, though the word hardly fits. Some of the troopers unsaddled to rest and cool the horses. Certain of the officers slept in snatches. But most of the people could not relax, being too restless. They knew they would be going on, or at least suspected it, though no word had been passed along.

Somewhere around eight, Custer rode back to the picket lines to tell the troops personally that the column would get underway in a few minutes. The officers were then summoned to Custer's tent for instructions.

They resumed march after dark and in five hours added another ten miles to the day's journey: The pace had become a crawl. On the twenty-fifth, there would be another twenty-three miles to get up to the battlefield. After daylight, the cooks would prepare coffee, then throw it away when the early risers told them that it was undrinkable. The water was so brackish that the horses wouldn't touch it.

The extremities of this rigor, and the reasons for it, require a closer look. On the afternoon of the third day, June 24, it had become certain that the Seventh was on a hot trail. There were forty-four Indian scouts with the column. Some of them had picked up the signs of a massive movement by the tribes, the hoof and travois marks in the soft earth being so clear and unmistakable that a recruit could hardly have missed them. The indicated direction was westward and into the valley of the Little Bighorn River. Major Reno's battalion had scouted the same area a few days before and read the signs, following which Reno had wisely retired.

The effect on Custer had been electric. With the discovery, his ambition came in conflict with his military judgment, which accounts for the equivocal pause, prior to the decision to march on. It was a capital blunder, the halt having been too brief and the air too stifling for there to be a replenishing of energy in man and horse. So again, he ran true to the form chart written on him by Major General John K. Herr, the army's last Chief of Cavalry, "He would lead his column on another killing ride, which left his officers and men staggering from fatigue."

The night was pitch-black. The troopers were already worn down. Going single file, the soldiers had to clank with their mess kits to keep direction, and despite Custer's urging, the column had to move at a creep. By 2:00 A.M. Custer was ready to give it up, probably because he felt spent. The Seventh pitched camp in a ravine next the divide between the Little Bighorn and Rosebud valleys, almost atop a low-lying and rather characterless range known as the Wolf Mountains. It is anything other than beautiful and refreshing country, being drab, featureless, and generally devoid of cooling waters or shade. Why it could have attracted the Indians, other than for the presence of the buffalo, is impossible to explain.

When Custer called the halt, his soldiers would get at best about three hours sleep. Where he camped, he was within less than ten miles of the ground where the Indians under Chief Crazy Horse had beaten off General Crook's column only one week before, though Custer knew nothing about that fight. Lacking the information, he could not foresee that he might engage an enemy fired-up by a victory and a euphoric surging of self-confidence. Had he known that night, he likely would have been too fatigued to appreciate the radical change in situation. Tired commanders think no more clearly than bushed orderlies.

There is an old army saying, that even a jug may become a door provided it opens. The meaning is underscored by one incident of the night march. During that troubled advance, when troopers were stumbling about, much of the time leading their mounts, and even so, occasionally losing the way, a mule lost its pack due to a loose cinch—a minor mishap that went unnoted until the camp began to bed down.

One Sergeant Curtis was ordered to backtrack and look for the missing bundles containing mainly hard bread—certainly no task for a faint heart. Just after dawn Curtis found more than he sought. Around the lost bundles, picking at them, squatted a small party of Sioux warriors. On sighting the lone soldier, they did the unexpected: They mounted their ponies and galloped off, leaving the loot to him. As he rode back to the camp, Curtis saw other Indians observing the regiment from the high ground, a fair measure of which side strove hardest to gain advantage through superior infor-

mation. The sergeant dutifully reported the bad news—
that the enemy must know that the Seventh Regiment was
threatening and knew the distance between its base and the
Indian camp.

What came ultimately of this intelligence leaves little room
to assume that even if Custer had known what had happened
to General Crook's force one week earlier, he would likely
have taken a more prudent course. He may have been thinking with a brain too tired to grasp realities. On the other
hand, the whole operation was at loose ends and courting disaster. The cumulative errors that blacken the campaign came
of an almost total breakdown in communications between the
supposedly converging troop bodies. None of its aspects was
in any way excusable since the failure left each commander, including Custer, operating blind.

The operating conditions, meaning ground and weather,
moreover, did not forbid the exchange of vital information.
More than sufficient time availed. It is a country of far horizons, with little cover for the springing of ambushes. Well-
mounted couriers, swinging wide of the Powder River country, could have maintained the flow of situational reports
between the three camps. The Indian scouts might have done
so. In the campaigns that quickly followed, such missions
were run consistently and successfully, with little or no loss.
Nothing should have been more important to the high command than the setting up of such a circuit to regulate movement and avoid blunders. It was not done; it was hardly more
than attempted in a halfhearted way that went wrong at
every turn, being requested rather than demanded.

Such deference to subordinates may be highly Christian,
but it is hardly military. General Terry may have believed in
gentility, truth, and beauty all of his life, but at this stage he
wasn't doing the army any good. Somewhere along in this interlude, we find him in his barge in the Yellowstone penning
these notes for posterity; "I hear nothing from General
Crook's operation: if I could hear I would be able to form

plans for the future more intelligently." Intelligently? It seems not once to have occurred to Terry that although Crook had failed to keep him advised, that lack did not stop him from sending forth a patrol to learn what had happened to Crook. He was proceeding as if the object of the exercise was to demonstrate that whoever said there is no glory in military stupidity didn't know the half of it.

No other lesson is as salient from the campaign. The enormity of the misfortune that dogged it may be understood only if we here stop the clock for a look at what had happened to Crook.

8

The Look of Crook

SOMETHING in the Montana air that June had to be intoxicating, making commanders feel more than a little bit mad with power.

It could have been the faultless weather and the charm of the countryside. Troops get high when the sun is bright and so do the leaders; their spirits sag under leaden skies, especially when there is mud underfoot. Decision comes easier when nature is kind; hesitation is the natural fruit of ugly weather.

The landscape in that season was radiant. The valleys of the Powder River, Rosebud, Little Bighorn, and Tongue were thick with blossoming groves of wild plum and chokecherry, and the fragrance lay so heavy that soldiers later swore it carried to them above the smell of explosives and the offensive stench of battle. One of those rare sweet-scented entries from the campaign, this one also has the smell of authenticity. Amidst danger, the senses seem to be keener, and the brain more impressionable to all that is beautiful or enchanting in nature. Bird song nowhere else sounds as lovely; the skies are never again quite as blue.

The Look of Crook

As with the soldiers, the warriors in the enemy camp were pervaded by a feeling of invincibility, a conviction unique to this time and this field that victory must lie ahead. From that spirit, their war might doubled. Setting and clime may have contributed to this phenomenon, though there were other stimulants. After torturing himself to bring on visions, the great Hunkpapa medicine man, Sitting Bull, called out that he saw soldiers falling and Indians riding over them. Yet probably more than from all else, the warriors became supercharged from the sight of their own great masses, an assemblage of fighting men from the Plains tribes in numbers without precedent. Indians are not unique in thus reacting to the sight of the human sea. It makes for euphoria in peoples supposedly highly intelligent. Hitler speaking at Nuremberg, Nasser dealing with the Cairo street mob to convince them of Egypt's invincibility, or Patton spellbinding a massed Third Army exemplify the magicianship. One is reminded of an old cartoon in *Judge*, wherein power is vaunted to an assembly by a spokesman in these terms, "We are rich. We are strong. Together we are many millions." But these were not humans exulting: These were cheese mites.

Of the strength that awaited to oppose them, these army commanders knew practically nothing and they made no sensible attempt to inform themselves. That they failed so to do affords some measure of their giddiness. They anticipated engaging at most about fifteen hundred braves, provided fortune favored them. Possibly someone had injected that figure speculatively at a conference and repetition thereafter had given it an official flavor. By their reckoning, a force of that size any one of the columns should be able to overcome. Even that assumption was reckless, there being nothing from the past to justify it. Yet here was the mistaken and overoptimistic calculation that clouded all judgments, superinduced carelessness, and made the army overreach.

That Custer was to be made the ultimate main sacrifice to all of this muddling may seem more appropriate than ironic, he always having been a headlong soldier, vainglorious, over-confident, and contemptuous of Indians. But Custer need not have become the victim of the campaign had it been in other parts properly conducted. The whole operation proceeded as if, rather than hunting Indians, the army was seeking a memorable catastrophe.

More astonishing than all else, General Crook had been unable to resist temptation one week earlier. For Crook was in many respects, and most of the time, the opposite of Custer. A deliberate and highly imaginative commander, he respected the red man as a fighter, did not expect to rout him easily once he had decided to stand, and tried to avoid killing him en masse if there was any happier alternative. Knowing full well about the ordered convergence of the columns and the anticipated time of arrival, Crook should have restrained his force so as to avoid full battle prematurely. Rather than being a question for his decision, this was a simple matter of complying with orders. Then to be doubly insured, rather than taking any chance of supply shortage, he should have moved with his train, lest his information prove wrong and there should ensue a shock meeting engagement with the Indian main force.

While facts about battle as often as not are ambiguous, in this case they seem clear: Crook did nothing he was supposed to do.

This fork-bearded man who looked as if he had been born to the saddle, though he preferred to ride a mule, has many times been praised as the ablest Indian-fighter of the western frontier. The encomium is likely deserved. Sherman among others rated him the foremost commander, though that could have been Sherman's way of praising him with faint damns. The rest of the Indian-fighting generals of that place and time were no sweet bunch of daisies, with the exception of Nelson Miles, who had flashes of brilliance. Original thinking was not for them, nor was average field-service prudence. They fared better than they deserved, for taken as a lot, they were flat bottoms that slid over the dew.

Crook at age forty was a confirmed posturer, almost an eccentric. He loved to be photographed in the Napoleonic stance, several fingers of his right hand in his unbuttoned tunic, as if he were scratching a fleabite. He went, however, for more than military trappings. A favorite pose was that of The Mighty Hunter, the camera getting him with sporting rifle at parade rest, pith-helmeted, one foot on an animal skin.

None of this was quite masquerade. He was indeed The Mighty Hunter, even as Teddy Roosevelt and Ernest Hemingway, whom he far outdid in chance-taking. With only a few members of his staff in attendance, he loved to venture on a shoot far in advance of his marching troops, this in Indian country, at the risk of getting scalped. Thus stretching RHIP (rank has its privileges) to the extreme limit, he probably worried his soldiers not at all, though it put one hell of a premium on staff loyalty.

His peculiarities were not put-on attention-getters. It was a case of the man expressing himself naturally. All else about him so attests. An original thinker on things military, an innovator and constant experimenter, Crook well understood that army regulations afforded guidance for sensible decision-making and were not written to be a block to action. A cardinal point, it is missed wholly by too many officers.

Except for the Civil War years, this unconventional soldier had passed his whole career battling and subjugating the most savage of the tribal groupings in the prickliest area of all—the extreme Southwest.

As his latest achievement, while commanding the Department of Arizona, he had brought the Apaches pretty well under control, without excessive loss of life to the tribes or the army. For so doing, one year before the Bighorn campaign, he was rewarded by being bumped from light colonel to brigadier, and at the same time was given command of the Department of the Platte.

One of his successes—and a quite new idea—he had raised and trained the Apache Scouts, using red men to find red men. The Scouts remained a useful adjunct to the army well into the twentieth century and fronted for it during the Punitive Expedition into Mexico in 1915. By the time of the concentration in the Powder River country, there were six hundred Indian scouts in the army, regularly enlisted and receiving the same pay and allowances as cavalry soldiers. They were distinguished by a hat ornament of two arrows with points upward. In time, a dozen or so of them would wear the Medal of Honor.

In Arizona, Crook had brought about the high mobility of his hitting forces in the harsh mountain country mainly through the employment of the mule—mules to carry his riflemen, their packs, and all field equipment. An idiosyncratic example of his thoroughness, he insisted on inspecting and handling every animal, and he personally culled those that his judgment said would not stand the long grind. He also fitted the aparejo to the beast. Due to his expertise and fastidious attention, Crook's mules could pack along 320 pounds, or almost double the load that regulations said would be considered average weight on an extended march. (The mean load for an elephant is only five hundred pounds.) By his striving, Crook won the title, "Daddy of the Pack-Mule Train." Since there are no longer army mules for anyone to father, his shade will wear that honor in perpetuity.

On taking over the northern command, Crook at once took steps to mount his infantry on mules. And it was just as well so. Many of the green rifle replacements had never been in the saddle before and the gait of a mule, while not quite as smooth as a rocking chair or the shamble of a single-footer, is a joyride compared to the walk-trot pounding jar of the typical cavalry remount. Getting past the first two days is the hardest part.

As for other adjustments, Crook had already discovered that while engaging the Sioux might not be more complex than fighting the Apache, the problems differed radically. In March, with his forces ill-equipped for heavy weather, he made his first go against the northern hostiles.

The approach was done under fair skies. Then as the column got to within one hundred miles of the Yellowstone River, it was struck by a blizzard. Temperatures plummeted below zero. The wagon train stalled in snowdrifts and was left behind. Frostbite casualties cut troop strength. Still, Crook carried on.

Next, the column came across some pony tracks. A battalion under a veteran cavalryman, Colonel J. J. Reynolds, was pared off to follow the tracks and act according to what it found. In the early morning it came upon an Indian village, went into the attack, killed as many people as could not get away, and burned the lodges.

For a number of reasons, that blow is rated a capital blunder. The victims were a band of friendly or at least allegedly neutral Cheyenne under Chief Two Moons. The chief and his people had met other of the outlawed bands of Sioux and Cheyenne in the country north of the Bighorns. Concluding that their mood was for war, Two Moons had turned his band about and was heading for the reservation. At least that is the story as pieced together later by historians and Indianophiles to explain why Two Moons was ever after a foe of the white man and would deal some hard blows in that role. Where the truth lies, one may never be sure.

If those were the circumstances, Reynolds swiftly got his comeuppance, and double. After burning the village, Reynolds and outfit pursued. The fleeing Cheyenne steadied on the same bluff from which the army had attacked. The pursuing troops, misled by their easy overcoming of a sleeping village, and suddenly dismayed by a storm of bullets and arrows, turned tail and fled in panic.

The mounted warriors took out after them and the harassment, along with the killing and scalping of any luckless soldier whose mount faltered or failed so that he either fell or lagged behind, continued until well after daylight the following morning.

To Crook, who had suffered no such mortification in Arizona, the affair was more than a passing incident. He turned the column about and marched it back to Fort Fetterman, where the southeastward-flowing North Platte River crossed his earlier line of march.

There, two of Reynolds captains were court-martialed for neglect of duty, and Reynolds was charged with conduct prejudicial to good order. The captains got minimum punishment, and although Reynolds was only suspended from command for one year, his career as an officer was finished. Crook could not forgive him.

If the result opened Crook's eyes to the fact that the standards of some officers were lower than his own, it was not a unique disclosure peculiar to his time. Though an awkward business, it still enabled Crook, near the beginning of the campaign, to put over the two command points that most counted.

He would show a hard time to soldiers who did not stand and fight.

If there were to be killings, it would be of warriors determined on battle.

When next Crook's mule-mounted host got in motion toward the appointed rendezvous with Terry and Gibbon, the troops were in fine fettle. The weather was salubrious, the morale high. That is, until the expedition got deeper into Wyoming. White settlers there had been hit by an epidemic that a frontier medico had diagnosed as inflammatory rheumatism. It spread to troops. The four ambulances soon filled. Crook used his supply wagons to haul the overflow, and kept going. The jolting was enough to speed either swift ruin or recovery.

During the column's crossing of the Little Bighorns from east to west, Crook daily was out in front of his troops with a few aides, shooting deer, elk, and mountain sheep, thereby to enrich the fare at the headquarters' mess. In this passage, one of his heavy patrols became hotly engaged by a band of hostiles and narrowly avoided extinction. Crook didn't so much as draw a ticket for killing big game without a license.

There was another oddity. Thirty prospectors followed along on the heels of the army to pan every stream crossed in the Bighorns. Covered thus by a protecting screen day after day, those miners worked in high style. But they found no gold.

When at last Crook bivouacked his command along the banks of the Rosebud (so called because of the ubiquity of the wild rose), there were more than enough hostiles right at hand. This was in the early evening of June 16. The camp was pitched in the immediate presence of the enemy, and moreover, Crook was fully aware of it. Another weird note from this peculiar campaign, there had been delivered to him a warning message from Chiefs Sitting Bull and Crazy Horse, "Come so far, but no farther; cross the river at your peril."

Crook was nearly over the line and not about to be stopped. His target was an Indian village a few miles farther down the Rosebud valley.

Such was the power under his command that Crook, still thinking in the limited terms of the Arizona warfare, saw no reason to draw up and wait for the columns advancing from the Yellowstone. Under him rode fifteen companies of cavalry and five of mule-mounted infantry. When to these were added almost three hundred Crow, Shoshone, and Snake scouts and the usual complements of civilian teamsters, packers and interpreters, the total force was 1,300 men. Except for one small group of teamsters and an infantry guard detail that had been left behind to cover the wagon train and tentage when Crook last broke camp, all of these, as well as a squad of correspondents, rode forth to hunt Indians when Crook gave the order to advance just after dawn on June 17.

They had not far to go and any chance for surprise had been lost. The Indian scouts had so warned Crook the night before.

The Sioux and Cheyenne under Crazy Horse were already drawn up in battle array beyond the bluffs on the other side of the Rosebud. Crazy Horse had charged up his braves with a war cry to remember, "Come on, Dakotas, it's a good day to die!" The hostiles, furthermore, had to stand to gain time for the withdrawal of their dependents in the village.

In all of Crook's experience with the Apaches, there had been nothing like this—massed Indians, more of them than were Crook's own numbers, drawn up for open battle, rampant to engage the army on its own terms. Nothing of that sort had happened before in the Plains wars, and after this campaign, it would never happen again.

A small screen of Indian scouts, fronting for the main body, topped the bluffs on the far side and vanished from sight. The sounds of sudden fire and of war whoops rang through the valley. Two Crow scouts, one of them wounded, came galloping back down the slope.

They were yelling, "Sioux! Sioux! Many! Many!"

Right after them came the mass of mounted Sioux and Cheyenne, charging the army front.

Crook's cavalry had already been deployed far over on the left and was now out of sight and contact. His mule-mounted infantry dared not await the full shock of that frenzied, downhill charge. Still under good control, these rifle units galloped off at an oblique uphill and gained the heights, though not without grinding collision and some loss along their flanks and rear during the spontaneous maneuver.

Before the Indians could check momentum and reverse course in large numbers, the soldiers had deployed on the commanding high ground in a defensive circle, or as it was called in later years, a "Custer ring." Done in the nick of time, it was also well done. When the braves regrouped to assault the position, there was a point-blank grapple and episodes of hand-to-hand fighting.

The perimeter broke. Its force became split into two groups, then three and four. But the individual soldiers did not break and their fire took heavy toll of the hostiles.

Then the Indians pulled away, but only so far as the skyline of the next ridge. How they behaved when they got there is told by John F. Finerty, correspondent of the Chicago *Times*, in words worth preserving for posterity, "Having rallied on the second line of heights, the Sioux became bold and impudent again. They rode up and down rapidly, wheeling in circles, shaking an indelicate portion of their persons at us." It was hardly a gentleman's war.

Crook was there to see these things when he might have been off with the out-of-sight cavalry, which in the meanwhile had become totally engaged by a body of mounted Sioux. There, too, the fighting was sparked and inspired by incidents of incredible individual and group valor, officers taking desperate chances and a number of them falling, enlisted men and Indian scouts risking and meeting death attempting rescue or trying to get through a message against hopeless odds.

Forever identified with this field is the name of Colonel Guy V. Henry. He took a bullet straight through the head and seemed to be dying. Henry had energized the fight and his fall should have been a dismaying loss. The troopers laid the still-conscious man, blinded in one eye, in the shadow of a horse, there being no other shade. A correspondent tried to console him. Henry said, "It is nothing; for this are we soldiers."

Still the battle as a whole could not be managed, though Crook, cool as ever, made the attempt. No order, no message, could recall in the critical time his cavalry wing, held as it was to its own field by the fury of the Indian attack.

When after two hours the cavalry was free to move and

come up to Crook, it was already too late to engage with joined strength the great body of Sioux and Cheyenne. Although the Indians had been pushed back to the third ridge line, one cavalry element still remained cut off and hard pressed. Most of the Sioux and Cheyenne that had given battle to the mule soldiers had already broken off the fight and disappeared. Many years later, one of these warriors explained why, "We got tired and we were hungry, so we went home." The question may have suffered in translation. Said more simply, they'd had enough.

Crook still had in mind the report of the Indian village, lying eight miles farther down what is called the Dead Canyon of the Rosebud. So he made one more try, only to think better of it.

At high noon, eight companies of cavalry under Captain Anson Mills were ordered forth to sweep the Dead Canyon and overrun the village if the situation looked favorable.

Then from the high ground a few minutes later, Crook scanned the countryside to the north and had a sobering second thought. Just a few miles ahead, the bluffs closed down tight to the stream, forming the constricted passage known as the Dead Canyon. To his eye, it looked like a natural trap, a perfect defile for the staging of an ambush.

Mills was already on his way. Crook sent his aide and one orderly galloping after to recall Mills, with the additional instruction that he should move to relieve the still-beleaguered cavalry element. They made it in time and Crook's clear thinking probably saved the army not a few additional scars. For as it worked out, the Indian village had already lifted and moved on. So there would have been ambush or nothing.

Decisions on the field are rarely clean-cut. Even the forces that engage often wonder whether they have failed or succeeded, and there are a number of ways of distinguishing defeat from victory, some of them quite unreliable. The Battle of the Rosebud raises such questions, none subject to satisfying answers.

If the side which first quits the field is the loser, then Crook was indubitably the victor and Crazy Horse the defeated. Crook occupied the battlefield and camped there that night.

There are no meaningful vital statistics as to comparable loss rates, such was the nature of the contest. The Indians were scrupulous about removing their dead and wounded from the field and would take unusual risks to that end. Yet they did not pick it clean this time. Correspondent Finerty railed at the Crow scouts for moving about the battlefield, emasculating the corpses of the fallen Sioux, pouching their trophies, and shouting in broken English about the unhappiness they would visit on certain Sioux squaws.

The records say that Crook's losses were "heavy," which in this instance was more an exaggeration than an ambiguity. His fighting line was fewer by only fifty men killed in action and wounded in action. The few dead were buried after dark fell and all traces of the graves were smoothed over, a hurried disposal that in itself cheated the records.

When Crook moved out the following morning, small parties of Sioux were observing him from the high ground, and they noted that he went south, away from the area of conflict. Such was the load of wounded encumbering the column, that coupled with the shortage of ammunition and rations, it left Crook, in his judgment, with no choice but to fall back on Goose Creek, where he had dropped his wagons. Goose Creek, near present-day Sheridan, was fifty miles to the south of where he had fought and another fifteen miles removed from the Powder River area, where his troops could have been of use in the ten days that followed.

As a temporary refresher, this move is understandable. Yet it was to be no brief interlude, followed by a fast leap forward again. From Goose Creek the wagons, bearing the wounded, were sent back to Fort Fetterman to bring up more food and ammo, this under heavy infantry escort.

Thereafter, Crook continued to displace his camp still farther southward, until he was almost bumping the base of the Bighorns, the object being to get in lush country where there was grass, good water, wood, and brook trout in abundance. In this manner, he sat it out through the high crisis of campaign, rating his own expedition *hors de combat*. If it was such, he had so made it through headlong action. He was the perpetrator of the crisis.

Crazy Horse, on the other hand, not only joined the great encampment on the Little Bighorn with his warriors already preparing to fight again on call: Their arrival and their chant of victory raised Cheyenne and Sioux war frenzy to an even higher pitch. Their performance and fervor gave an uplift to the community and made the fighters feel indomitable. Crook's retreat, in effect, certified the claim. No stake to be won on the battlefield counts more than this.

If the difference between winning and losing is reflected in how the two sides react in spirit to the experience of a common field, the Rosebud had to be an Indian victory, though it is usually termed a "drawn fight." To call it such is to overlook or discount everything that came of it and to mock the most basic military values.

Warrior bands rode southward beyond Goose Creek, following up Crook to foray and feint around the edges of the camp, ambushing patrols and water and hunting parties, setting the fields afire, running off the stock, and in general, making sure that Crook and his soldiers would get little rest. Whether he was so preoccupied by this marginal harassment or temporarily engaged in such pained reflection over his one day on the Rosebud, Crook failed to do the one thing that a sense of duty and of situation should have compelled: Send a message north to Custer or anyone else, reporting that his column had engaged the Indian battle order and found it to be in such strength that the army had to withdraw from the zone of decisive operations.

There is no explanation for this lapse on the part of a dedicated commander of whom so many favorable words have been spoken. Of the omission, much evil was to come, though it is unthinkable that Crook, whose character is unassailable, would let it occur for personal reasons. He was a good hater at times. He despised Sheridan, his overall commander in the West, and let it be known that such were his sentiments. That bias was by no means unreasonable. Crook rated Sheridan far too vindictive. Still, Crook was not a man who, out of deviousness, would have contributed to a wanton sacrifice of troops. He cared about the soldier too much for that.

Crook stayed south of Goose Creek and was lethargic and silent during the week that Custer was moving up, and on through the six weeks that followed. It is an aberration, an enigma in a career otherwise generally lustrous, though it is not strange that he survived it, as did his reputation.

The irony is that everybody was playing dum-dum. Crook kept beefing to his staff that he was getting no word from Terry or Gibbon, and they were no less touchy because they heard nothing from Crook. This being the common plaint of the seniors, they must have been equally willing to let George do it, and George was intent on special business of his own, unconcerned about spreading the word.

Here we have the fugue theme of a memorable campaign. The army was playing that it didn't need communications anymore.

9

Custer's Last Stand

᠍᠍᠍᠍᠍᠍᠍᠍᠍᠍᠍᠍

CUSTER on that fateful morning remains an enigma. There may be relative certainty only about what he did; there can be none about his thoughts.

What Sergeant Curtis had learned on his lonesome round was conveyed to the regimental commander. It was some time later that the scout party returned after reconning the Indian camp from the heights at a distance of around fifteen miles. The spot was later dubbed the Crow's Nest. The object was much too far away to reveal important detail, the light was thin, morning haze draped the valley, and the line of poplars and willows along the sinuous course of the river effectively hid from view the village lodges. The Indian scouts, however, reported observing an enormous horse herd on a ridge west of the river and were markedly impressed by its size. There is no doubt about the correctness of their report, for that is where the herd was located, although Custer later went to their same observation point and saw nothing.

While the collation of the two reports afforded full reason for caution, there was none in the one man who counted. Custer was bent on seeing more, though it cost him a black eye. Sometime later, he called his officers together to tell them what he had learned and what he intended. Whether he regarded the intelligence as an excuse for violating General Terry's stricture not to attack until the other columns were upcoming—an accusation made by his critics—that is precisely how he used it. The argument as to whether Terry had given him an order or an instruction is made trivial by the consequence.

Custer said to the assembly that the Seventh had to prepare to attack as soon as possible, either that or the tribes might get away. If anyone hearing this declaration of intent, other than several of the scouts, either questioned or protested, there is no record. A kind of gloom was rising from the bellies of the Ree and the Crow.

Yet with Custer's pronouncement of the order had come a plan of attack wholly inconsistent with his discussion of the situation. Here was the irreparable blunder made right at the start. For if the information was correct, it said clearly that the hour for surprise had passed. Either the enemy would be in retreat or if he was willing to give battle, he would also be ready, prepared, and probably standing on ground of his own choosing. It was therefore too late for shock action by Custer and the regiment, aimed to erupt the encampment and panic its people. The warriors, unencumbered by their dependents, should be set up outside the perimeter of the camp, not merely to fight but to ambush on the largest possible scale.

Inasmuch as their numbers and exact placement remained unknown to Custer, the problem required that he keep the regiment together and under tight control until he could measure the danger. Common sense and tactical logic demanded nothing less. Moreover, he had given the Indians an additional half day in which to refine their preparations, or so he should have reckoned it after being apprised of the surveillance.

All of these prime considerations were either discounted or brushed aside as Custer launched on a wholly opposite course, whether because his faculties were impaired, or because ambition made him reckless, or because earlier success had filled him with contempt for the Indian as a fighter. To do that which invites defeat is in any circumstance foolish, and in this instance would be ruinous, in that while disregarding what higher command had directed, he would be prolonging a war. Still, he did it! Right at the start, he divided the regiment into three columns, each of which would advance on a different line, out of sight and beyond sound of the others—a sensible arrangement only if Custer had been conducting a reconnaissance instead of seeking all-out battle.

Could he have had any such thought in mind? General Terry wrote later in his official report that Custer must have believed that the Indians were already getting away. These gentlemanly words spoken for the defense are the one possible kindly interpretation to be made of his motive and action.

The morning advance was slow and cautious. It was about high noon on June 25, or approximately three hours after the Sioux got the full warning, that the pace quickened as the Seventh became irretrievably committed. The regiment was then approaching the divide from where it could see the Little Bighorn valley.

The average company counted forty men or a few more. Each trooper had been ordered to carry twelve pounds of oats for his mount, an extra handicap that must have run these chargers into the ground before they entered upon the combat field.

One battalion of three companies under Captain Frederick W. Benteen, an old hand, steady and war-wise, rode west as instructed to scout out the South Fork and continue on to the creek beyond, prior to turning toward the enemy encampment. Taking approximately the same line as Benteen was the pack train, escorted by one troop under Captain Thomas M. McDougall, which contingent counted 130 men, or twenty percent of the regimental strength.

The reason for this oblique, major diversion remains a mys-

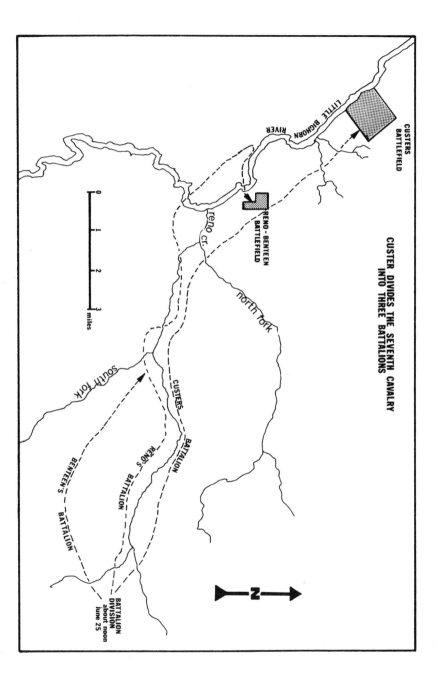

CUSTER DIVIDES THE SEVENTH CAVALRY
INTO THREE BATTALIONS

tery. If the object was to make certain that the Indians were not getting away, the mission still became a wild-goose chase. Furthermore, if that was to be the situation, the 130-or-so men under Benteen and the troop with McDougall would perforce be operating as blocking force, and confiding to their care the pack train with the reserve ammo was therefore outright recklessness. Of this mission, wherein his vaguely defined task was to wander from valley to valley, Benteen would later make this biting comment, "I understood it as a rather senseless order . . . Carried out, I would have been twenty miles away."

The rest of the regiment split in twain soon after crossing the divide to begin the drop into the Little Bighorn. The circumstances in which the two battalions parted company to go their separate ways were almost ridiculously melodramatic and must have pained Clio, the muse of history.

Fred Girard, a civilian interpreter who had been cantering along in the van, on coming to a knoll, sighted forty to fifty warriors galloping tight down the valley along the flat, far bank of the river. They could have been racing to the village to spread the alarm.

Gesturing grandly, Girard shouted to Custer, "Here are your Indians, running like devils!"

At that point Custer, through his adjutant, the Canadian, Lieutenant W. W. Cooke, relayed to Major Marcus A. Reno the words by which Reno's three-company battalion became committed, "Charge after them and you will be supported by the whole outfit."

Uttered on spur-of-the-moment impulse, seemingly without thought, those several phrases were to determine the fortunes of the day. Did they then constitute a competent order? No more so than had the loose instruction given Benteen. No object was defined for the Reno battalion; no limit was fixed on the depth to which it might involve the regiment. Reno was simply to run after Indians. Here was military operation being conducted in the spirit of the paper chase or the huntsman bawling, "Tally ho! There goes the fox!"

Theirs was not to reason why. Reno perforce swung left on the chase that took him to a ford, over the river and through the trees that soon screened him from Custer's sight. To begin, it was a free gallop on a flat floodplain to run down a few braves. Custer, at the same time, after holding briefly in place to see Reno on his way, was swinging his five companies wide and over the fairly even ground of the reverse slope of the ridge line east of the river.

It simply had to be Custer's intention to attack the Indian encampment from the far end. The almost clifflike sheerness of the bluffs east of the river forbade an earlier practical strike against the enemy flank.

By the time the two battalions were out of sight of one another, they were also beyond signaling range. They could exchange information no faster than a horse could cover the ground between. If either battalion became critically compromised, reinforcement was minimally thirty minutes away, with the interval rapidly lengthening.

For Reno, there was first the chase in which he was outrun. To begin the action, there was initially a scattering fire from a few casual resisters off the flanks that hurt no one. This fire thickened as the battalion galloped unscathed to within practical carbine range of the first lodges. No ambush, it had all of the enticements of such, for the prime effect was to suck the battalion in deeper. A first illusion of easy success, it was sustained just long enough to prove ruinous.

We have here beyond any doubt a dramatic example of surprise followed by countersurprise. Chief Runs-the-Enemy gives his clear account of it. As the cavalry thundered along in hot pursuit, the Sioux leaders together sat talking and smoking their pipes. Then they heard the sounds of small arms fire. They ran from their tepees. Bullets whizzed through the camp. A scream was heard from lodge to lodge,

"Woo, Woo, hay-ay, hay-ay!"—roughly, "Warriors to your saddles, the white soldiers have come." Runs-the-Enemy dashed for the upper end of the camp. He thought he was quick, but he found hordes of Sioux warriors boiling out ahead of him. Many of them were naked, but all were armed. So seeing, Runs-the-Enemy checked.

The explanation for the Sioux complacency before Reno came on firing is little short of amusing. The warriors who scouted the Seventh Regiment early that morning had never reported. That part of it, though it precipitated the attack, was a false alarm. But a homing band of Sioux had seen the cavalry camp, then turned about, and by 9:00 A.M. had brought the warning to the council. It lit no fire under the chiefs. After mulling over the information that the army was at hand, they decided that there need be no rush, since no enemy, red or white, had ever dared attack a full mustering of the Sioux in broad daylight. They went on with their pow-wowing and smoking, and no one moved to bring the horses from the ridge until the bullets began to fly.

The only lesson that appears to stand out in this battle is that appearances deceive only persons who mistrust them along with incurable simpletons. It was bad enough and sad enough that Reno, if not his scouts and his troopers, was wholly misled by an initially weak resistance from an enemy who also had taken far too much for granted. Far worse, the quite accidental deception must have contributed to the undoing of the whole Custer operation. Everyone was in such a hurry that one fleeting wisp of intelligence came to be treated as the final word, which has happened in many battles.

Two very able officers, Captain Myles W. Keogh and Lieutenant Cooke, were the instruments thereof. They belonged with the Custer battalion. When Reno peeled off, they rode along with him to get a feel of the situation. There could be no other reason for their going—one a troop commander, the other the adjutant. Reno lost them at the ford when he signaled for an extended pace. But they must have stayed long enough to encounter the weak and unorganized fire from the fringes of the enemy camp. It might have been better all around had they not gone at all.

The quick, the superficial glance convinced them. They spurred back to Custer to report that all was going well, which was truth as they knew it, though not true whatever. Custer was fully disposed to believe them, if only because wishing had made it so.

There is a tale that when last seen by Reno's soldiers, Custer, mounted, was atop the bluff on the other side of the Little Bighorn waving them on. Then he vanished from sight and right after that the Sioux lowered the boom on Reno. This yarn is accepted. A plaque marks the spot. It is still to be doubted. The source is one of Reno's lieutenants, a spinner of tall stories. From where Custer is said to have waved, the distance to where Reno's soldiers had to be, owing to the westward loop in the river, is so far away that recognition would have been impossible.

At about the time the two battalions came even, Custer dispatched a mounted messenger, Sergeant Daniel Kanipe, who galloped to the rear with the request that the mule train be rushed forward with the reserve ammunition. Far from being a call for help, the message and all else confirm that Custer was anticipating a field day killing Indians. The time was about midafternoon and it would take Kanipe almost an hour to get to Benteen and then to McDougall.

To make doubly sure, another messenger was sent within a few minutes, probably at about the time when the battalion checked at the one deep notch in the straight-running ridge. This time the courier was Private John Martin, serving as Custer's trumpet orderly for the day. Until lately, he had been Giovanni Martini, a newly arrived immigrant who spoke little English. A good soldier this one, a Martini without a twist. Still, there was such concern that he might garble an oral message, that Lieutenant Cooke wrote it out, "Benteen come on. Big village. Be quick. Bring packs. P.S. Bring pacs."

Ponder the message. Cooke rightly passed to Benteen, the senior, the responsibility to get McDougall forward. The rush must have frazzled him a bit. He scrawled and he misspelled. The reference to the big village is almost irrelevant. What Benteen needed most was a firm fix on Custer's location. That Cooke's emphasis is on ammunition rather than human reinforcement reflects an unbounded optimism, and there is much more of that from the witnesses Kanipe and Martin.

During the same interval in which these messages were going off to Benteen, Reno and his soldiers west of the river were fighting for life on the brink of disaster, though neither Custer nor any of his elements were in position to observe it, all having cantered on north.

The warriors came swarming on and firing in such numbers that, in his first attempt to save the command, Reno had his men dismount to skirmish as infantrymen, using whatever cover the nonundulating ground afforded. The floodplain is markedly free of brush or boulder beyond a few yards to either side of the stream line. Still, it was not the effectiveness of the Sioux fire that chilled Reno. Only one man had been thus far lost. Superior numbers, this and this only, stopped him. As if arising out of the earth, hordes of Sioux appeared on his left flank and rear. There was no thoroughfare to his right, due to the twisting of the river. Steadily expanding, the mounted movement must in time cut off the battalion, encompassing its destruction.

So for the second time in the action, Reno was having to exercise an independent judgment, though now it concerned a change from the direction in which Custer had launched him, with men's lives at stake. A quite unsteadying situation, it could have been much easier for Reno had he, over time, become closely identified with his units, their leaders, and especially with Custer. But he was a man emotionally pretty much at sea, tossed into action as carelessly as one might discard a shirt, with no confiding conversation between him and the regimental commander. Had Custer been bent on pushing Reno beyond his depths, that was exactly the way to do it. Here was the fatal flaw in Custer's makeup that has been so greatly overlooked. He virtually arrived at decisions according to the striding of his mount. His failure to discuss his operational ideas with his subordinates has few exceptions. Practically nothing is revealed about his manner of thinking in what they said of him.

Here we have an altogether too familiar figure in military literature—the man isolated from his lieutenants because he is at the top, though the need of the fullest possible understanding is mutual. Weep for such a character if one must. For free exchange, there is no substitute. Nothing else so well lubricates the wheels of higher command. But Custer couldn't see it. Hungry for adulation, with a pack of devotees ever in his train, he still must have been a very lonely man.

Unprepared for a head-on collision with the Sioux nation, shaken by surprise, Reno, even so, ordered the one logical and semiresistant maneuver still within his options. And it might have worked had the five Custer companies still been standing in place as a back-up force. The men were told to withdraw to a shallow wood copse on the right flank, within a bend of the river. To that cover, some of the less doughty soldiers and scouts had already repaired out of fear, as had the horse holders with their spans of four. The move was a temporary expedient and nothing more, so numerous were the warriors and so unpromising the cover. Reno was in fact already defeated.

The fall-back, not orderly but pretty much helter-skelter, was made in time at little cost, except for equipment abandoned on the field. It succeeded only because the Sioux were not pressing close. In contrast to the head-on tactics of the cavalry, the enemy swarms were moving elusively, circling beyond effective carbine range to keep down casualties, extending the trap while awaiting the ultimate collapse of the defenders where they stood. With so many fleeting targets dashing about within the sights of the troopers, sooner or later it was certain to happen.

At the position in the river bend, the defense—and it is a euphemism—was extremely short-lived. Although some of the soldiers were dogging it and taking no part in the exchange, and some of the recruits were blasting away blindly, among the veteran active firers ammunition had already begun to run low before the retrograde movement.

That in itself doomed the brief attempt to hold on to something, though the position itself was no good. The battalion left flank dangled in air, since the wood cover did not afford room for a fire line with refused (turned back) flanks. Also, the enemy could finally take the line in rear by coming across the river.

The choice left to Reno too quickly became one of sticking it out in the wood copse until the last man was killed or seeking any escape from annihilation.

Reno was no last-ditch diehard, and the situation was one that would have frayed the nerves of many more resolute commanders.

He shouted to his men to move to their horses.

Some didn't get the order, or so they said later, and in one way or another, seventeen men became abandoned in the wood.

As Reno gave the order, "Mount!" a large party of Sioux dashed toward him, firing.

The enemy had seen the moves prior to a breakthrough attempt.

From the Sioux fire, Bloody Knife, one of the Ree scouts,

took a bullet that shattered his skull. His brains spattered over Reno's face and jacket. The shock of it, so goes the story, did Reno in.

Failing wholly to give the follow-up order, Reno spun his horse and spurred for the nearest bluffs, one mile to his rear and eastward. Most of his men followed. No retreat, it was mad, panic flight.

For so acting, Reno was later accused of cowardice. Whether he deserved such a slur is to this day a good question. A fair slice of his battalion was already *hors de combat* from death, wounds, malingering, and stark fear. Amid the tumult, with his command scattered, Reno's bolt for high ground might have been the best way to let his men know what he wanted. Quite possibly, had Reno been killed while trying to be the last man off the field, no one would have been saved. It is so very easy to condemn when one was not there. Yet an attempt at orderly withdrawal, while honorable, could have been fatal.

Though Reno did not know it, when he galloped for the high ground on the shortest line, there was another ford directly in his path. The swarming Sioux raced on ahead of him. As it worked out, the worst ordeal by fire for the fugitives, the heaviest losses, and the most heart-breaking scenes were at this juncture where the cavalrymen ran the gauntlet of shooting, screaming Sioux. The passage of torment has been described in detail in numerous, highly readable books and is here best passed over.

The Indians did not follow beyond the river. The slope of the east bank is cruelly steep. Somehow, they made it, stumbling, staggering men; their minds almost blank, pulling at weary horses. What was left of the battalion got together again atop the bluff. By then, these soldiers were clean spent. Had the Sioux but followed up, there could have been no organized resistance. Heaven briefly was merciful.

There are many ifs in this battle. For example, had Keogh and Cooke but stayed with Reno a little longer, or had Custer tarried a while atop the bluffs or stationed there an observation party with couriers, the day might have been saved. Custer could have used some of his companies to outflank the Indians who were attacking Reno, then covered his withdrawal, and at that point decided whether to go on the defensive on favorable ground or to use the regiment as a whole in a blocking movement toward the northwest. Benteen's battalion could have been brought up in an hour or sooner. That column, during this time, was about six miles away and to the southeast, and was accomplishing nothing.

The supreme tragedy of the Seventh Cavalry on that day was that its commander did nothing right, behaving as if the book had never been written. Soundness in procedure being absent, the play had to unfold as if the Indian chiefs had read Custer's mind, or Fate had written the lines. The Reno attack and withdrawal might have pulled the hostile force off balance, drawing its preponderant strength to the southeast; nothing of the kind happened. It simply alerted the mass of warriors. Most of the horse herd was still on the ridge; given time in which to arm and mount up, the bands of Cheyenne did not follow the Sioux up the valley. They waited as if they knew what was coming. The theme here is not unlike what happened to General Douglas MacArthur's forces on the Chongchon River in Korea seventy-four years later, when again forces were divided in anticipation of quick, easy victory. While generals have to remain overly hopeful, ever to count on such is hardly generalship.

Somewhere around the time that Reno's men fled from their well-blooded field, Custer and the five companies, having ridden twelve miles over fairly smooth ground in about ninety minutes or so from where they had split from Reno, came to the tapering end of the ridge on the east bank of the Little Bighorn. At that point the van of the regiment came even with the lower end of the enemy camp.

There, with horses and riders strung out over more than

three-quarters of a mile of trail space, they entered upon a prepared battlefield. Reno, though unfortunate enough, had escaped that unkind fate. He owed his repulse to the speed of the Sioux reaction and not to their forethought. As to what happened to Custer and his people after they galloped into a deadfall, historians have continued to speculate. The Indian witnesses are all said to be unreliable, which is only partly true and more than a bit snobbish, in that the same may be said fairly of almost any combat hand. If ten Custer men had survived, we would have ten quite different tales of how the battle went. The mute evidence of the field is also moot. There are, however, some fairly definite guidelines.

The most commonly held view among historians who have tried to reconstruct the battle, few of whom know combat in its multifarious aspects, is that Reno's battalion was held, turned, and routed by an Indian force under Chief Gall, the Hunkpapa war leader, who then doubled back to fall upon the rear of Custer's battalion and begin the second action. This thesis contends that a second and larger body of Indians then closed on the front of the Custer battalion from the lower end of the village. Here it should be noted that the whole camp was on flat ground and that "lower" and "upper" refer only to the running of the Little Bighorn.

All of this is a pipe dream. From any rational view of tactical action and reaction under the stress of combat, and of human capability in these circumstances, that story of the fight cannot stand up under critical examination. It is inconsistent with logistical tables and glandular truths. The actions had to be independent of one another. Hence, the tale is interesting only as an example of how myth, once loosed from the bottle, becomes sky-filling.

For one thing, Custer's column was going on too fast to permit it, even if the horses were moving at a trot. By the time the warriors had chased Reno to the river, they were almost six miles from where Custer became stopped. Also, they had fought a thirty- to forty-minute, wearing action. The ground between the two scenes of engagement was not too rough, but the serpentine line of the river was a restricting obstacle to the east. On the west, the populated lodges intervened. Even charged-up Indians are not so endowed that they may accomplish superhuman feats and the harassers of Reno were tired Indians.

What we know for certain is that Custer charged deliberately into a neatly rigged trap, though it is likely that the trap came about empirically rather than through preconceived design, there being no centralized Indian leadership. The trap was far enough removed from the Indian noncombatants that it endangered them little or not at all.

Some of the chiefs knew, or thought they knew, that Custer would go for the village at the lower end. This was not great wisdom, the ground making it all but inevitable. So largely by accident, one chief and another moving his band to the point of threat, they established a front or blocking force of mounted skirmishers to turn him that way. But they would hardly have taken the risk of turning him toward the village unless the blocking force was in fact the base of a large ambush in the shape of an inverted L. The cavalry forming the base of the hostile L simply blocked Custer from entering upon the lower end of the village.

This same kind of trap was turned many times against Americans fighting in Vietnam, only there it was by deliberate design.

That the battalion's ultimate fire line extended so very far speaks loudly. The force was unequipped for any such deployment. When relatively few men are spread out more than one thousand yards and are armed only with short-ranging carbines and revolvers, they cannot be of support to one another, especially in hill country, where the folding of the land provides defilade to flat fire. The killing zone of each group would be well under fifty yards. Infiltration between groups would engage little danger. None but an idiot would

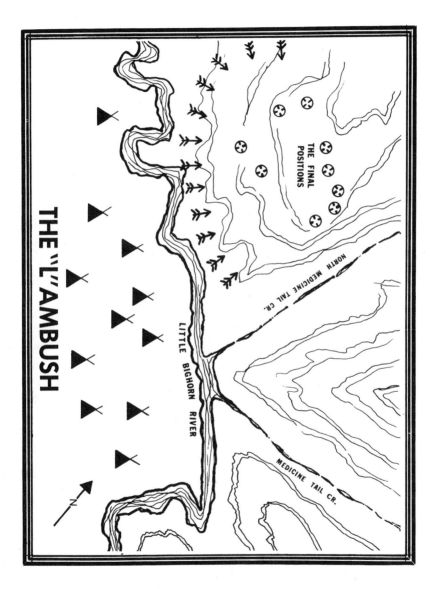

THE "L" AMBUSH

THE FINAL POSITIONS

LITTLE BIGHORN RIVER

NORTH MEDICINE TAIL CR.

MEDICINE TAIL CR.

N

order things that way, purposefully overextending. Mutual support is the imperative of any formation in the attack, being no less desirable in the defense.

On the other hand, this same distance of about three-quarters of a mile is approximately the natural extension of a battalion-size horse column in rapid movement over rough ground in unfamiliar country. The longer the march, the more cavalry, moving in twos or fours, strings out. Except in flat terrain, its stretchings and collections are accordionlike. Furthermore, the forward elements of the Seventh were later found bunched up around Custer, while those of the rear were more evenly spaced, bespeaking that the front had come to a sudden and jarring stop, as in a chain reaction on an expressway, while the rear was given more time and space in which to brake. Old horse soldiers have witnessed this phenomenon on maneuvers and are well aware that modern man's reaction time in a motor vehicle is no better than that of a horseman trying to avoid collision.

All of these signs point to the conclusion that the deployment of the doomed battalion could not have been voluntary. Custer was stopped and turned by volume fire in the moment when such change of direction had to be ruinous. When it happened, or a few minutes later, his strung-out column became a line as its individuals faced left and started moving downslope toward the village, still having little or no measure of the resistance from that quarter, the way seeming open to their senses. In extremity, the troopers continued to respond to the gravitational pull of the target. For men in combat, the attraction is downhill, not up. The flow is as of water.

The changes of direction and of formation from column to line, however, must have been for lack of alternative, due to the presence of a block on the south-to-north axis, for it was exactly the wrong way to go about attacking the village. The battalion's one chance rested in staying collected as long as possible, and where it fronted, the river was a barrier.

Two fairly evenly sloped ravines that cut toward the river

were in the battalion's foreground. Where they bottomed out onto the shelf at the base of the ridge, the Indian main force was already spread in strength, or fast gathering. A minor bank there, which is hardly a subridge, served as a natural earthwork for the Indian skirmishers, who in any case were beyond effective carbine range. These hostiles were neatly positioned to rake Custer's thin line with rifle fire of sufficient intensity that the cavalrymen, already dismounted, could not advance afoot. The warriors of this deployment on the low ground had crossed the river afoot. They fought like infantrymen, advancing cautiously from dip to dip and hummock to hummock. The slope was otherwise pretty barren of cover.

Whether there remained at this stage any possibility of Custer's backing away is a question. The blocking force most likely had already closed on his immediate rear. It is enough to say that he held with his plan of desperation. The rearward companies, there are reasons to believe, could have pulled out. They stayed with the fight.

The aforegoing appreciation of what happened was arrived at by deductive reasoning, based on my knowledge of tactics and logistics. Afterward, when I was looking for illustrations for the book, in an obscure file in the National Archives, I chanced to come upon Chief Runs-the-Enemy's account of how the battle turned.

Toward clearer understanding, what Runs-the-Enemy saw and said is best related in the third person. He and his band of two hundred warriors were all hidden behind the first rise of ground, just east of the river, which I have earlier identified as the location of the Indian main force. Sitting Bull had briefly moved among these people saying, "Make a brave fight!" fulfilling his obligation as head cheerleader. Runs-the-Enemy looked and panned toward the high ground. A band of Cheyenne, mounted, had stopped the Custer column by fire from the front, then hooked around the column to the eastward. There were other Indians on the west, north, and east sides of the column, which left a gap to the south that was quickly if only partly filled in by Runs-the-Enemy and his warriors, thereby almost completing the envelopment.

Until Custer and the battalion were all but surrounded, there had been little shooting by either side, except for the initial volleying by the Cheyenne of the blocking force. The Cheyenne were probably led by Chief Two Moons. To begin the pinching-out action, a band of Sioux then charged the already dismounted battalion from the rear, shooting a few men and stampeding some of the horses. The return fire from the soldiers was so strong that the line of mounted Sioux had to retire to the high ground. Worried by their departure, fearing that the envelopment might be collapsing, Runs-the-Enemy left his band and went in person to reconnoiter the situation to the east. He found the Sioux line already re-forming. When he returned to his band, Custer's soldiers were still fighting. Shortly they made a rush down the two ravines toward the river. The rush was met by the Indians' firing, then advancing from behind the earth bank that had served them as a shield.

The relatively few surviving soldiers then backed away uphill. After that, according to Runs-the-Enemy, they "made a stand all in a bunch." Thereafter cavalrymen and braves got all mixed up in a hand-to-hand grapple. The Indians became so overwrought when they closed in from several sides that they accidentally killed or wounded not a few of their own people.

When the resistance ended, so says Runs-the-Enemy, they threshed the field, looking for soldiers wounded that they might shoot them dead.

In the final scene, the bodies of the cavalrymen were stripped and their uniforms were piled high and set ablaze while the warriors danced about.

This is about how Runs-the-Enemy remembered the battle. It is the only Indian account that seems to be consistent with the evidence from the field itself, as with what is known about the physical resources of man and horse, and is the more credible due to Runs-the-Enemy's modesty about his own role.

In this famous encounter, approximately 225 cavalrymen, and some well-marked civilians, died. The toll included three of Custer's blood kin and a brother-in-law, as well as a news correspondent. The precise number of American dead cannot be stated due to faulty records-keeping by the army. (Lest too much be made of that, it should be noted that the same kind of blanks occurred in the Korean War.) They were slain by 5,000 Indians, more or less. The estimates of the hostile strength run from 1,800 to 9,000. Runs-the-Enemy guessed it at 4,000 warriors.

At least 40 percent of the soldiers were raw recruits who had not previously faced fire. Some had mounted a horse for the first time on starting the ride West. Many were without any formal range training.

Saved from the slaughter were Custer's Crow and Ree scouts. Alone among the members of the expedition, they had warned Custer that he was taking on too much and risking destruction. So when the column began its approach to the low ground, they held back atop the bluff, and before they had a chance to see how things were going, they rode away. This was greater wisdom than shone elsewhere on that day. The youngest Crow, seventeen-year-old Curly, did a complete circle around the Reno and Benteen battalions, then rode north toward the Yellowstone to carry the news, and doing it not too well. He told General Terry that the whole Seventh Regiment had been wiped out.

Bravery counts for little once weapons go empty, unless an ammo reserve is handy. Therefore the result of this fight was never in doubt once the commitment was made. Many of the horses that had carried the troopers four hundred miles or so to the engagement were shot by their riders to provide breastworks. But a dead horse affords protection in only one quarter and the hostiles were moving in from all directions. They, too, ran short of rifle ammo and shifted to bow and arrow. So the horse-killing was a pitiful but vain sacrifice that simply extended for a few more terrible minutes a fight that could hardly have lasted more than forty minutes.

The braves kept coming up the gullies and crowding closer as they wiggled from cover to cover. In the end, the Indian losses from army fire had to be insignificant. Carbines and revolvers are poor tools in such a contest. As the dust cloud rises and chambers foul, such weapons go out, and men spread too far from one another on a stricken field too soon lose steadiness of aim, however dauntless their courage.

Seventy dead cavalry horses were later found on the battlefield; the others had been taken live by the hostiles. Yet there were only two dead Indian ponies on the ridge. It is perhaps the truest measure of the relative fire effectiveness of the two sides.

On this field, the earth bank near the river and downhill from where the Custer men made their last stand figures conspicuously in the lasting legend, as in Runs-the-Enemy's story. Covering the main body of skirmishers concealed there, it barred the way. The legend has it that in the final scene when army ammunition ran out and resistance all but ceased, from behind the earth bank Chief Crazy Horse and his warriors swarmed upward for the kill. By that time, Chief Gall and some of his warriors had closed on the left of the Custer line. But Gall certainly had not redeployed from the Reno battlefield nor had he initiated the attack on Custer.

Of the numerous other chiefs in the action, the best-known name is Sitting Bull, and his role was exclusively that of prophet and exhorter. Chief Red Cloud's son, Jack Red Cloud, fought with Crazy Horse's band, and it is suspected that the old man gave his blessing to the enterprise. Red Cloud was a very wily Indian.

Jack, the son, gives the vaguest account of the action, "The

Sioux kept circling around Custer and as his men came down the ridge we shot them. Then the rest dismounted and gathered in a bunch, kneeling down and shooting from behind their horses."

Here is a view of the battlefield as a man hugging earth might see it. Adding nothing, it is therefore beyond cavil.

One truth of that day, concerning which there is no dispute, is that every man with Custer was killed. Some few of the dead were scalped or their bodies otherwise mutilated. Later it was said that the warriors were guiltless and that some of the squaws did the dirty work. Who knows? Custer's body, apart from two bullet wounds—one in the head and the other in the heart, either of which would have caused death—was unmarred, though like the others stripped of all clothing. When asked why Custer had not been hacked up, Runs-the-Enemy responded with two mutually exclusive answers: The Indians respected him as a valiant foeman, and besides, no brave was able to recognize him, due to his having recently shorn his locks.

About one century later, U.S. forces fighting in the Central Highlands of Vietnam in June 1966 were directed to name their large-scale operations after famous Americans, such as Nathan Hale, Nathaniel Hawthorne, or Paul Revere. As it happened, the largest and most difficult campaign of that summer was called Operation Crazy Horse. The Seventh Cavalry, still going strong, though it was riding helicopters instead of Front Royal remounts, wished that honor on him, feeling that he deserved to be hailed as a great American. From among the chiefs who had zapped their regiment in 1875, they had made a highly proper selection.

The fight that legend says Crazy Horse and his warriors closed out is known to history as the "Custer Massacre." Though as a national milestone, the incident is no less prominent than the Alamo, Bastogne, and Pork Chop Hill, the title is wrong because of one word with malice misapplied. There was no massacre. The terms of the battle had been predetermined by Custer's decision, and its fully mournful ending was the all but inevitable consequence of the headlong nature of the attack.

That the argument persists until today as to whether Custer was right or wrong—and it is hardly less impassioned now than when widow's weeds were sprouting in the wake of the wake—suggests only that people try to get their fun that way in lieu of something better to do.

So to get along with the story, we return to the two messengers dispatched by Custer to bring up the rear. They were anything but mad gallopers bathing horses in lather out of sheer desperation. How they acted reveals much of what Custer was thinking on that day.

Take the first messenger, Sergeant Kanipe, a veteran. He had been sent along after Custer made his snapshot appraisal that Reno was getting along OK in his assault down the valley. Sent to give his message to the commander of the mule train escort, he tried to pass it to Benteen, a not uncommon failing in combat couriers. Benteen shooed him along to McDougall, whom he had left well behind in the act of trying to regather the train of scattered jugheads that had become enamored of a bog. But before posting off, Kanipe sang out to Benteen's soldiers, "We've got 'em boys, we've got 'em." He had to believe it from what he had seen or heard. Combat cheerleading does not go so far as to permit deception of uncommitted troops by NCOs, although high commanders sometimes try it. So Benteen was given no cause to feel alarm, though from frustration he had already changed direction and was heading toward the fight.

Then about fifteen or twenty minutes later came the second messenger, Bugler Martin, a recruit but not green, having seen military service in Italy. Martin had followed along with Custer perhaps half the distance to the end of the village before being pared off to serve as courier. On his ride back, some Sioux out of ambush put a bullet into the withers of Martin's mount, and the wound bled badly. Here was a first-time experience likely to unnerve a well-seasoned trooper.

By then, Reno's battalion must have been in heavy trouble. Had Martin stopped to look, he might have seen. That he did not do so implies that instead of riding the skyline, he was wisely posting along the reverse slope. Still, Bugler Martin, whose knowledge of the language was so slight that he could not be trusted with an oral message, after handing Cooke's note to Benteen, said to troops, that under the pressure of the Reno-Custer assaults, the hostiles were "skeedaddling." A slang word that today finds its place in the dictionary, it must have been passed to the newly-arrived American, Martini, alias Martin. The message in itself conveys that Cooke thought of the battalion and the pack train as one force under Benteen's leading.

There is no more eloquent testimony as to the high hopes, excessive expectations, and false judgments of the situation that must have been in Custer's mind when, after concluding that Reno would hold his own, he led the overstrength battalion to its doom. He was not trying to pull Reno out of a hole or running out on him, although both of these motives have been imputed to him. He was intent on demonstrating to all concerned how the superior Indian-fighter had won his reputation. Time and distance so far separated the two points of attack that only a novice at war could imagine that the second would ease the pressure against the first.

Though Benteen, on getting the second message, became a badly worried soldier, in a sense decision was taken out of his hands; he had to quit the pivot and get going. One of his companies, without being given the word, was already raising a dust cloud as it pounded north. The slow-moving mule train was at least one hour to the rear. Still, without waiting for the packs, believing that McDougall would get the message and do his best, Benteen hurried along with his three cavalry companies and at last put them to a gallop, his troopers riding with drawn pistols. Benteen could hear heavy firing in the distance and he may have expected to encounter the Sioux around the next bend. Exciting stuff, it is ideally suited to TV.

The trail they rode of itself delivered them into Major Reno's position—along the bluff east of the river—in the nick of time to begin a salvage operation. Reno, not yet beleaguered, the Sioux having lost a golden opportunity, had called the roll and found that he was missing three officers and forty men. Those with him were still shaking and in no condition to fight. But at first, Benteen had no time to worry about Reno. The company under Captain Thomas B. Weir had pushed on, looking for Custer, and the others made ready to follow.

About midway between Reno's position and the lower end of the Indian village, Weir's company came to the high point of the ridge crest. From there, two miles off, they could see a field of action. Many Indians were moving about eccentrically and seemed to be shooting into the ground. Fitting Runs-the-Enemy's description of the coup-de-grace exercise, it is a partway fix on the sequence of events.

Of what Weir had sighted, however, Benteen's soldiers stayed unaware, for immediately their own problems became horizon-filling.

On observing Weir's approach, the Indians broke off their orgiastic celebration of the victory and galloped south to cut off the lead company. The cavalrymen dismounted, formed a skirmish line, and started to engage. It was an instinctive but foolhardy reaction, as they quickly realized.

What was left of the Seventh Regiment was now strung out over five or six miles of trail space. Reno's men were in no condition to come forward and the ammunition train was far to the rear. Attempt to hold the forward ground, and each element would become isolated and destroyed in detail.

The order was given to fall back on Reno. It was done just

in time. As Weir's company closed, hordes of warriors surrounded the position and the position on the bluff became fully besieged until nightfall. The troopers dug in with knives, tin cups, and mess kits, while ammunition cases and ration boxes were thrown up as barricades.

Most of the Indians retired to the lodges when dark came, leaving the bluff outposted. But the command was in no condition to attempt a break-out. The Indians renewed the attack on the following morning and fighting continued through most of the day. There was gallantry in the defense that slightly redeemed the blunders of the campaign. The garrison grew desperate for lack of water and the suffering of the wounded became acute, a mixture of evils more demoralizing to troops than their battle deaths. Nineteen men volunteered to run a patrol to the river, moving out with kettles and canteens on what seemed to be a hopeless mission, while covered by the fire of four sharpshooters. They made it without loss, although the slope is bare and the climb was strenuous. All were later decorated with the Medal of Honor.

In late afternoon of June 26, the Indians fired the hay fields in the valley, and through the cloud of smoke the soldiers watched with relief the departure of the whole enemy encampment. The great procession of people and ponies at first moving slightly north of west, then turned south to vanish within the Bighorn Mountains.

Wary of ambush and exhausted from the fight, the survivors still did nothing to find Custer, though the corpse-littered field was but a five-minute gallop down the ridge. During the two days of siege, the two battalions had lost thirty-two men killed and forty-four wounded. The horses and mules had gone unwatered since the start of battle. So there was essential work to be done at the base camp and full reason to exercise caution.

On the morning of June 27, the 450 men under General Terry and Colonel Gibbon, marching southward up the valleys of the Bighorn and Rosebud, drew even with the Custer battlefield. One patrol under Lieutenant James H. Bradley, who one year later would die bravely at Big Hole, had been scouting to the east of the Little Bighorn. It was Bradley who discovered the blood-drenched slope, first counted the bodies, and carried the shocking news to his military superiors, from whom it went to the outside world. A detail under Benteen was given the task of surveying the field. Next day the Seventh Cavalry moved up to the site of Custer's last stand to locate, identify where possible, and bury the dead.

There remained on the field one living thing, a badly wounded charger, the mount of dead Captain Keogh, named Comanche. The troopers nursed him as gently as they might a child, and by their ministrations saved him, despite multiple bullet wounds. Comanche lived to a ripe old age, and while never ridden again, became the center of attention in military reviews and other ceremonies.

The wounded men from the other battalions were littered to the steamer *Far West* at the mouth of the Bighorn. It was a tedious journey, the expedition not being equipped to handle a heavy burden of casualties. Not until the morning of June 30 were all of the sufferers boarded. The *Far West* docked at Bismarck in midday of July 5 and swiftly thereafter the news of the inglorious battle, along with the story of how the other two battalions had fought, was flashed to the world via a telegraph key under the hand of one J. M. Carnahan, who sat at his task for twenty-two hours.

The general reaction of the public to the story was one of shocked dismay and demand for vengeance, Custer having been a hero of the people. President U. S. Grant commented in his accustomed heavy fashion that the defeat on the Little Bighorn was an "unnecessary sacrifice of troops," which snap judgment is probably a flawless verdict on the operation. Yet Grant himself was not without fault. Of his decision had come Custer's restoration to military favor and to the command of the Seventh Cavalry, after Grant had been given more than sufficient reason to doubt that Custer was a responsible leader of fighting forces, but was instead a clumsy operator and a power-seeker in the realm of politics. If there is anything truly heroic about Custer, it must be read in his service in the Civil War.

There is call here for a reprise. Absurd though it be, unto the present day, no battle fought by Americans has been as fiercely debated as this one and none has received as much superficial attention from the writing armchair experts. Custer cultism is a phenomenon all the more baffling in view of the fact that the battle was hardly more than a ripple in the flow of the national history and its lessons, all negative, are equally redundant. So it perforce must be the mystery rather than the importance of the event, or for that matter, its tragedy, that accounts for its unique fascination. For in recent years in Vietnam on at least four occasions, whole infantry platoons were wiped out, and more to the point, ambushed and massacred, without stirring even a passing public interest in the question of what happened and why.

As is true of practically every other combat field engaging American arms, at the Little Bighorn there were minor phenomena defying explanation. To mention but three, there was the body of the lone cavalry sergeant found on the bluff about one-half mile to the rear of the rest of the slain, the few corpses found next the river, some of them decapitated, and the four Americans, including one doctor, who simply vanished into thin air.

In the immediate wake of the news, however, and through the years that followed until the present, main controversy between Custer adherents and detractors arose, heated, and persisted around two questions, the answers to both of which seem palpable.

Why did Custer make Reno a promise and then let him down?

Why did not Reno, having withdrawn, ride to help his chief?

Regarding the plaint of some inveterate cavalrymen, that if

Reno had but sustained the charge instead of dismounting his soldiers when confronted by superior numbers in the bottoms, he would then have routed the Sioux, one may only smile. It at least establishes that such delusions did not die with Fetterman, and may be taken seriously only as an example of professional lunacy in a mild form. Had Reno tried it, the whole regiment would have been wiped out. Let it be filed then with the boast of at least two modern commanders of armor, who said that if their divisions had been loosed at the Elbe in 1945, they would have taken Berlin before the Russians got within smelling range.

The notion that Custer reneged on a promise to Reno deserves closer scrutiny. Custer, via Lieutenant Cooke, had assured Reno only that, once committed, his battalion would be "supported by the whole outfit." That we have only Reno's word for the transmission is less relevant than that Custer may have meant one thing while Reno, to suit his purpose, construed it as meaning something else. In modern military parlance, "support" does not mean reinforcement on the same line when the need arises. The sense of it is that the nonengaged element will in proper time be committed against the common enemy. The words would not have limited Custer to moving on the same axis as Reno, while serving as his reserve. Though mistaken, Custer rode to his death keeping his promise.

On the other hand, that Reno was derelict, once he was beaten back, in not pushing north to help Custer, is a thought for simpletons. Any experienced observer of the impact of combat stress on men's powers must hoot at the idea. When troops hit bottom, knowing the extreme of physical and emotional exhaustion, no act of will may restore energy or superinduce group action. Only rest, with preferably a few winks of sleep, will initiate recovery. Reno was incapable of doing other than he did and so were his people.

Because the Reno battalion beyond doubt was immobilized by exhaustion, the question of the time element—whether on becoming non-engaged it might have advanced to support Custer and thereby averted the disaster—should not even arise. The controversial point is here noted only because the Custer cultists make a large issue of it. The chronological relationship of the two engagements, however, is the key to the problem of distinguishing between myth and fact in what has been written about how the hostiles performed.

Colonel W. A. Graham, U.S.A., though he was a judge advocate rather than a tactical specialist, probably devoted more years to researching the battle than any other person. His general conclusion as to the chronology is best stated in his own words:

> The logic of the whole situation, its time element, the distances traversed and the fact that fully three-quarters of the Indian force was waiting for Custer at the end of the village to ambush him as soon as he turned toward the river, impels the belief that the attack upon him commenced some time before Reno's retreat.

I find the common sense of this passage distinctly soothing. Little need be added to it and nothing should be taken away. Graham's words were called to my attention some months after I had reached and written almost identical conclusions after taking the logistical approach to the problem. The distinction here is that logistics implies the mathematics of movement whereas Graham's "logic" is the process of analysis and deduction. To be as accurate as possible, the combat historian needs both.

It is mainly Chief Gall among the hostiles who becomes the instrument by which the two widely separated fields of action are joined as if they did indeed interreact. Gall is thus made the superchief, the heavy smiter who also possessed decisive mobility, an unbeatable but rare combination. By thus accrediting him, the myth-makers not only have an argument; they have a good plot. Gall was burning for vengeance. Reno's sortie had come to within arrow-flight distance of the first lodges. Loose carbine fire had killed two of Gall's children and one squaw.

So Gall is pictured as energizing, if not commanding, the counterattack that routed Reno, then wheeling about, charging north and getting on Custer's rear in time to start the action that destroyed Yellow Hair and all of his men.

Now if the Indian had been capable of doing a bending race in and out of several hundred lodges in such way as to become a principal on both fields, they would have been in fact joined not only as to terrain but as to time sequence, and Reno should therefore have been able to support Custer. The nuances of the role accorded the Indian may not therefore be scored too lightly, since the hypothesis not only divides all of Gall into two parts but makes of Reno's cavalry a horse left at the post.

Either Gall has to be confirmed in his part as superstar in the Whirling Dervish manner or the play goes out of joint; the two fields stay unconnected and there remains no reason to assume that Crazy Horse was not again the superior tactician, as on the Rosebud. Gall's own statement, many times repeated, that to get personal vengeance he forayed with a hatchet and clove as many cavalry skulls as came within grappling distance, casts a first doubt on his prowess as a director of fighting forces. Still, that is not enough.

Apart from that bit of claiming, Gall was no braggart. Though most of what is credited to him on the red-letter day has to come from post-battle interviews after a long lapse of time, which is said to react on the imagination of the average ex-fighter like a triple martini, Gall never once reached for the laurels gratuitously tossed him by kindly historians. Like not a few non-Indian VIPs, his memory seems to have grown increasingly muddled out of the pressure contacts with newsmen and other recorders. Either that, or the press did him wrong, another not uncommon failing. Every interviewer credited himself with eliciting the first, full, and only truthful account of his doings from Chief Gall, leaving the skeptic to comment that these valiant clarifications still find us groping.

To a Chicago reporter on June 26, 1886, after saying somewhat vaguely that "Sitting Bull and I were at the point where Reno attacked," which remark probably referred to the location of their tepees, Gall gave the Custer fight a hasty onceover in the third person, never once implying that he was a main battle leader, the weight of his comment being that "those Indians ran out of ammunition and they then fired arrows from behind horses."

To a reporter of the St. Paul *Pioneer Press* on July 18, 1886, he discussed his role, largely with sign language, in greater detail. He said that when Custer first appeared with his troops on the ridge above the end of the village, he, Gall, along with three other Indians, was sitting on a mound six hundred yards away, within full sight of the soldiers, and stayed so seated as he watched them dismount and move down the ravines of the slope. It was also made clear by Gall, the reporter said, that the Cheyenne did most of the "bloody work" against Custer. Next, "then Gall described how he brought some of his own warriors on in time to kill the horse-holders and capture the horses of Keogh's and Calhoun's companies," this toward the rear of the column.

Thus to himself, Gall ascribes no outstanding role, none as a salient captain among captains, and makes no claim to having begun the attack on Custer, but to the contrary. Not less pertinent and to the same end were the questions and answers at the tail of the interview.

"Where was Sitting Bull all the time the soldiers were being killed?"

"Back in his tepee making medicine."

"Did he fight at all?"

"No, he made medicine for us."

"Did you fight Reno?"

"No, I only fought the white soldiers down this way."

Here Gall pointed to the Custer field.

"Then you know nothing of what happened at the other end of the village?"

"No, I was down among the Cheyenne looking out after our horses when the first attack was made."

When a coup-counting Sioux war chief is thus so abnormally modest about his deeds on the one day he shines in history, he might be allowed to have the last word for himself.

Gentlemanly courtesy virtually demands it.

Then there was one other thing. What made possible the speed of Custer's advance was that it was all over high but fairly even ground with comfortable footing, except where the trail drops sharply down into the coulee of North Medicine Trail Creek, a break shaped as if an ax had cut straight down through the ridge line.

The creek bed there is wet in dry season, and hardly a rivulet, though it runs a flowing stream when the snows melt. Where it threads the notch, the stream is about to empty into the river and the drop is only a few feet.

Come to that point, Custer had both a window opened toward the enemy camp and a possible sally port toward the village. He might have turned 90 degrees due west and launched his attack.

Of late years, Park Service historians have made much of this feature and its possible attraction on that day. Mainly because of the finding of combat metal on the spot—slugs and casings—which cannot otherwise be accounted for, they have Custer making an abortive move there, turning west into the constricted passage with the expectation of using it as his jump-off point, only to meet resistance coming up from the river. Thus confronted, it is theorized, Custer felt compelled to reverse himself, and thereafter the regimental column resumed its canter along the reverse crest of the ridge.

This legend appears in lately published government literature, which rather sprinkles the tale with holy water. There is still an earlier source. General Phil Sheridan in his writings alludes to the possibility, it having been reported to him that the grass at the mouth of the coulee had been beaten down as if the regiment had turned west.

Battlefield archaeology is a valuable corroborative and on occasion an essential corrective to other sources and findings. It is so used at Big Hole, Montana. When, on the other hand, it threshes about wildly only because battlefield rubble has been kicked up where little expected, while at the same time ignoring every valid tactical consideration, it is playing small games in the name of science.

A cavalry column at any pace above a walk which attempts to turn left at the foot of a steep slope while shifting from fours to lesser numbers due to the narrowness of the passage is already in deep trouble. To imagine that on then meeting resistance, it may turn in orderly fashion within the narrow defile and resume march in the prior direction is to credit it with the nimbleness of the pronghorn and the mountain goat.

Rather, here is what must happen. Oncoming horses, while braking on the downslope, still clog en masse the passage to the rear of the leaders. There ensues within the defile a melee growing worse by the second, men cursing and shouting orders, mounts milling and mauling. It is worse than bedlam. All control vanishes as units become scrambled. Toward unscrambling, riders must individually take to the banks of either side for the sorting out and reassembly. Most of this is terribly demoralizing and time-wasting, the work of an hour or more, causing a loss of all momentum.

A modern battalion of paratroops, jogging to an anticipated contact, would not fail to be thrown by such a mistaken maneuver. Something quite like it, though on a larger scale, happened at St. Come du Mont in Normandy and the entanglement lasted through a full day. It is altogether possible that a troop at the rear of the Custer column made such a move and did at that point engage briefly. As for the column front, no, it could not have happened. When historians have cavalry whip through any such exercise without losing stride, thereby proving that Custer legends, unlike old soldiers, never die and far from fading away, come on ever more strongly, it is time to concede that the pen is mightier than the sword.

Their positions are defended with excellent arguments that any tactician can throw into the garbage can. They dispel myth by seeding the clouds with muck. So doing, they make Chief Gall shine, not so much for his hatchetry as for his honesty.

10

Dismal Aftermath

Except on an extremely local basis that was rarely successful, reconnaissance was at no time systematically practiced by the Indian-fighting army.

In hostile country, scouts worked at most only a few miles out in front of the maneuver battalions. There was rarely any deep penetration of the enemy territory by agents or well-mounted patrols having the sole task of sizing up the strength and location of opposing forces and reporting back.

What explains this aberration? One may only speculate that the risks were deemed so great that friendly Indians could not be recruited for such missions and soldiers would not volunteer. From whatever cause, here was a conspicuous omission of what in our other wars was considered SOP, a normal safeguard and the *sine qua non* of combat intelligence.

Nothing else accounts for the recurrent surprises, the massive ambuscades, and the waste motion, as time and again the army of the frontier aimed a mighty blow, only to have it land in air. It was commonly said at the time that the cost to the United States for every Indian killed by its forces was one million dollars, and it may not have been an exaggeration, if spoken of warriors only.

Without doubt, the vast assembly of tribes, on breaking camp and departing the field of the Little Bighorn, at once split apart into small bands and hunting parties, and scattered in many directions. The dispersion had to take place, if for no better reason than that the families had to be fed and the pony herds moved into uncropped grassland.

By making a military virtue of necessity, however, the fanning-out of the tribes denied the army any worthwhile target. When there is little or nothing to hit, a war perforce winds down. Unlike the army, the Sioux and their allies consistently practiced long-range reconnaissance. While they had missed Custer's entry prior to the final day, they had scouted and harassed Crook's camp, and they were aware when Gibbon's cavalry-infantry column reached the Powder River country.

Here again the parallel between Indian tactics and the Viet Cong way in warfare is striking. Always after engaging in main battle, an NVA or VC regiment dissolved into small units and deployed to hidden and well-separated base camps to foil or to minimize any main counterblow. Yet their scouts lurked ever at the edges of our base camps and in many instances penetrated them.

Nothing about the campaign is more ludicrous than the climax to the sad story of fouled-up communications. On July 9 Terry at long last decided that he must try to get in touch with Crook. Three buck privates of Company E, Sixteenth Infantry, volunteered to serve as couriers. They traveled by night and lay doggo by day. On July 14 they got to Crook and delivered the dispatches. Five days later they were back at Terry's headquarters with messages from Crook. They had not seen a hostile face or heard a shot fired in anger. Still, each was pinned with the Medal of Honor. It is the only example in the record, of three heroes being decorated with the nation's highest award for doing that which should have been routine, but doing it one month late.

Even so, the belated exchange altered nothing. The army

in Montana Territory simply did not react as if its generals had made the slightest effort to understand the Indian mind or believed other than that the bands captained by Crazy Horse and the other chiefs would hold the field and continue to challenge after their famous victory. Either it was unwilling to go along with Shakespeare,

> Farewell the neighing steed and the shrill trump,
> The spirit-stirring drum, th' ear-piercing fife,
> The royal banner, and all quality,
> Pride, pomp, and circumstance of glorious war!

or its campaign planners were wooden-headed.

His few casualties replaced and column strengthened, General Crook marched north and down the Rosebud Valley during the first week of August. Toward this host of 2,100 soldiers and 250 Indian scouts, advancing from the Yellowstone, came General Terry with 1,600 soldiers, moving up the Rosebud. The only real risk they ran was that they might shoot one another by accident. That, they avoided. They met face to face and front to front, having accomplished nothing, neither having sighted one hostile. One fleet and venturesome scout could have saved them all of that bother and an average employment of common sense should have done so. There was no possibility that the Indian mass would have held in place for almost two months, waiting for the blow to fall.

The remainder of the campaign was hardly less idle, a vain threshing about that foundered mounts and frazzled troop nerve, while supply bottomed out and soldiers subsisted on the flesh of broken-down chargers. There is nothing heroic about sacrifices out of damn-fool bad management. Terry's force backtracked to the Yellowstone and worked east along the valley, only to find the bag empty. Crook's column made almost directly for the Dakota country. By the completion of about 200 miles of march, the force had become so desperate for food that a company of 150 cavalrymen, commanded by

Captain Anson Mills and mounted on the fittest horses, was peeled off to ride south to Deadwood for resupply.

In Reva Gap at Slim Buttes, just a few miles north of the Black Hills, Mills came upon a Sioux village. Not certain that his force was strong enough to overrun it, he dispatched a courier to tell Crook to come up fast. Then without waiting for Crook's arrival, though he held his command reined-in through a hard rain that lasted the night, Mills attacked at dawn. Now almost forgotten, Mills was a superb fighter.

Stampeded by surprise, the Sioux withdrew into a dead-end ravine and prepared to defend, under the leadership of Chief American Horse, among the ablest of the Plains tacticians. Before pressing the fight further, Mills' soldiers searched the lodges and found them well-stocked with buffalo meat and other foodstuffs, the main object of their ride south.

In this relative calm before storm, American Horse sent one of his braves riding with a come-up-quick message to Crazy Horse, whose band was not far away. So it became a race between the two sides as to which would reinforce first, Crook or Crazy Horse.

Crook won. Some of his hungry soldiers on arrival broke away to raid the food stores in the lodges, while others pressed the attack against American Horse in the ravine.

They had scarcely begun when out of the pines that rimmed the village charged Crazy Horse and his six hundred warriors. The soldiers were there in too great numbers. Pickets had been placed and an outguard of skirmishers had been thrown around the village. Crazy Horse had arrived just too late to have any chance of crashing so solid a defense. For some hours, before Crazy Horse drew off in defeat, Crook's soldiers were fighting both ways, defending against Crazy Horse while attacking American Horse in the ravine.

The brawling had ended there before Crazy Horse quit the fight. American Horse's few survivors surrendered; there was no massacre at the finish. Quite a few fighters and not a few horses had been killed or wounded during the engagement, including American Horse, who died too soon.

Crook made no attempt to chase after Crazy Horse; he knew that his men, like their mounts, were too dead beat. They had been pushed to the verge of starvation. The food from the lodges was barely enough for one sustaining meal. While the main force rested and licked its wounds near Slim Buttes, Mills and his scratch force rode on again for Deadwood, to return several days later escorting a wagon train laden with hardtack, bacon, flour, and coffee and grain for the horses. Crook buried his dead on the ground, then marched his whole command over the graves to hide the signs.

This limited and chancy success at Slim Buttes was the one solid accomplishment out of the summer campaign. A fair-sized field army had been outfitted, maneuvered over great distance, and pushed to exhaustion to bring off the sacking of one Sioux village and the killing of fifteen warriors. At that point, General Sheridan, who wasn't too bright about fighting Indians, decided it was time to call off the Bighorn Operation. He hardly had any other choice, due to the condition of troops, though the pursuit of Crazy Horse would not be given over.

It would resume, following a rest period, in a wholly different form—a winter campaign under the general direction of Crook, with the specific aim of putting down both Crazy Horse, who is sometimes described as America's greatest cavalry leader, and Sitting Bull, the bitterest intransigent and most forceful rallier among the Sioux.

Crook set up headquarters at Fort Fetterman. Sheridan promised him that he would get everything he needed in troop numbers and equipment to energize his campaign however brutal the weather. For once, that promise was kept. The thoroughness with which Crook prepared—his highest virtue as a commander—was in keeping with the new opportunity.

Equally important, his staff gave a new dimension to intelligence operations. There would be no more aimless sweeping of the countryside. Prisoners would be worked over for information. Indians who knew the territory would be screened into the scout companies. Long-range reconnaissance was instituted.

Out of Fetterman in November, Colonel Mackenzie, the same man who had tracked after Satanta in Texas, took the field.

Mackenzie already knew where he was going. A captured Cheyenne had given Crook the fix on the target.

The expedition counted ten troops of cavalry, four companies of infantry, four batteries of artillery, whose gunners would fight as riflemen, 400 Indian scouts, 168 wagons, seven ambulances, and 400 pack mules.

Here for the first time the scout battalion included friendly Sioux and Cheyenne recruited by Crook's direction.

The troops were warmly clad against the winter rigor, with such extras as buffalo-skin coats, fur caps, and fur mittens.

In late November Mackenzie's advance scouts located what they had been seeking. It was a Cheyenne village in the canyon bed of Crazy Woman's Fork on the Powder River. The gorge, at 3,500 feet elevation, was already icebound, and the numerous frozen tributaries made it all but impossible for the scouts to follow the main channel.

Still they were doing the work that shielded the main body from another possible disaster, and they were working far ahead of the column. Here was the decisive change. When at last they had the village fixed, they sent word to Mackenzie, and the column marched all day to come up even.

When Mackenzie closed on the scouts after night fell, he heard war drums beating. The Cheyenne under Chief Dull Knife, one of the tribe's ablest battle leaders, were celebrating their success in raiding a Shoshone village. When shortly the village quieted, Mackenzie knew that his presence had not been detected.

The attack went at dawn. The surprise was complete. Some of the Cheyenne fled naked from their tepees. Others cut slits in the sides of the lodges and returned fire. Amid the tumult, any number of braves who had first panicked and fled naked, returned to the cover of the lodges and still naked, fought back. Stripped to the buff, small children and squaws carrying babies kept going to get away from the fight, and scores froze to death in the blizzardy cold.

The tide of battle surged back and forth through the day, the Cheyenne resisting with a terrible tenacity in the worst of circumstances. One band broke away and took a defensive position six miles up the gorge, from which the soldiers could not dislodge them.

Crook had marched through the night, almost thirty miles in twelve hours over frozen trails, to be with Mackenzie. By the time of his arrival in late evening, the fight was over, though what he saw told him that the Cheyenne had been dealt a mortal blow. Most of Dull Knife's people were already either dead, dying, or homeless fugitives.

By that time, Sitting Bull was already a fugitive, so driven by a separate force under Colonel Nelson Miles, a future chief of staff of the army.

It had happened in October when Miles, with only five hundred soldiers of the Fifth Infantry Regiment and some pieces of artillery, invaded the Powder River Country, starting at the mouth of the Tongue River. Sitting Bull had this time made a mistake, having concluded that when Terry and Crook had together marched east, doubling back to the old battleground would be the best way for his people to evade them. Whether it was a mark of genius or a stroke of sheer luck, General Terry sent Miles back for one more check. Before there was any contact, four companies of the Twenty-third Infantry and another artillery piece reinforced Miles. His force was now 850 strong.

More has been written about the exchange between Miles and Sitting Bull when at last the confrontation occurred in the Powder River country than of any like episode. How much is legend and what part is truth, it is impossible to say.

The story goes that as Miles' column moved up, the scouts found a message on the path, which was delivered by them to the commander,

> I want you to know what you are doing traveling this road. You scare all the buffalo away. I want to hunt in this place. I want you to turn back from here. If you don't I'll fight you again. I want you to leave what you have got here and turn back from here.
>
> I am your friend,
Sitting Bull
>
> P.S. I mean all the rations you have got and all of your powder. Wish you would write me soon as you can.

Certainly a very courteous man, though one who is also in somewhat of a hurry.

The story continues that as Miles' column overtook Sitting Bull's war party, there was a preliminary face-to-face parley between the two, each having only a few of his closest followers present.

Sitting Bull repeated that Miles and his force had better leave. Miles told him, "You must surrender and return to your reservation," meaning the Great Sioux Reservation in Dakota.

Sitting Bull's answer, if true, is Indian eloquence at its best, fit to be bracketed with that of Red Cloud.

He said, "God made me an Indian, but not a reservation Indian."

From the view of Miles, that was Indian small talk.

He gave his ultimatum: "You may have fifteen minutes to think it over; surrender or fight."

Along with his retainers, Sitting Bull wheeled his pony and galloped back to the tribesmen.

Although there were around three thousand Indians in this body, that is not a warrior count. The fighting season, from their view, was well over. The dispersion having achieved the desired result, there had come about a reconvergence of some of its parts, including many noncombatants, which made the mass vulnerable. Another thing, Sitting Bull was a spiritual leader and not a fighting chief.

So the odds were not what the numbers would seem to say. The fighting weight was with Miles. His people attacked, and the prairie fire started by the Sioux to deter them had hardly more than a nuisance value. Miles placed his cannon and kept it firing so as to discourage organized counterattack and to demoralize the Indian mass.

If not a glorious victory, it was decisive. Twenty-six hundred Sioux and Cheyenne surrendered. Sitting Bull and several thousand followers managed to get away from the debacle, outrun pursuit, and escape to Canada, thereby achieving nothing except survival. Sometimes, the supreme achievement.

Miles could not afford to encumber himself with prisoners, because he had no way of feeding them. Leaving them armed so that they could hunt on the way, he told them to deliver themselves to the Spotted Tail or Red Cloud Agencies. With Sitting Bull no longer present to rally them, many so did.

The hunt next turned to Crazy Horse, though Crook, for personal reasons, would have no part of it, and so quit the field.

Believing that the situation now left Crazy Horse with no real hope and certain that he could convince the Indian that further fighting was folly, Crook thought it wrong to achieve with killing what he might better accomplish with talk.

Miles took a different view. An ambitious soldier, regarding himself as a rival to Crook, Miles was determined to take or kill Crazy Horse in the field.

While Miles continued to flail the ridges south of the Yellowstone in search of the Sioux's greatest battle leader, Crook sent word to Crazy Horse, using Chief Spotted Tail as his messenger, that if Crazy Horse would come on in peacefully, Crook would assure his band a homeland in the Powder River Country.

Crook seemingly meant what he said, believed that the Government would support his pledge, and was banking on his reputation among the tribes of being a man of his word. Having little faith in anything but his own prowess, Crazy Horse continued to hold out.

On January 7, 1877, acting on information supplied by a captured Cheyenne, Miles' column stood outside Crazy Horse's village in early morning. There was no surprise: The thousand warriors within the village had seen the army come up. As the soldiers took their meal before action, the taunt came from the village, "That's the last breakfast you'll ever eat."

Miles didn't think so. He had made his presence obvious because he had prepared a different kind of surprise. In two of his wagons were concealed mounted cannon, Napoleon guns, ready to fire: Indians invariably broke under artillery fire.

The direct assault was made up an ice-covered and slab-sided slope, there being no other way to surround or penetrate the village. It was an exhausting and costly climb for skirmishers loaded with ammunition and cramped by heavy winter clothing. At the top, there was briefly a hand-to-hand grapple, though luckily for troops, the red line was already wavering under the shelling from the two Napoleon guns. The Indians broke with the killing of Chief Big Crow in the forefront of the defense. The surviving warriors under Crazy Horse got away through the far end of the village. But they had abandoned all of their food stores and much of their fighting supply. It was another decisive defeat.

In May, Crazy Horse, responding at last to Crook's appeal, turned himself in at Camp Robinson near the Red Cloud Agency in Nebraska. But he did not come like a broken, contrite chieftain. At the head of eight hundred warriors all wearing their war paint and bonnets, lofting their weapons and chanting war songs, he rode like a proud man. The show served notice that he would bear careful watching.

Although it is said that Crook tried hard to make good his word, the pledge he had given Crazy Horse was ignored by a government that had already burned its bridges in the indicated direction. One year earlier, while the war was in full flood, a national commission had persuaded the Sioux and Cheyenne chiefs already living on the reservation to sign a new paper yielding the Black Hills, the unceded Powder River country, and a large tract of the Great Sioux Reservation. It was outright trickery, going through the motions of legality, since it ignored that part of the Fort Laramie treaty requiring that any such transaction would have to be approved by the vote of two-thirds of the males in any tribe. Indian rights were pernicious abstractions, since through pretension they were aimed to deceive.

Even so, though he believed that Crook had tried to persuade the Government to reverse course and keep the bargain only to fail, Crazy Horse remained tractable for a time. Lieutenant W. P. Clark, who had accepted his surrender, wrote of him as being "remarkably brave, generous and reticent . . . a pillar of strength for good or evil." That was while Clark waited and wondered what might happen next.

The army's main concern of that summer was not Clark's unpredictable prisoner but its unexpected humiliation at the hands of the peace-loving and progressive Nez Percé. A David on the loose was trapping and snaring Goliath while millions cheered. Army ineptitude has seldom been so harshly ridiculed. Whereas Crook, who had always respected the Indian as a fighter, might better have viewed this puzzling spectacle unblinking, such prestige as remained to the army was so much at stake that practically all brass from Sherman down had to get into the act.

Crook's role was to recruit and train a large band of Indian scouts to assist in the campaign against Chief Joseph's people. He even sought the support of Crazy Horse, asking him by letter if he would lead his band westward to fight the Nez Percé. Legend has it that Crazy Horse replied that he would fight until every Nez Percé was dead, then when his boast passed through the interpreter, that worthy garbled it, quoting Crazy Horse as saying that he would battle until every white was dead. Be that a likely story, the suspicion did grow in the mind of Crazy Horse that Crook, rather than sighting on the Nez Percé, was about to mount an expedition to go after Sitting Bull, a manifest absurdity, since it would have entailed invading Canada, and the army was wholly occupied with stopping Chief Joseph.

The eccentric moves of Crazy Horse at this time suggest that he had not been misnamed. Saying nothing to anyone, he pulled his band out of the agency and slipped away. Believing that he had turned hostile, Crook, at Omaha, dispatched an order for his arrest. Eight companies of the Third Cavalry and four hundred Indian scouts took up the chase, one of the Indian leaders being American Horse the Younger, whose father had been killed at Slim Buttes. Before this overstrength expedition could make contact, Crazy Horse showed up at the Spotted Tail Agency. Whether he did not understand his danger or no longer cared, he was brought back under guard to Camp Robinson in compliance with Crook's order.

Because he had submitted quietly, Crazy Horse had not been searched and disarmed at the Agency. He may not have understood that he was under arrest, or he could have been in that emotional state where obscure motives possess and agonize the brain. When he was brought to the office of Lieutenant Clark, who commanded the scouts, a soldier started to frisk him and one of the Indian scouts, Little Big Man, pinned his arms.

Breaking free, Crazy Horse came up with a knife and stabbed Little Big Man. There was a brief struggle. Either Crazy Horse turned his knife on himself or someone else bayoneted him deep in the belly. There being no official verdict, one can only pay one's money and make one's choice of these two accounts.

That night he died of his wound, the warrior who was always in a hurry or in a dream. Chief Touch the Cloud, whose name makes him fit the spot, stayed with him to the end to say his few words for history, "It is good. He has looked for death and it is come."

As eloquent a postmortem pronouncement as any, it still draws the veil over a shamefully awkward business and a wretched finish for the greatest battlefield plunger of his race and time. No other Plains war chief matched him in skill and audacity. His designs were his own secret and they passed on with him, as did his image. He loathed the camera and would never pose for a picture, which may be taken as a sign either of his daftness or of his superiority.

Even the story of his finish is moot, one account making it an official murder. Major H. R. Lemly, who claimed to have been there, is the quoted source for his deathbed statement, "The Gray Fox (Crook) sent soldiers to surround me and my village. But I was tired of fighting. All I wanted was to be left alone. So I anticipated their coming and marched all night to the Spotted Tail Agency while the troops marched on my camp. Touch the Cloud knows how I settled at Spotted Tail Agency. The agent told me I must first talk with the Big White Chief of the Black Hills. Under his care I came here unarmed. But instead of talking they tried to confine me. And when I tried to escape, a soldier ran his bayonet into me."

The death of Crazy Horse coincided with the expiration of the fighting spirit of the Plains Indian, though not because the embodiment of that spirit was gone. It simply so happened. Men do not fight unless they believe or imagine there is something to be gained. Like Crazy Horse, the older chiefs, almost without exception, had had more than enough of war. There was no longer anything of promise with which to give battle and nothing of value worth the fight. No free Indian bands roamed the land between the great river and the tall mountains, and the ravaged but roaded prairie had no support for the old way of life.

It fell to the Gray Fox, Crook, to round up the stragglers with his cavalry and escort them to the designated reservations. He did it, we are told, as gently as possible, though sometimes gently is too gentle a word. If in the course of this operation, Crook again roamed fore and aft, shooting the elk or whitetail and trying to hit the elusive pronghorn during his ingathering of confused humans, nobody made notes on it and Crook missed a great opportunity.

Here was the sideline that might have given his outing the sporting touch.

11

Thunder in the
Mountains

OF one Indian leader—and one only—nothing but good
has ever been written. There is more praise, however, for the
nobility of his character than for the brilliance of his generalship, numerous of his biographers indeed questioning whether
he was truly a battle chief.

Chief Joseph of the Wallowa band of the Nez Percé, although his story has been debunked and rebunked almost
endlessly, still stands higher than his legend. His fame as a
warrior, not unlike his place as a major figure in Plains warfare, is nonetheless a paradox. He and his tribesmen came out
of the far mountains of the Pacific Northwest. Devoted to
peace, without prior military experience, he became the central and leading captain in the most trying and skillfully conducted Indian war ever to engage the United States Army.

Whereas Chief Crazy Horse out-generaled the military in a
few spectacular episodes, a day of fighting here, another brief
battle later on, and Chief Red Cloud's reputation is based on

two actions, in one of which his role is obscure while in the other he was roundly beaten by a meagre force, Chief Joseph held to the field longer, by out-maneuvering the army his only time on the warpath, than any Indian leader in history. Like Napoleon or George Washington, Joseph had natural gifts as a military manager and a moral force that are not to be explained in terms of environment and training.

He was born to the Indian name of Hin-mah-too-yah-laht-ket, meaning Thunder-Rolling-in-the-Mountains, an almost prophetic choice. His father, who was also a man of peace, had been renamed Joseph by a missionary, following a conversion to Christianity that proved to be quite temporary. So Thunder-Rolling-in-the-Mountains became Little Joseph, and when the father died in 1871, the son became Chief Joseph. His early years as leader of the band, according to the historian, Alvin M. Josephy, Jr., won him credits as "the soul of wisdom, eloquence, goodness and mercy immeasurable."

The Joseph people had as their ancestral home the Wallowa Valley along the Snake River, where today's Idaho, Oregon, and Washington come together. There, like other Nez Percé, they farmed, raised cattle, and specialized in breeding the appaloosa, the blue-toned horse with the black-spotted rump that is still highly favored in the West. No other tribe boasted as fine horse herds. Captain Meriwether Lewis, of the exploring expedition that bears his name, visited the tribe in 1806. Noting that some of the people wore a small seashell as a nose ornament, he picked up the name fixed on them by French traders, and on returning East reported that the Nez Percé employed stud skills that were "superior to both American and English practices." They consistently used selective breeding to improve the strain. Much of the tribal pride centered in superior horses and superb horsemanship.

In the years when North and South approached the impasse from which came the Civil War, prospectors, ranchers, and other settlers invaded the Nez Percé country in large numbers, drove a wedge into it, the focus of which was near present-day Lewiston, and stayed rooted. At first, there was little trouble. The Indians, due partly to Old Joseph's influence, overlooked a number of provocative incidents and held to their ancient customs. When a warrior died, his favorite appaloosa was killed and its head, tail, and hoofs were used to decorate the grave. To the Nez Percé, there was something almost sacred about the horse. Youngsters sang chants about the animal, one of them running like this, "You are my god and I will take care of you."

In 1863 when Abe Lincoln was so busy looking for a good general that he had no time to reflect on honesty being the best policy in dealing with Indians, Government agents superimposed a chief with the unlikely name of Lawyer over the Nez Percé. Lawyer proved to be the shyster type. Neither the man nor the treaty that he signed, ceding much of the tribal homeland, was palatable to Old Joseph and several other legitimate band leaders. Refusing to yield their pleasant valleys for life on a reservation in accordance with the paper signed by the double-dealing factotum, they were tabbed Non-Treaty Indians. Other bands accepted the deal because their homeland was in the area set aside for the reservation. These differences split the Nez Percé into two quarreling factions in Old Joseph's time. Most Treaty Indians cut their hair short to conform to the white man's style. The Non-Treaty Indians let it grow as an expression of contempt.

When Young Joseph took over as chief of the largest Nez Percé band, there was at first no direct pressure on him to give up the Wallowa Valley and move to the Lapwai Reservation. Then in the spring of 1877, Government agents, backed by the army, made their move. Brigadier General O. O. Howard, the regional commander, didn't like his orders: He argued that the displacement was unjust and that it would breed trouble. But he went ahead. Reluctant to yield the Wallowa, Joseph nonetheless agreed to cooperate rather than risk a war.

While some of the Indians were packing for the migration,

white raiders moved in on them and ran off several hundred of their most prized horses, including some stud stallions. That fresh outrage, coming in an hour when tension among the younger warriors was near a breaking point, might well have loosed the lightning, but for the restraint of the Non-Treaty chiefs.

Howard had set June 14 as the deadline for the move. On June 10, there was an assembling of chiefs and their bands at Tepahlewam, a meadow near Grangeville, Idaho, the traditional meeting ground of the Nez Percé. Joseph was not present. Then age thirty-seven, he was at home in the Wallowa, dressing down beef while awaiting the birth of another child. The principals at the conclave were White Bird, seventy-year-old chief of the Salmon River band, Toohoolhoolzote (Pile of Clouds), a few years older than White Bird and head man of the Snake River band, and Looking Glass, chief of the Clearwater River band. Looking Glass was forty-five.

All three spoke up for peace and compliance with the government order. Belligerent and spoiling for trouble was a young warrior from White Bird's band, Shore Crossing, whose father had been murdered by a white several years before. Demanding war, he was backed by his cousin, Red Moccasin Tops. The chiefs tried to soothe this pair and seemed to have succeeded.

When the conference ended and the warriors dispersed to the lodges, Shore Crossing, high on whiskey, rode his horse blindly across a tray of camas bulbs that a squaw had set to dry. Her man, Yellow Grizzly Bear, yelled at him, "You talk big. You say how brave you are. But you scatter my wife's food. Why don't you go after the man who killed your father?"

Here is another incident as trivial as the butchering of the Mormon's cow or the theft of the farmer's eggs. Yet the taunt and the whiskey together exploded another war. Taking with them another young buck, Swan Necklace, who was just old enough to be a witness while holding their horses, the two cousins rode off on a killing spree. They couldn't find the murderer they sought, so they slaughtered two other whites and wounded a third. At sundown Swan Necklace rode into Tepahlewam lofting the trophies from these crimes and carrying the news of the killing from lodge to lodge. Mounting up, White Bird rode among the lodges calling on other warriors to arm and strike at whites. Quick to respond was Toohoolhoolzote, who burned over a recent jailing by the army. Joining seventeen of his warriors with the two killers, he charged off on another raid, slaying white settlers and plundering the ranch houses.

In this way the die was cast. Seventy-one years after seeing their first white man, the Nez Percé made war. The opening blow was an inexcusable atrocity, most of the victims being innocent of any offense against the tribe. But the basic motivation, far from being anything new was the familiar behavior pattern, the product of land hunger and the young buck's boredom.

For Chief Joseph, these deeds placed a clumsy finger on an already aching wound. Speaking for his people, he said, "Rather than have war, I will give up my country. I will give up everything." Still, on getting the news, he saw no way out of the trap for the Wallowa band. When a kinsman argued that the band could still square things by moving quickly to Lapwai, since it was not involved in the violence, Joseph replied, "I can hardly go there; they will blame it on me." And true enough, Howard did regard him as the main influence among the Non-Treaty chiefs.

It is commonly said that there is no more dangerous figure in war than the man who has done his best to avoid it only to find that no other choice is left, and it may well be true. Regard Joseph, a figure not to be pitied, being much too big for it. Once this Indian had decision taken out of his hands, he turned iron. A more dramatic transformation than his is hardly to be found in the annals of warfare. The marvel is that he had been patient for so very long and that after patience died, there remained such awesome dignity.

Many of the Nez Percé were shocked and appalled by the killings. Some families fled south to White Bird Canyon, hoping thereby to escape retribution at the hands of the army. Joseph tarried for a few days until the infant was born. Then he packed his family and with his thirty-five-year-old brother, Ollokot, followed the others to White Bird.

On getting the news of the limited outbreak, General Howard, then at Lapwai, on June 15 sent two troops of cavalry to either punish or bring in the guilty Indians. Howard expected no real fighting due to the nigh-unblemished record of the Nez Percé. That was his first miscalculation; the expedition was understrength and it was pushed too hard. It took along as a civilian guide one Ad Chapman, which was a much greater mistake.

Captain David Perry's force of 110 soldiers from the First Cavalry reached the White Bird camp site in early morning, the mounts blown, the troops dog tired. Perry was pretty much of a fool. He insisted on closing when his force was in no condition. Joseph and the people were in defensive position, there being about sixty warriors present on the floor of the canyon. Perry reckoned that a charge from the ridge top would scatter them.

As the cavalry appeared, a small truce party of Indians came forward bearing a white flag. Ad Chapman, a reckless rascal, fired on the flag and wounded one Indian. Another Indian returned the fire and drilled Perry's orderly-trumpeter through the brain. With the music silenced, Perry could give no commands above the tumult of the action. The Indians knew the terrain, the soldiers didn't. Some of the jaded mounts collapsed, throwing their riders. A few minutes of wild and disordered action was followed by panic flight. Though less than half of the braves bore rifles, thirty-four of Perry's soldiers were killed and four were wounded. Only two of the braves were hit, neither fatally. The dead cavalry-

JOSEPH'S
COUNTERATTACK

PERRY'S CHARGE

FIGHT AT WHITE BIRD CREEK

men were neither mutilated nor stripped. The Nez Percé doubly armed themselves from army hardware dropped on the battlefield, sixty-three rifles among other loot.

Here was a startling development—the army encountering for the first time Indians who worked rifles with the accuracy of Deadeye Dick, and the warning should have been perfectly clear. Once openly challenged, however, the army had to make it a war despite the dismal showing by its marksmen at White Bird.

General Howard, on getting word of the rout, at first hesitated. Joseph picked up strength, being joined by Chiefs Five Wounds and Rainbow with their bands when they returned from a buffalo hunt in Montana. Chief Looking Glass, so called because he wore a plated tin mirror on his chest as an ornament, was peacefully encamped with his band on Clear Creek, having sent word to Howard that he was not hostile and would soon report.

Howard's response was to send Captain Stephen G. Whipple with one troop of cavalry and a party of civilian volunteers to round up the Looking Glass band as a safety measure. It was a capital blunder based on the misinformation that forty of Looking Glass' braves had slipped off to join Joseph, whereas Looking Glass had only forty braves and they were with him. Further, Whipple was more than a little bit thick in the head. During the opening parley, one volunteer with an itchy trigger finger fired into the Indian camp, killing a child. Thereon Whipple loosed a Gatling gun to fire on the camp. The warriors and their 150 or so dependents fled in the other direction, heading for the woods. The soldiers then burned and looted the lodges.

With a large and righteous hate in their hearts, Looking Glass and his people joined the war party, and it was a respectable reinforcement. Like Joseph, Looking Glass was instinctively a skilled hand in directing fighting operations, physically tough, courageous and quick-thinking. With his coming, the Nez Percé had about two hundred warriors ready for the field, all but a handful armed with rifles. This maneuver force, however, was encumbered by about 450 dependents, not a few of them either ailing or aged. Some of the Treaty Nez Percé were already serving the field army as scouts and guides in the war against their brothers. If this fact struck Civil War veterans as a betrayal typical only of a savage, they could not have been thinking very clearly.

The war bands moved to an assembly ground on the Clearwater River, not far from where Whipple had stampeded Looking Glass and his people, this after sideslipping General Howard, who spent several weeks vainly searching for them in the churned-up country below the Salmon River, about one hundred miles to the southwest. Once again, they had come to rest on sound defensive ground. Because this feature is characteristic of the campaign from first to last, the credit must go to Joseph.

With Howard were about five hundred soldiers and two hundred Indian scouts, teamsters, packers, and other civilian oddments. The main body caught up with the Nez Percé on the Clearwater on July 11, by which time more than three hundred warriors awaited them. The army attacked with full surprise under a covering fire from one cannon and two Gatling guns. Before the infantry line could get well started, a

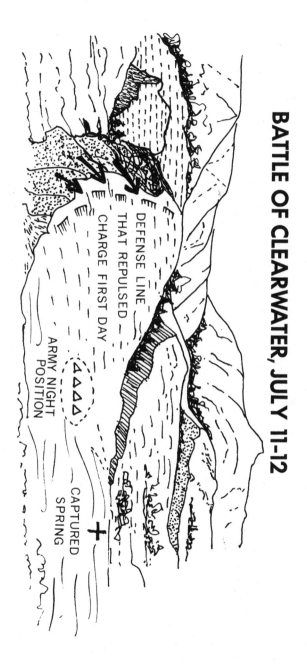

BATTLE OF CLEARWATER, JULY 11-12

DEFENSE LINE
THAT REPULSED
CHARGE FIRST DAY —

ARMY NIGHT
POSITION

CAPTURED
SPRING

counterattack by a small party under Chief Toohoolhoolzote caught the skirmishers in an enfilading fire from the high ground and pinned them until another force of Indians could get on the army rear.

But tactics as such had relatively little to do with the steady buildup of pressure. It was a day of deadly heat. The Indians had access to a bubbling spring. Too soon the army ran out of water. That one extremely critical difference in supply situation pretty much evened the odds of the day-long, but thereafter lackadaisical fight, along with one other unhappy though not unusual development.

Early in the game, Howard and his staff had halfway secured their command post by piling up pack saddles in a circle round about them, which did not make for the best possible observation. When the attack along the bluff and at the edge of a small ravine was mounted, a section of the Fourth Artillery under Captain Marcus P. Miller was ordered into action. Under the pressure of the movement, everything was being done too quickly. Shortly, Miller's guns were firing into the infantry and his gunners were getting nicked by bullets from the friendlys in that kind of exchange that never uplifts morale, save possibly in the enemy camp. From such experience, it is learned mainly that combat is managed less easily and safely than the July 4 fireworks show at the country club.

Night came, as it usually does, and the two sides broke it off, not the night but the engagement. On the following morning, Howard's force captured a fresh-water spring on the plateau overlooking the Clearwater River, the bluffs and banks commanding which were still held by the Indians. We are asked to believe that this conquest saved the day for the troops if only because potable water enabled the mess sergeant to boil coffee, and the soldiers reacted to Arbuckle's Best as if to a needle in the forearm. For that matter, so did the scribes working on the official journal.

In mid-afternoon the Indian line broke, and according to

one contemporary record, the defeated, routed warriors along the bluffs above the Clearwater "fled incontinently," whereas they retired in good order to rejoin their families on the other side of the river, their weapons still in hand. The officer who tried to burn these fugitives with Parthian fire from the Gatling gun later wrote honestly that he didn't believe he had hit anybody.

What we know for sure is that the battle could not have been half as confused as the various accounts of it. When the firing ceased, the Indians were well on their way, and Howard decided he was in no condition to pursue, although it wasn't Sunday. A very pietistic soldier, Howard would not move or fight on the Lord's Day. This prohibition no doubt nettled the hard chargers among the officers, while warming the hearts of the more veteran sergeants, Sunday being as favorable a day for fishing as last Tuesday.

The hostile loss was ten killed and wounded. Army casualties were thirteen dead and twenty-three wounded. The field had been littered with Springfield rifles, spade bayonets, cartridge cases, canteens, and meat ration cans. The Nez Percé had not abandoned them, but they certainly gobbled them up.

So who was the victor? He who claimed victory, in this case the army, the Nez Percé having no interest in the propaganda value of a drawn fight. They were much too busy and too ignorant to engage in such calculations. The play had to continue if only because certain men in military suits believed that honor, the national goals, and other major considerations such as preferment, prestige, promotion, pay, and public plaudits remained very much at stake. Up to this point, however, the response of the army had been unbelievably awkward, nonunderstanding and delayed, main forces reacting as if the one great object in war is the drawing of blood.

Until after Clearwater, the several bands of the Nez Percé had been little unified, even as their coming together had been haphazard rather than systematized. They were having to learn about the conduct of war in the hardest possible school, which is sometimes an advantage.

During the retreat from Clearwater, the chiefs got together to plan the next move. Of that meeting came the decision to strike east across the snow-capped Bitterroot Mountains, one of the most spectacular ranges in America, thereafter to join their friends of the buffalo hunt, the Crow, in Montana. They truly believed in all innocence, that once they had made the passage, having left Howard behind, that would end the war.

Chief Joseph was wholly opposed to the flight. He wanted to make a showdown fight for the countryside that was their homeland both by tradition and treaty, a position that would have been unassailable, had the Government and the army respected either.

When Joseph was outvoted, Looking Glass was made war chief of the combined force for the trek through the Bitterroots. In crossing the mountains, the warriors not only took along their families but drove before them about two thousand horses. This was their capital and their reserve food supply when there was nothing else. They would need it wherever they set up store. Still, the trick of keeping a herd of that size collected during a long march through a rugged, forest-clad highland must baffle the imagination of white men who know the way of a horse.

Going down the eastern slope of the Bitterroots, when barely over the Montana border well south of Missoula, the Indians found the Lolo Pass blocked by a hasty fortification. Behind it were thirty-five army regulars of the Seventh Infantry and two hundred militia volunteers. When Joseph rode forward to explain to Captain Charles C. Rawn that he had no quarrel with anyone and asked only for freedom of passage, the citizen-soldiers backed off, the regulars became downcast and Rawn quickly saw the light of day. It was no time for a game man to prove that he could also be foolish. Montanans at once dubbed the spot where Rawn stepped aside "Fort Fizzle," and so it is called today, being better known to more tourists than most of the bloody fields.

General Howard, catching his second wind, followed along slowly, seldom less than one hundred miles behind. His officers and soldiers didn't sweat out the chase too much, hugging the illusion that on coming to the Montana line, they would about-face and return to base, the Territory being in a different department.

Members of the expedition wrote letters to their families describing how they had successfully worked a trout stream, bagged an elk, or gone on a shoot for prairie chickens and grouse. With every Sunday came a rest, and the sportsmen deployed.

Howard moved well ahead with his cavalry. Marching about seventeen miles a day other than on Sunday, the infantry was neither overpushed nor given cause to complain about the monotony of hard rations.

But if it was some better than the worst possible, it was still well short of idyllic. A fair percentage of the riflemen were already marching barefoot, their boots having fallen apart, and no resupply was moving with the train. In that season, at that altitude, however, there was no memorable suffering. For the common soldier, it was one more thing to gripe about. The medicos and the quartermaster continued to pull at Howard's coattails, protesting that flesh and blood could stand no more, which was a slight exaggeration. Howard kept returning the stock army reply that wherever Indians could go, soldiers could go also, and that was another exaggeration. In no mood to enjoy the landscape, the troops were only slightly comforted by the fact that at least half of the way they were walking downhill.

Those rough Nez Percé aggressors next moved on Stevensville, Montana, and with the town in their hands, instead of pillaging it, replenished their supplies through purchase in the local stores at boom-town prices. One thing they didn't buy was firewater. Joseph ordered the purveyors of booze to lock up their joints. Strange Indians. Odd chieftain.

When they got over the Continental Divide and dropped down to Big Hole Valley, where the plains take over from the mountains, it was the decision of their combined chiefs that right there they should tarry a while, pitch and patch their tepees, cut fresh timber from the Lodgepole pines, clean and grease their weapons, rest their families and deliberate on what next was to be done. Joseph and the others believed that time and distance had immunized the camp for at least a little while.

In that wishful thought, they were wholly mistaken. The telegraph was exclusively the ally of the army. At Fort Shaw, Montana, that grumpy old warhorse, Colonel John Gibbon, had received an urgent message and report on situation from General Howard.

It was a pivotal happening in the Plains wars, more revealing than others of the character, spirit, and limitations of the army commanders. Howard could not properly order Gibbon to attack the Nez Percé, if for no other reason than that he could not know Gibbon's force limitations and operating problems. Moreover, Gibbon was in Terry's department and Howard had no whip over him. He could, however, request cooperation toward turning or checking the hostile movement, leaving the implementing decisions to the man on the spot.

Here again, however, as in the Custer fight, we have the instance of the headlong, impulsive commitment so typical of commanders in that period. It is never enough to do a sound military job; there must be the intrepid, all-out attack to reaffirm gallantry. Courage more than brain must be proved by battle test. Custer was by no means unique. His was the common ailment along the frontier and we need ponder why. These commanders had enjoyed higher rank during the Civil War. Then their stars had passed into eclipse. They were in hot competition to rewin glory and higher pay and felt they could not risk that a thinking conservatism would be mistaken for a want of boldness by their superiors. It is sadly true that the brooder who has been cut back from flag rank is far more apt to drink deeply of the Bitter Tea of General Yen than the colonel who never made it.

Once he got the word, Gibbon was off like a shot. Anyone who has traversed this route in a motor car must marvel that he could put foot soldiers and wagons over unroaded and thickly forested mountains at such speed. His was a masterpiece of improvisation and command determination. Gibbon had to pick up reinforcements as he moved along, a necessity that determined his march path, which was by no means the most favorable avenue. Among the additions were thirty-seven civilian volunteers who went along with no reasonable expectation that it could profit them.

At the end of this exhausting but heroic march, piece by piece, the operation began to fall apart. No monumental blunders occurred, though the cumulative effect of many small misjudgments became nigh disastrous, which is usually the way it happens in battle. Gibbon could have made the decision to circle to the southeastward, avoid contact with the Nez Percé, and set up in a blocking position on high ground to the east along Joseph's probable line of march. The ground made such a move feasible, provided the wagons were brought up. By waiting for Howard to come along, thus trapping the Nez Percé front and rear, he could have brought off a bloodless surrender.

Whether any such maneuver scheme was ever contemplated, Gibbon proceeded as if he had no option but to do it by himself. Moreover, luck was with him to begin, though it swiftly ran out. For what he planned, he was using the right methods, though systematic procedure may never offset over-extension of force. The small Battle of Big Hole is therefore still today an object lesson in tactics, its main point being that soldiers, like nippers, must not bite more than they may later have to eschew.

Gibbon halted his column on high ground within what he reckoned was strike distance of the Nez Percé camp. It wasn't an inspired guess. Big Hole was almost certain to be the place, due to its confluence of fresh waters and the abundance of lush grass in an otherwise parched and tawny countryside. There was one prospector among the volunteers who could tell Gibbon all about Big Hole. He had vainly scratched for gold along the slopes above the river. Rising sharply from the trench of Big Hole River's north branch, that mountainside was the last ground for the cutting of lodgepoles. To the eastward for miles stretched a sear, relatively flat plain, interrupted here and there by low ridges, mostly barren. Great for cattle, this landscape affords no hiding place to more than a picket post. Given these conditions, Gibbon had to know as a tactician that either he would overcome Joseph at Big Hole or his force would become unhinged, with no line of escape to the eastward and hardly more to the westward. Still, he made the hard choice. In command of what today would be rated an understrength battalion, he was thinking as a deployer of troops in regimental numbers.

From his base camp, once he had come up, Gibbon sent forward Lieutenant James H. Bradley (who had volunteered for the task) and two other gallants to reconnoiter the valley flat, where he thought the Indians had made camp. A nonpareil among soldiers, Bradley was ready for extreme risks. Getting to the cap of what is now called Battle Mountain, Bradley shinnied up the tallest Lodgepole pine on the skyline to look down on the Nez Percé, little more than one-half mile away, his eye to the nearest tepee. All that he could see was reassuring. The Indians were going their customary rounds and in general behaving like a human antbed, though the squaws were doing most of the physical labor. Bradley could hear them calling to one another as they hacked away at the pines on the slopes below. To his view, the base of the mountain looked like an ideal springboard for an assault on the Indian camp, the foldings of the ridge and the intervening pine stands hiding the truth of the situational problem.

The facts are that there was no such open road. The serpentine-like meander line of the north fork and what the loops enclosed imposed a forbidding barrier. Bradley could see the camp but he could not scan either the river line or the median between the base of the mountain and the solid ground on which the camp was set up. The bends were thickly overgrown with stunted poplars, willows, and brush, much of this growth impenetrable, while to either side of the flowing stream, there were marshes, stagnant pools irregularly bottomed, and patches of tule and thornbush. All of it was treacherous, tedious footing. The final 250 yards were certain to be for Gibbon and his soldiers the most trying test they were ever to know. It was not Bradley's fault that he missed the most significant military feature of the landscape. From his coign, it was not to be seen.

Bradley sent one of his companions back to Gibbon with the report. The main body came forward. On the following night, guided by Bradley, Gibbon brought his soldiers and civilian volunteers up, over and down, under the cover of dark. Most of the way, they marched along the bed of Trail Creek. A more chance-taking approach is hard to imagine. The body of fighters descended to the tree line near the mountain's base, where they were not more than one-quarter mile from the Indian camp or more than thirty-five feet above the trench of the north fork. There placed, they looked straight at the dimly lighted ground they would assault at dawn, but still had no measure of the torment they would experience in negotiating the bottoms in between. Legend has it that Gibbon shifted his fighters by the left flank, out of the pines and onto a treeless and grass-grown sector of the ridge slope, though this affords room for a healthy doubt. Even on a dark night, a bald slope so cluttered with troops must have revealed itself to the Nez Percé camp, black mass profiled against a whitened hill. Yet there was no alarm. The Seventh Infantry Regiment's soldiers had already worked a miracle by getting so close, unheard, unobserved.

Miraculous, and still a forlorn hope, made so by the colonel. Gibbon had marched his 170 men five miles over trackless ground, boulder-strewn, cluttered with fallen timber, steep, laced with icy streams, and this with practically no rest, although he had begun in late evening. The remainder of his force, which totaled 191, was rearward with the wagons, the ammo reserve, and the one gun. Most of the line was made up of Seventh Infantrymen formed in six small companies. It was about 2:00 A.M. when Gibbon at last settled his troops on their designated line of departure for a heatless, foodless, and largely sleepless bivouac. The men stretched out on the dry grass of the mountain slope. A few dim lights dead ahead and about one-quarter mile away marked the location of the hostiles. It is not the kind of sight to lull a soldier to sleep even though he be worn down. Gibbon's men in the greater number remained awake and shivering hard until just before dawn. At Big Hole, even in the hot season, sojourners either burrow under layers of blankets or they do not sleep.

Not realizing it, Gibbon, by his procedures, had caused his soldiers to dissipate most of their combat energy, while preparing to ask of infantry more than it may well give. The rifle and ninety rounds of ammo that each man carried would weigh doubly. Every step forward in the closing stretch would terribly drain the fighter's resources of will and effective response. By what he had ordered, Gibbon, in effect, had beaten his own troops.

Then Gibbon further compounded these ill effects by extending his people in line for at least eight hundred yards, with the civilian volunteers at the extreme left. Due to the meandering of the north fork, the uneven footing in the marsh, and the harsh variations of the passage from one small unit to another, the formation would not only put a maximum stress on individuals, making each man feel pretty much alone, but would make it certain that the assault force would enter upon the target area raggedly. To have any chance of exploding the camp, Gibbon needed heavy, controlled volleying to begin. Spread as were his men, they would be unable to deliver it.

One-half hour before first light cracked, the riflemen of the six light companies slid down the last fifty or sixty feet of slope and began their floundering advance through the muck, the chest-high icy water, and the willow thickets that bestrew the bottoms. Gibbon was right along with them, though mounted, as they strained and stumbled along this tortuous passage, a 250 to 300-yard march into misery that must have taken them one-half hour at least. Soaked through, shaking from cold and tension, they emerged in twos and threes onto the solid ground of the flat meadow where the Nez Percé still slept. If any made it still poised and eager for the kill, they were supermen.

Some part of the horse herd was grazing at the east end of the meadow beyond the 89 lodges. An older warrior, short of vision and hard of hearing, his name Natalekin, was out early that morning of August 9, working his pony, and heading for the horse herd on Battle Mountain. This enterprise won him a place in history. Not seeing them at all, he almost rode down one knot of soldiers. They shot him and his steed dead, and that is how the fight began, haphazardly and before anyone was truly set for it, Gibbon having earlier given the direction, "When the first shot is fired, charge the camp with the whole line."

A simple direction, like ten years in the penitentiary, it was easy to say but hard to do. Gibbon's troops were in no physical condition to make a charge, and they were still two hundred yards from the lodges. Instead, from this irregular and far-extended line of skirmishers came an insensate and scattering fire that did not so much panic the Nez Percé as serve on them a last-second warning. Most of the warriors ran for the tree cover in the river bends at either end of the camp. They got away naked, such was their hurry, but they also ran armed. Soldiers remarked, and perhaps sniggered a bit, at the sight of these scurrying nude fugitives, little aware that the flight left them no less naked to the consequence.

Many of the families trailed after the warriors, some seeking safety in the waters of the north fork. Other squaws and

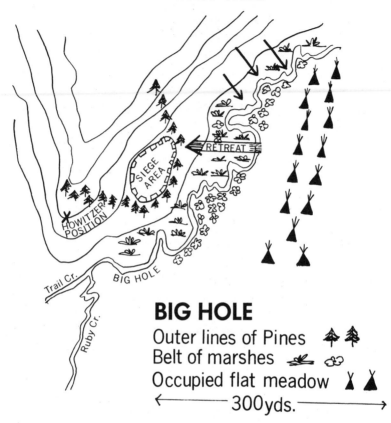

BIG HOLE

Outer lines of Pines 🌲🌲
Belt of marshes ⚚ ❀
Occupied flat meadow ⛺ ⛺
←——— 300yds. ———→

children—far too many for it to have been simply a tragic accident of war—were shot and killed before they could get away.

Lieutenant Bradley and his scouts were the first group to enter the village, this at the extreme east end. A brave popped out of a thicket and shot Bradley dead before he could raise his weapon. The scouts riddled the Indian with bullets. Another warrior rushed Captain William Logan, who snap-fired his Colt and drilled the Indian through the head. The dead man's sister leaped to his body, wrested his revolver from the limp hand, and shot Logan dead. Logan's men in a frenzy almost blew her body apart.

The opening exchange was replete with such incidents, personal, bitter, brutal, but of organization there was at first no sign on either side. The infantrymen tried to fire the lodges; the poles and hides were too green to burn. Even so, within twenty minutes or less, the army was in full control of the village area, and as the firing began to fall off, these infantrymen had a first illusion of victory, hardly noting that most of the bodies lying about were those of noncombatants. About sixty such lay dead.

The Nez Percé had just begun to fight. Chiefs Joseph, Looking Glass, and White Bird were rallying to the counterattack the warriors who had fled to the willow copses. But there was to be no desperate headlong assault, nor would one be needed. Again, Joseph and his lieutenants had a better sense of situation than the military. Their riposte would be a steady and calculating fire from under cover by marksmen of such precision that at 150 to 200 yards, they would zero-in mainly on officers, including Gibbon himself. When Gibbon's men tried to get at these snipers' nests with short rushes, they were either driven back with loss or the Indians withdrew to the tules and willows of the next bend.

There is small profit in discussing the tactics of an action that was already lost due to mistaken decisions before it opened. Gibbon must have read the lesson quite early. Even without the bullet in his hip, which added to the pang of defeat, he had to sense that his position had become hopeless. His men had won nothing. They couldn't stay in the village, the ninety-round issue of ammo was wearing thin and the expedition's rear was dangling in thin air. It probably occurred to the doughty old scrapper in those dark minutes that Custer, the ever-impetuous, had hardly done worse. When at last he ordered his men to get out, they really had no place to go.

They scrambled back across the north fork because that was the way they had come; there was no chance to the eastward, and Indian fire corked the valley at both ends. When they came to rest among the Lodgepole pines on a fairly level bench at the foot of the mountain on which they had roosted the night before, close by and exactly at a level with their jump-off point, that was because they were bushed, blown, bruised, and beaten and not because the position was any good. Flesh and blood could take no more, so it had to be Hobson's choice. Common sense, as well as every valid military consideration, would have dictated continued withdrawal up the mountain to the trains.

FROM EAST BIG HOLE

1. Jumpoff   2. Indian Camp   3. Seige

The stand could not have been a matter of choice. In staging it on what is now known as the Siege Area, the Seventh's elements asked to be exterminated, and nothing more saved them than that the Nez Percé tacticians were either obtuse, played out, or slightly merciful, though nowhere else did they muff opportunity. Had their skirmishers interposed upslope in strength between the army and its base of supply, Gibbon and his people would have been compelled to resume the attack under conditions that foredoomed them. Moreover, the horse herd might have been used to flush the game. There was a covered approach all the way to the slopes above the siege area, and the field of fire upslope from the ground where they reassembled was only a rod or so.

As they settled in, they could hear the screams of the Nez Percé braves as they reentered the village and found their innocent dead. It was grimly, chillingly foreboding.

The forest-shaded bench on which they deployed, formed perimeter, and dug is about sixty by thirty yards in area. Hasty pits and trenches were scratched out with mess-kit spoons and on-trial spade bayonets sent to some units of the Seventh for field testing. Under the forest duff, the soil was loose. The prospector-volunteer found himself defending with a rifle the same hole that he had dug some years before while after precious metal. Taking a rifle, the wounded Gibbon fitted himself into the defensive circle more to hearten his men than because every weapon counted. Almost immediately the force was out of water and as the men thirsted, the sight of the cold-running north fork glimmering a stone's throw distant but added to their torment.

Still, the Nez Percé did not come on in any meaningful strength, and why not stays one of the mysteries. There was no concerted and directed action against the besieged, no disciplined sortie aimed to wipe out the garrison. More than enough warriors and several of the chiefs, panting for vengeance, worked up through the tree line and pressed in at such close quarters that the force had to stay pinned. Rifle fire was exchanged at less than ten yards. But it was an individual thing. More soldiers and a few Indians died in this arm's-length grapple. At the end of fighting, Gibbon had lost thirty-one killed and thirty-eight wounded, a large proportion of which casualties were sustained in the siege area. The Nez Percé loss in dead is reported at eighty-nine, the greater number being women and children.

During the siege, the Nez Percé did not muster the strength to break in, and Gibbon's people stayed so harassed through the first day that they could not attempt to break out. Many colorful legends, doubtless grown larger and made more romantic by time's passage, shroud this stage of the operation. One story goes that in midafternoon of the first day, the Indians fired the grass at the mountain's base. Carried by a strong wind, the flames raced upward and were about to roast Gibbon's people, when magically at the last moment a shift in the wind brought salvation. It reads like an intervention by Providence. Anyone who looks at the stand of grass on this steep lower slope in that same season and notes that the ground under the lodgepole pines is clean of growth helpful to arsonists must doubt this tale of a heavenly deliverance.

Engagement, being under fire, and the rise of fear de-energizes men no less than hard labor. When night fell, though the close-in attackers eased the pressure, most of them returning to the village, Gibbon and his people could not pick up and go on. They were clean spent by a day of battle.

Gibbon was doing what he could to get help. One courier was dispatched eastward to sound the alarm in the settlements. Another went northwest to look for Howard, who was seventeen miles back at Ross's Hole. The howitzer and the wagons came forward that same night to bivouac somewhere atop Battle Mountain, the wagon master (a civilian) torn with anxiety about what was happening to Gibbon. Joseph was far ahead of Gibbon when it came to precaution. All along, a Nez Percé scout party had been shadowing Howard and sending reports about his rate of movement. Out of the several intelligence ventures, Joseph only would reap some profit. Gibbon, by the way, was saying to Howard that he had killed a hundred warriors and held an advantageous position.

Although Gibbon in his official report confuses the events of the two days (a not uncommon failing of commanders under combat pressure), with resultant confusion to the literature, there can be little doubt that the garrison's water supply was replenished the first night. The terrain made that feasible. Once dark fell, there was no possibility of the Indian snipers interdicting the steep but clean slope to the bank of the north fork. What is to be doubted fully is the story that the besieged continued to rake the village with fire, killing more Indians. At that distance, even with modern rifles, it would have been an outright waste of bullets. The defenders had no ammo to spare and further aggravation of the Nez Percé would have been an extreme folly.

With morning came a wholly futile attempt at intervention, more bold than wise. A motley crew of six gunners, led by an Indian scout, came down the mountain with the howitzer. This clumsy piece was sited on a south-running flange of the hill, where it was approximately three hundred yards off the flank of the besieged and one hundred feet upslope. What followed, though dramatic enough, is often described as a fatal turn to the fortunes of the defenders.

It had no such importance. As placed, the howitzer could not lift the pressure on Gibbon but could only shell the village, the occupants of which would at once scatter to the protection of the river banks. So the advancement of the howitzer was a gallant if reckless gesture, though little more.

While it was being unlimbered conspicuously on the skyline, about one-half mile above the Nez Percé camp, the hostiles spotted it. Thirty of them mounted and took off at a mad gallop over the river and up the slope right past the flank of the siege area, the intervening forest screening the movement. The scared gunners had time to fire only two harmless rounds. Under the fury of the charge, two privates panicked, their flight ending only when they reached the nearest settlement. Two sergeants were wounded by rifle fire as the Indians closed, a corporal was shot dead, and one Private Bennett, the driver of the team, became pinned under a wounded horse. Even so, on later extricating himself, Bennett beat the wounded sergeants back to base camp, perhaps the most prodigious feat of the day.

Not only did the Nez Percé dismantle the piece and roll its parts down the mountain; they captured a pack mule laden with two thousand rounds of rifle ammo intended for Gibbon. For the thirty braves it was the climactic coup of an action already tapering out. The soldiers by this time were dining on raw horse meat, while Ollokot and the relatively few warriors who had pressed the siege turned their attention elsewhere.

In early evening Chief Joseph and the people broke camp and moved out. The scouts had brought word that Howard was only a few hours away. At about the same time, a courier got through to Gibbon with the word that relief was coming. Howard arrived early next morning; with him was only one small troop of cavalry. Although the Nez Percé were still within reach, there could be no immediate pursuit. Getting Gibbon and his men mending and mobile was a duty that had to come first, along with making a return to the meadow to bury the dead.

Either these soldiers were less than crack shots or the ferocity of the siege is a myth. Only twelve warriors were killed during the two days. The toll included Chiefs Rainbow and Five Wounds. Also dead were Shore Crossing and Red Moccasin Tops, the two young rascals who had touched off a war by a spree ending in murder. Because one of the dead braves was nicknamed Looking Glass, the demise of his namesake was reported prematurely. Chief Looking Glass survived in temporary disgrace. The other chiefs blamed him for the slack security that let the Big Hole camp be taken by surprise and deposed him as battle leader.

Some historians report that his place was taken by Chief Lean Elk. Actually, the honor fell to Poker Joe, a half-breed with a marked talent for fighting, an encyclopedic knowledge of the countryside, and possibly a genius for palming cards. The post in any case was secondary. The controlling mind was Joseph's and something more should be said on that score. The long campaign had markedly the same characteristics from start to finish because it had one strategist, one overall director of operations. Looking Glass, then Poker Joe, was the fire-fight leader, taking charge when battle was joined. The cornerstone of generalship, however, is not tactics, an elementary subject, but the mastery of human nature. Joseph was the great unifying force, the best brain, the logistician. His was the command presence. General Howard recognized him as his central antagonist, and in so doing, Howard was right.

Following the line of the Continental Divide that curves out to the east from Big Hole through a rolling and almost treeless prairie with far horizons, the Nez Percé headed for Yellowstone National Park. Set aside as such only five years before, the park was already attracting sight-seers and campers in considerable numbers, though then there was less gawking at the bear and the elk.

At this stage the war turned doubly bitter. The Nez Percé raided the ranches to provision themselves and waste stock that might otherwise sustain Howard's forces. Whites who resisted were killed. The Nez Percé aged were left behind with water and some food. When Howard's Bannock scouts came up to them, they were killed and scalped.

Having delayed only long enough to give Gibbon's battered-and-down command essential help, Howard then came on so hard that he almost foundered his force. In the next few rounds of the feeling-out game, he had reason to repent his haste. He sent a platoon of cavalry under a lieutenant to block at Targhee Pass, the western entrance to the park, toward which he felt certain Joseph was heading. Not only was it a bad guess: When the Nez Percé stay-behind scouts reported that Howard had halted in place to rest the main body while waiting for the blocking party to do its work in the defile and make the Indians rebound toward him, Joseph and the others saw their opportunity.

About forty braves mounted up for a night raid on Howard's camp. The outpost heard them coming and thought it was the lieutenant's detachment returning. So the sentry did not challenge and the camp stayed unalerted until one brave, contrary to orders, fired his rifle. Then, war whooping and

CAMAS MEADOWS

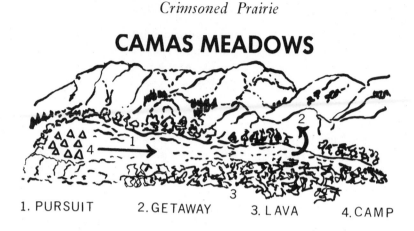

1. PURSUIT   2. GETAWAY   3. LAVA   4. CAMP

shooting as they departed the area, the raiders ran off all of Howard's pack mules, missing the horses only because that night they had been tied to a picket line.

Three troops of cavalry rode off in pursuit only to be stopped short just outside the camp. More of the Nez Percé were waiting to ambush them at a place called Camas Meadows. Two troops recoiled from the shock and the third became cornered in a lava bed, where the horse soldiers dismounted and fought in a Custer ring to save themselves, the action ending when the ambushers slipped away through a nearby canyon.

Having spent his alloted time at the Targhee Pass and found nothing, the lieutenant obediently returned to the main body. The Nez Percé then pushed on through the unguarded pass. Howard again had to hold up while waiting for more pack mules.

Here we see tactics advanced far beyond anything within the imagination of the Plains Indians, a superior employment of mobility, deep penetration reconnaissance, employment of rear and advance guards, collection during night attack, bold feinting, swift disengagement, and the devising of complex ruses and deceptions.

During the enforced halt, Howard deployed in person to Virginia City, feeling the need of aid and comfort, though he found little of either. Some of the civilian volunteers who had been with Gibbon had already returned from Big Hole and were spreading the word that Howard was an incompetent procrastinator. The local editor was relaying this assessment to the country, while at the same time lauding Chief Joseph as a "splendid military intelligence" leading a handful of men, women, and children. As if determined to confirm these judgments, Howard on August 24 wired W. T. Sherman, "My command is so much worn by overfatigue and jaded animals that I cannot push it much further." Sherman, smarting because the army was coming in for so much criticism, replied, "If you are tired, give the command to some young, energetic officer." Back went Howard's answer, "I never flag. You need not fear for the campaign . . . nor doubt my pluck and energy."

Here was a childish exchange of rabbit punches between two aging professionals who should have had more dignity. The battlers then came out of the clinch and returned to their corners. Howard managed to buy some shoes, clothes, and medicines for his men while picking up a few mules and a string of unbroken ponies, though even as a shopping tour his sortie from Henry's Lake was no howling success. Still his troops remembered it fondly, being rewarded with three extra days of rest while they awaited the boss man's return.

Howard was not dragging his feet. The army remounts and the regional supplies were not equal to the demands of any such campaign. Still, somebody had to be skinned and Howard was the most obvious target. Hardly the reincarnation of Hannibal when it came to traversing tall mountains, Howard still belongs among the better half of the Indian-fighting generals, if only because he was a gentleman rather than a fire-eater.

The Nez Percé had to continue their march unhelped. Their fair-weather friends of the buffalo hunt, the Crows, refused either to receive them or to provide any assistance. Further, the Crows in large numbers joined up to serve as scouts with Howard's column. It is another sad chapter in the story of Indian betrayal of Indian. They had no quarrel whatever with the Nez Percé. But having bedded down all along with the army, they put that interest above a traditional loyalty, and this act of picking the winning side at the right times has served them quite well ever since.

"Beauty is happiness," wrote the philosopher, "the only happiness of which we are never doubtful." Oh, well. Going through Yellowstone Park at what is usually the finest time of year to luxuriate in its wonders, smelling the sulphur springs, timing Old Faithful, feeding the bears, and drinking Apollinaris spring water, the Nez Percé made their march as nearly as the terrain permits on a straight west to east line, the only side excursions being for scouting purposes. The saying that anything that gurgles in a wearying land is worth a taste was not for them.

They were in a hurry, so much of a hurry that they missed General Sherman, who was holidaying amid the geysers and lakes while keeping a weather eye on the campaign.

Some of the younger braves wantonly attacked several nonoffending parties of campers, killing two white men and shooting up a Negro cook. There had been some military excuse for the bloody aftermath to Big Hole. For this there was none, except that the older chiefs could not control all points in the extended column, and the young braves were still fired up about the slaughter of the women and children.

Joseph had used his influence to keep savages from acting less savage than civilized men, but it didn't always work.

Once Howard knew that the Nez Percé had entered the park, by using the telegraph to order forced marches, the army set troops to block every exit. Both Howard and Sherman were confident that the entrapment was final and the campaign all but over. The news was flashed to the public at about the time that the Nez Percé, having crossed a ford in the Yellowstone River, emerged from the mountains through an unguarded hole in the wall to the northwest of present-day Cody.

Once more footed on open prairie, the column veered sharply north and quickened its pace. Joseph and the other chiefs were heading for Canada by the shortest route, or the "British line" as it was called in that time. Various troop bodies were beating out the country in search of the hostiles, the Fifth Cavalry out of the Little Bighorn region, part of the Seventh Cavalry advancing west along the flat Yellowstone valley, and Howard's mixed force still pushing up from the rear.

For once, the Nez Percé scouts went wrong. What they thought they saw was ballooned into false information. One of the main columns, they said, lay directly athwart the path on the short line to Canada. So Joseph swung out on a wide detour to the westward, this to avoid contact with a small cavalry patrol under Lieutenant Hugh L. Scott, many years later the army's chief of staff. But for the added miles, the Nez Percé might have made it.

At Canyon Creek, Montana, having pursued the Nez Percé for seventy-five miles, Colonel Samuel Sturgis and 350 cavalrymen of the Seventh Regiment came to contact and gave

CANYON CREEK FIELD

battle. It is the same Sturgis who was titular head of the Garry Owens when Custer mishandled them. Whether they might have done better under his hand remains a guess. There is only a glimpse of him as he steps from the shadows.

The meeting ground was between what are now the communities of Billings and Laurel. Some miles up the creek and thirteen miles west of where Billings lies occurred the clash. Although the cavalry was beaten into the ground by too many forced marches before the shooting began, it made a brave try. Losing a fight by asking too much of man and horse had virtually become a regimental tradition.

Howard had almost come up to Sturgis at the time of battle. His troops on coming abreast would bivouac beside a stream called Careless Creek, and not badly named. For during the engagement, Sturgis sent word to Howard that his men had cut into the Indian horse herd, and if Howard would just make a flanking movement, he could bag the rest. It was not the sort of incident to increase confidence in the worth of command estimates. Howard was still well outside any possibility of closing, though most of his officers did not realize it. Nothing odd about this. The same happens in every war.

Against Sturgis, the Nez Percé, with most of their column still moving north, were given time to deploy their rear guard along the rimrock of a sharp ridge that covered the trail. The resulting encounter was by nature a delaying action, drawn out over a full day. An inconclusive thing in which for the first time the Nez Percé suffered disproportionate loss (twenty-nine Indians KIA to three for army), it was equally costly in that the tribe lost about three hundred of the remaining horses. With the cut-down force, there were just too few warriors to cover all of the critical points.

But the defenders of the passage accomplished their object, the getaway of the main body, and the attack up the rocky ridge took too much out of the cavalry muscle. Sturgis had to conclude that his men were exhausted and could not pursue. Joseph and his main body marched on to spread their camp on the open prairie seven miles to the north of the foot of the Bear's Paw Mountains. What was left of the battered rear guard followed along. They were now only thirty-five miles from the Canadian line and fourteen miles south of what is the present town of Chinook.

Once again, Joseph halted for a rest, either because he thought that he had time or reasoned that he must take it. His people were pretty well spent. During the respite, the buffalo would be hunted, the sores on the horses would be swabbed, meat would be dried, and equipment would be repaired.

While the Nez Percé regirded themselves, they out-guarded and scouted to the south, lest Howard or Sturgis come on again. But there had been a change in strategy; more than ever in a punitive mood, the army was bent on trapping Joseph rather than permitting him to escape. So Howard and Sturgis were held on leash.

Out of Fort Keogh, Wyoming, Colonel Nelson Miles and a column that included six companies of infantry, five troops of cavalry, a hundred Indian scouts, two field guns, and many wagons were moving on Joseph from the east, following a track that wound next the Little Rockies. Sturgis had kept a flow of information about Joseph's movements going to Miles by mounted couriers and Miles was performing accordingly. With the colonel cracking the whip, these combined arms had covered 260 miles in twelve days, which would be a good rate for cavalry moving independently.

There was more pressure on Miles than that of the basic desire to continue proving himself. He had married W. T. Sherman's niece, quite likely because he loved her, which would in no way ease the itch to outdo his uncle-by-marriage if a small war afforded any such opportunity. Being a Sherman in-law could not otherwise hurt him, but might cause him to accept inordinately the risk of dying too soon. Miles was rather careful about that. Unlike Gibbon, when he went for a headlong plan, it kept him at respectful distance from the danger center, an attitude routine and honorable rather than foolishly heroic. Also, he consistently kept an anchor to windward, which is not a bad idea.

Joseph, who eschewed the almost exclusive preference for high ground that is the fetish of most professional infantrymen, once again saw tactical advantage in making the best possible use of low ground. In large degree, the Bear's Paw field was Big Hole repeated. The two positions were remarkably alike, except that in the final scene there were no high mountains immediately off the flank. The setting should more properly have been called Snake Creek, rather than Bear's Paw, the channel of that stream being the most conspicuous terrain feature. Whereas this new camp, set in a grassy hollow, was surrounded on all sides by higher ground in the form of gently ridged and treeless prairie, such had been the aspect of Big Hole only in three directions. Too much could be made of this comparison in defensive features. Conceivably the Nez Percé could have chosen both sites because of the running water and concern for their remaining horses. But if in so doing they accidentally chose ground enabling them to repulse the United States Army, that is either an ingenious coincidence or proof that fighting men had best think like horses. Joseph's choice of ground, wholly unorthodox, invariably worked out.

The lip of the cup in which the Indians sought to recoup was a rounded, exceptionally smooth crest, devoid of tall grass, shrubs, rocks, or any cover satisfactory to a rifleman. To the east and south, the land fell off gently with no accident or natural growth, except for some sage and the bland stretch of dried grass. From any direction, a horseman might gallop dead on to this perimeter. The enclosed hollow was at the heart of good buffalo country and the thundering herd had worked it over. The bottom of the cup or hollow was bisected diagonally by the narrow trench of Snake Creek, joined midway by the equally deep coulee of an on-and-off tributary. Both of these sharply walled dirt ditches were thickly furnished with scrub poplars, willows, and bullrushes; the haunts of red-winged blackbirds and magpies, their ribands of green afforded the one touch of color relief to the otherwise austere and tawny prairie.

Seasonal rainfall around this vale averages thirteen inches per year, which makes the countryside semi-desert. The hollow is about 150 by 600 yards and is treeless except for the water courses. The rim of the roughly oval perimeter is not more than thirty feet above the floor of the bowl, the low-lying ridge line being cut through by three draws on the south and west. Otherwise the crest runs quite even around the oval, and the ground is perfectly clean of rimrock, boulders, and shrubs. Hence the defensive possibilities, while they may have looked good to Chief Joseph, would never have attracted the eye of a Fort Benning graduate.

Having ridden hard and pushed his column to the limit of endurance, Miles came up early on the morning of September 30 with worn mounts and men near exhaustion. Still he chose that hour to close and by hasty decision created his own dilemma. Several of his cavalry troops were peeled off to go into a blocking position along a high ridge line more than two miles to the northwest of the hostile camp, while a smaller contingent was detailed to run off what was left of the Nez Percé horse herd. The main body of cavalry was to charge right on from the southeast via an earth bridge that provided level galloping right to the lip of the bowl. Elsewhere the approaches were relatively steep.

Self-evidently, Miles anticipated that the cavalry charge would of itself panic and stampede the Nez Percé, following which the blocking force, serving as the dustpan to the broom, would gather them in. Although the tactics seem to be elementary, the flaws in Miles' line of reasoning should be laid out in order:

. . . The Nez Percé had shown no such susceptibility, but

to the contrary had proved to be phenomenally steady under surprise pressure.

. . . Under the conditions, the prospect of achieving surprise was negligible.

. . . If the Indians did not flee from the charge, any attempt by the horsemen to descend into the bowl could bring disaster.

. . . Miles had no notion of what awaited him within the bowl or whether the horses could find a footing there.

. . . If the army was getting the word about the deadliness of Nez Percé skill with the rifle, no one seemed to be listening, for it was certainly no factor in battle planning.

. . . Miles had Joseph defeated without a fight, if he simply interposed his force to the north on ground of his own choosing.

But of course, there had to be a cavalry charge to begin and everyone knew it. With the infantry playing spectator at safe distance, pride of service virtually demanded it. Furthermore, the level and rockless prairie was nature's gift to hard charging and the cavalry had been trained for little else. To pass up such an ideal setting would have been little short of ignoble.

The stakes and forfeits of the cavalry charge, while sufficiently dramatized at Balaklava and at the Little Bighorn, have never been more eloquently stated than by Winston Churchill following his ride into the melee at Omdurman.

> In one respect a cavalry charge is very like ordinary life. So long as you are all right, firmly in your saddle, your horse in hand and well armed, lots of enemies will give you a wide berth. But as soon as you have lost a stirrup, had a rein cut, have dropped your weapon, are wounded, or your horse is wounded, then is the moment when from all quarters enemy rush upon you.

Miles, who should have been warned by things past, still

proceeded uppidee-uppida like the hero of the poem "Excelsior."

Even the elements seemed to be in tune with his decision. That is to say, the thunder rolled, the clouds grew big, the lightning flashed, and the rain came down not as a gully-washer but as a horizon-shrinking sod-soaker. Amidst this junior twilight of the gods, Miles launched his cavalry from four miles off, a far piece of galloping for Canonero on a clear day and a sudden-death handicap to run-down troop horses in any weather. These luckless skates were already at the end of their tether.

Romance writers will have it that the thunder of their mighty hoofs as they approached alerted Joseph's sleeping camp in time so that volunteer outguards sprinted to the ridge crest, spread, flattened, and poured out a withering fire. A pleasing story, though the fact is that a small Nez Percé boy had earlier sighted some of Miles' Cheyenne scouts skulking about in the distance. This juvenile communicator ran back at once and spread the word. There had to be sentries flattened around the south end of the rim and they were the linchpins of a preconcerted scheme of defense. Here I mean to say only that the Nez Percé were not taken unaware, knew what they had to do, and still more to the point, were afforded a sufficient time in which to do it. The consequences of the charge speak to that point. Come to within 150 to 100 yards of the hostile perimeter, the forefront of Miles' cavalry was stopped dead and turned by Indian volley fire, though momentum carried a few riders on to the perimeter rim where braves and troopers crumpled and died from point-blank fire.

Not as gory or as spectacular as the Charge of the Light Brigade, it came pretty close and was nigh as ghastly a folly. From these relatively few seconds of going against aimed rifles, 53 out of 115 Garry Owens, or almost 50 percent of their committed strength, were killed or wounded, officers and noncoms accounting for most of the toll. The Seventh rolled back leaderless. When from the repulse the Seventh limped to base camp, one lieutenant cried to Miles with pardonable hyperbole, "I am the only damned man of the Seventh to wear shoulder straps alive." He was in fact the only officer unhit.

Miles later wrote of the attack, "The gallop forward, preceding the charge, was one of the most brilliant and inspiring sights I have ever witnessed on any field. It was the crowning glory of our twelve days of forced marching." Warmer words than these have rarely been so chilling.

The dismal consequence of this eye-popping attack was that Miles was almost out on his feet without knowing. The spectacular try that is bloodily beaten back in the common sight at the start of battle is a crusher to combat morale. No one is willing to try again in the same way and a commander would be a fool to ask it.

Miles' horse raiders had done much better and his blocking force remained unhurt. The roundup detachment of Second Cavalrymen under Captain Tyler not only succeeded in running off about eight hundred head of Nez Percé horses and mules; one company from this force intercepted, engaged, and killed or scattered a column of eighty or so mounted hostiles who were packed up and heading north. Some few of the Indians made it to Canada. Still, there was little glory in these things, the main idea having failed at center.

When the pressure on the perimeter eased following the repulse of the Seventh, the warriors dug frantically to improve their positions around the southern end of the rim, and they used any tool that would make dirt fly. Even so, maintaining the defense of the camp along the outer crest was from the beginning a hopeless task, made so by the disparity in numbers. Joseph did not have enough men to spread around the oval ridge and cover all of the approaches. So the door was open for the infantry skirmishers to probe for the unguarded places, crawl to the top of the ridge line, and pick off from flank or rear the Indian snipers who were outguarding at the same level.

Miles made one more abortive try to penetrate and over-run, this in early afternoon, using infantry. Two companies of the Fifth Regiment under Lieutenant Henry Romeyn attacked along the draw where Snake Creek cuts through the ridge to enter the bowl, with the object of blocking the Nez Percé water supply. This sortie got as far as the western end of the village and died among the first few lodges, by which time Romeyn had lost 35 percent of his people. Joseph was caught up in what became a hand-to-hand melee before Romeyn was routed. Trapped in one of the struck lodges, he fought back with a rifle, coming out of the fray with his clothing shredded by bullets and his horse wounded, though he was otherwise unhurt.

The greater number of Nez Percé line responded more sensibly and less vulnerably to this suddenly imposed threat against their interior. They jumped down into the straight-banked ditches of Snake Creek and the tributary dry coulee. The rushes and overhanging bush gave them concealment; the banks served as protecting breastworks. From this experiment they learned something. The screened ditches were a natural second line of defense when the high ground of the ridge could no longer be held. From the lowest of the low ground, they could draw a bead on any enemy skirmisher as he came over the skyline, whether walking or crawling. So was it done during the remaining days of battle.

Two trys on the first day, two bad beatings, and that was the end of direct assault. The army settled down to siege, which was an admission that its mobile and moral power was no longer up to the task. In lieu of knowing what to do, Miles did what he knew, which was the application of gradual strangulation to the Joseph camp, made possible by his own larger numbers, the war-weariness of the Nez Percé families, and the wide-openness of the range. Both Joseph and Miles were trapped, though in different ways. The Indian finally had become immobilized; he would have to fight it out on the ground where he stood, and his heart was no longer in

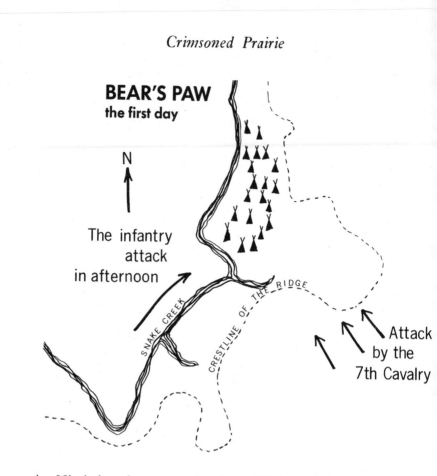

BEAR'S PAW
the first day

N

The infantry
attack
in afternoon

SNAKE CREEK

CRESTLINE OF THE RIDGE

Attack
by the
7th Cavalry

it. His beloved younger brother, Ollokot, had been killed during the day's fight and so had Toohoolhoolzote, and several other chiefs. As for Miles, he had to come out victor in some way, but without killing more of his people uselessly or crossing them in such way as to make himself notorious.

The storm had continued, the weather turning cold, and heavy snows fell that night. High winds made it a blizzard, with acute suffering to both camps, a condition that persisted. Miles was still waiting for his wagon train to come up bringing medical supply, tents, blankets, and food, which shortages he should have thought about before invaliding one-third of his soldiers.

BEAR'S PAW looking south

Miles sent couriers to tell Howard to bring up his soldiers fast, a sufficient measure of his discouragement.

Joseph dispatched some of his warriors afoot to Sitting Bull, who was idling in Canada's Cypress Hills just over the line from Belton, Montana. It was a call for help. There were three thousand Sioux with Sitting Bull and not a few scalps taken on the Little Bighorn. But Sitting Bull was no El Cid or Cyrano. His response was to move a few miles deeper into Canada.

Half-hearted attempts were made to negotiate, the details being unimportant since they came to nothing for lack of sufficient trust on either side.

The little war went on, hardly a siege, little more than half-siege, but a nasty, though intermittent exchange between belly-down snipers. More Indians, more troopers, died in this senseless dueling. Most of the people in both camps stayed out of it, responding to the will to survive, if possible, a battle coming to an end already certain. The experience is hardly less demoralizing to the indicated victor than to the vanquished.

Near the end Chief White Bird and a small party of followers were able to elude Miles' circle of outposts and make it to Canada. There was no chance that the main body could make such a getaway. Most of the horses were dead and the warriors were bound to the spot by their women and children. Like Looking Glass, White Bird had wished to keep on fighting. Joseph had said to them that his decision had to rest on what was best for the dependents.

After their "joint chiefs'" council, as they turned their separate ways, each to choose his own course, a stray bullet hit Looking Glass in the head and struck him dead. With Joseph for four months, he had helped lead a small army of Indians more than thirteen hundred miles, always defeating the United States Army until his last moment. It was not a good way to die, though possibly he would have welcomed it.

By Joseph's order, a flag of truce was raised above the village. There remained to him 87 warriors, 40 of them wounded, 184 squaws and 147 children, many of them with open wounds, some abscessing from malnutrition and the pounding of the march, and all pitifully weakened by stress and hunger.

When General Howard arrived on October 3, Miles was at first frigid and formal with his superior, though when Howard explained that he had not come up to take the honors, and would leave such as were to be had from this dubious field to Miles, the colonel became all sweetness and light.

The next day the two rode forward together to receive the surrender. Joseph rode toward them unescorted, jumped from his horse, and walked forward to the meeting. From under the blanket in which he was wrapped, he pulled a rifle and prepared to hand it to Howard, who motioned that Miles should receive it.

Then addressing the gentler and more senior soldier who had opposed him from the beginning, Joseph said through an interpreter,

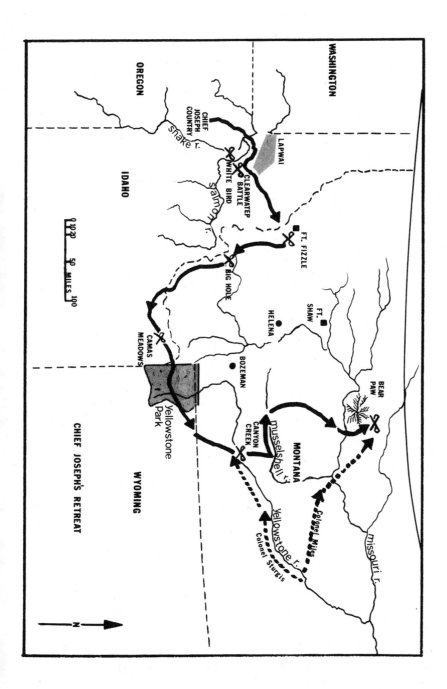

CHIEF JOSEPH'S RETREAT

Tell General Howard I know his heart. What he told me before in Idaho I have in my heart. I am tired of fighting. My people ask me for food and I have none to give. It is cold and we have no blankets, no wood. My people are starving to death. Where is my little daughter? I do not know. Perhaps even now she is freezing to death. Hear me, my chiefs! I have fought. But from where the sun now stands, Joseph will fight no more forever.

Howard and Miles were gentle. They knew the goodness in this man and respected his brilliance and honorable conduct as an adversary. Much of civilian America felt the same way, having followed the campaign closely. After the prisoners were escorted to Bismarck, they were cheered and fed by a surging street crowd, and later a group of church women banqueted Joseph and the few other surviving chiefs.

The two commanders had promised Joseph that they would have him and his people returned to their own country in Oregon. And they did their best to make good on that pledge, fighting the War Department and the rest of the bureaucracy all the way. But two days after the Bismarck banquet, the Nez Percé were on a train headed south, with Indian Territory as their ultimate destination. Within a year, one-third of them had perished from malaria or other ailments. In 1882 Joseph and a few of his following were allowed to return to the Pacific Northwest, largely because Miles had continued to fight for them. Even so, for Joseph it had to be a sorrowful journey. None of his children was along. One by one he had buried them in Oklahoma soil.

General Howard's aid at the Bear's Paw surrender had been Lieutenant C. E. Wood. Later, as Charles Erskine Wood, he became a nationally known writer. His biting words epitomize the tragedy of the life of the greatest of Indian leaders, "I think that, in his long career, Joseph cannot accuse the United States of one single act of justice."

12

On Wounded Knee

In 1890 the Chief of the Census Bureau announced to the American people that on the basis of population distribution, it could be established that the western frontier no longer existed.

Still remaining unfixed, however, were the boundaries of the homelands to which the tribes had been shifted; although in theory they had been drawn permanently, it did not work out that way in practice.

When in 1873 every tribe had finally been assigned its reservation, Indian lands had a peak of 150,000,000 acres.

By 1887, through one fast deal or another, this total had been cut to 139,000,000 acres.

In that year the Allotment Act was passed by the Congress. By its terms the Indians were treated as a race that had to die. No provision was made for an increase in population. As their numbers shrank the allotment would be reduced, the land left over could be declared surplus and opened to white settlement.

Most of the land was unsuitable for farming and the Plains Indians did not make good farmers even when conditions were ideal.

Still, the act premised that in twenty-five years, the Indian would have adjusted as satisfactorily as the average white settler. For that length of time, his land would be held in trust, untaxable and nonalienable. Thereafter the land would be his by title, liable to taxation, and he would be free to sell, rent, or lease it.

The Indian had no preparation for this way of life. Devotion to a small homestead that he could call his own had no such importance to the red man as to the white. He knew little of real estate values or of mathematics, which made him an easy mark for a sharp trader. Still, he did know when he was going hungry, and when poverty hit, with it came the pressure to sell his allotment. So general and continuous was this pressure that within thirty-five years after the passing of the Allotment Act, less than 50,000,000 acres remained in Indian hands. In 1890, during the preceding two years, more than 12,000,000 acres, or about 12 percent of the original holding, had been taken from them for return to the public domain. The steady shrinkage, coupled with hard times, darkened every future prospect.

So as obvious as it may have been to men in government that the western frontier was no more, equally unmistakable were the signs reading that the scars and hurts caused by its passing remained.

The reservation people did not so much brood over wrongs at the hands of whites as sorrow for themselves. Self-pity was the mood of the day and its causes like its symptoms were numerous.

There was too little food, warmth, and comfort in the new environment; freedom of choice was denied them, almost no work opportunity existed for the males, and the children were left bewildered and wretchedly uneducated.

Whether done with good intent, the thrust of agency policy was to make over the Indian in the image of the white man.

As young as it was possible to take them, the children were

separated from their parents and sent to boarding schools distant from the reservation. The schools were usually denominational. At school the Indian boy was given a Christian name, was required to wear his hair short, became dressed in a work suit, and was assigned to an overcrowded dormitory. The average food allowance was eleven cents per day per child. As part of their vocational guidance, the children scrubbed and swept floors, did the dishes, made the beds, and tended the yards. The excuse given for this enforced Oliver Twist-like regime was that Indian children, in their former state, had no real home life.

The process was supposed to "civilize" them. Its effect was to make them feel ashamed of their tribal culture. Agents and missionaries worked to the same end on the reservations, discouraging the wearing of long hair and the use of blankets, buckskin shirts, and moccasins as symbols of savagery.

All of the old tribal ceremonies, such as the war dance, were taboo, and in some instances, prohibited on the reservations, lest incitement come of them. It was done as if the Bill of Rights was never intended for the red man. To practice any of the ancient rites, the Indians had to do it in secret and out of sight.

Urged to house themselves like the white man, they dwelt in quarters made of shoddy material, less warm and no better lighted than the tepee. Their annuities from the Government almost invariably arrived late and were usually short, or so it seemed. Of the new religion, they had acquired only enough knowledge to compound their confusion.

Such were some of the fundamental causes of their mass depression. To recover from it, to find the road back, they needed a voice of hope, a major prophet, a new messiah, and as 1890 opened, it seemed that he had arrived.

The prior year had begun with a solar eclipse, mystifying and terrifying to the tribes who could not understand it. They called it "the day the sun died."

But to a previously inconspicuous Piute living at Mason Valley Nevada, it was the day of ascension. Wovoka, or Jim Wilson as he was known to the whites, was then about thirty-five. On the day of the eclipse, he renamed himself Kwoh-itsauk, which means Big Rumbling Belly. Fortunately or otherwise, that alias did not take hold, and it is as Wovoka that he made his niche in history.

The story goes that Wovoka was running a high temperature when the sun quit, and the two things in combination reacted on him as if he were high on mescaline or peyote. He came out of the eclipse and the fever tinged with divinity and claiming that he had been transported to heaven while the earth was dark.

God had told him to make it a round trip because it would be his destiny to lead the Indians out of their reservation misery into a new order of things purged of white men, where again the buffalo and antelope would play plentifully. The Indian dead would arise when he gave the signal. Though he was to speak only the language of brotherly love, these promised wonders would somehow be accomplished.

Wovoka caught on. Almost overnight his message swept from Nevada through the Oklahoma flats and Dakota hills, wherever Indians lived colonized. His following became not a cult but rather impassioned believers in an original, if short-lived faith, halfway between the missionary's God and the less positive Indian worship of the Great Spirit.

With Wovoka's great claiming, there was also great showmanship. That modern faith healers have to combine the two if they are to be successful suggests that Wovoka, despite his absurdities, had a Barnum's understanding of human nature.

If the Indians were to win the new utopia here on earth, in which all things would become theirs, they must practice his ceremonial that came to be called "the ghost dance." Though the movements of the dance were as eccentric and as variable as modern rock, the sanctification came of the dancer working himself up into such a state of ecstasy that in the end he collapsed from exhaustion. No doubt it was barbarous, as much so as what white couples had to do to win a marathon dance forty years later.

Yet there was also much breast-beating with it, a crying aloud for the old days, the wearing of sackcloth and ashes over the wretched state into which the Indian had fallen, as when the Arapaho ghost dancers sang,

> Dear Father, have pity on me,
> I have nothing to eat;
> I am dying of thirst,
> Everything I owned is gone.

From the Indian's view, conditions may have been almost that bad, though privation unlimited be not the right tune-up for marathon dancing. Like the Arapaho, the Sioux and Cheyenne of the Dakota reservations sent delegations westward to sit at the feet of Wovoka and partake of the new wisdom that they might return with the chart to deliverance.

Although he was the fat-faced and jowly type, looking more simple than sage, Wovoka must have possessed charisma before it became patented. The missionaries homed to their bands to spread the word that Wovoka was a supernatural being. Where they preached the true gospel, they led the dancing. The orgiastic exercise would last through one night at least, ending with many of the dancers flat and in a catatonic state. On reviving, they would seem to arise from the dead. The spell cast by Wovoka became swiftly as pervasive and as powerful as that of the Sudan's Whirling Dervish in the same era.

Here was Indian incitement in a wholly new form. The contagion took firm hold and spread so rapidly that governmental authority was not only alarmed but baffled and hesitant about how to cope with it. Government can hardly be firm about that which appears to be wholly cloud cuckoo.

One extra load on its back in this hour came of its own capering. Chief Sitting Bull, by this time in his late fifties, had returned to the United States and was living on the Standing Rock Reservation in Dakota. The medicine man was still so hostile to white Americans that he would not speak to the agent.

Why the United States wanted Sitting Bull back is a good question. His semivoluntary exile in Canada had not been to his liking, in part because his several thousand warriors had deserted him one by one, and also Chief Gall and other leading Sioux would not answer his letters. For a man who had to be seen and heard because his ego demanded it, his isolation had become intolerable. That way, it might have been left. But seemingly some point of honor between nations, such as led to the negotiations decades later over the Bomarc missile, was at stake with Sitting Bull at center. So there took place at Fort Buford, Canada, in 1881, a conference of dignitaries from both sides of the border. General Terry, who had yet to bag one big Indian, led the American delegation. Sitting Bull held the stage. Insulting Terry and his colleagues, glad-handing the Canadian commissioners, he proclaimed his love for Canada and his hatred for the United States, which he said had continued to wrong him, adding that he wanted his children to grow up in their own country.

It cannot be said of this deal over one body that Canada's loss became the gain of the USA. Sitting Bull crossed the border and yielded to the U.S. military while singing a new song,

> A warrior I have been,
> Now it is all over,
> A hard time I have.

If he meant one word of it, he didn't act that way. For several years in the 1880s he toured the country, performing in a Wild West show produced by William F. (Buffalo Bill) Cody, who like himself was part warrior and part thespian. Due more than all else to his connection with the circus, and out of fulsome acclaim from its barkers, Sitting Bull achieved far more fame than he deserved, eclipsing that of Red Cloud and Crazy Horse. So it remains today.

But if actor he was, he was also a bad actor, and much of the medicine man was bad medicine. He continued to agitate and stir trouble like a man whose hunger for power never dies.

Sitting Bull swung over to Wovoka not because he believed in his nonsense but because he saw another chance to hit back at whites. The Ghost Dance religion was one more opportunity to make mischief on a large scale. With no reasonable use for any such following, the old rebel had about five hundred devotees clustered around his cabin some forty miles from the agency, and they became the foremost disciples of the faith. A warlike tone was not missing. Some of the young warriors went through the ritual swinging rifles with crossed bandoliers over their shoulders, while wearing "ghost shirts" that they chanted would turn back any white man's bullet.

Other notable chiefs such as Hump, Big Foot, Little Wound, and Big Road pronounced for the new religion, and in all five of the Dakota reservations, there was mounting tension and excitement among the Sioux and Cheyenne and a rise of fear felt not exclusively among the white staff. Agents reported to Government that at least half of the Indians were ghost dancing and that control of the situation was rapidly slipping from their hands.

As for Chief Red Cloud, his attitude was as usual inscrutably mixed. When his son, Jack Red Cloud, joined the ghost dancers, he neither demurred nor gave him his blessing. But on the other hand, when a white man dressed in Indian garb showed up one day, claiming that he was the new messiah and was bound for the Badlands to proclaim the gospel, Red Cloud spit in his eye, saying, "You go home! You are no Son of God." The would-be savior proved to be a loony strayed from an Iowa poor farm.

Amid the crisis of emotion, in the worst possible hour,

Government blundered. At the Pine Ridge Reservation the old agent was allowed to resign in protest because the promised beef ration was not coming through. His place was taken by one D. F. Royer, who lacked both the intestinal fortitude and common sense that a highly delicate and possibly explosive situation required, "a gentleman with not one qualification in his makeup," as one contemporary put it. From the start, Royer's nerves frayed and he was soon begging Washington to send troops.

The national press was already playing the new war scare to the limit. The public was caught up in the excitement. When Royer at last wired Washington, "Indians are dancing in the snow and are wild and crazy . . . We need protection and we need it now . . . The leaders should be arrested and confined at some military post," President Harrison had already made up his mind.

By mid-November the army had taken over control from the Interior Department and some three thousand soldiers marched into the Pine Ridge and Rosebud Reservations. More out of fright than from rebellion, several thousand Indians fled the reservations for the South Dakota Badlands, a pinnacled, fantastically eroded, and almost inaccessible fossil bed off the corner of the Pine Ridge reserve and in prehistoric times the pasture of little four-toed eohippus, the remote ancestor of the horse.

Two chiefs, Short Bull and Sitting Bear, had earlier led a march of ghost dancers from the reservations into that strange region, a setting as eerie as the cult itself, wholly lacking in sustenance for man or beast.

Except for the last mass exodus, the prime effect of the army occupation was to quiet the scene, so that ghost dancing almost stopped. For the time being, the military, like the agents, worried less about the fugitive bands that had trailed after Short Bull, since they would be forced to return by starvation, than about the possibility that Sitting Bull would foment violence at Standing Rock.

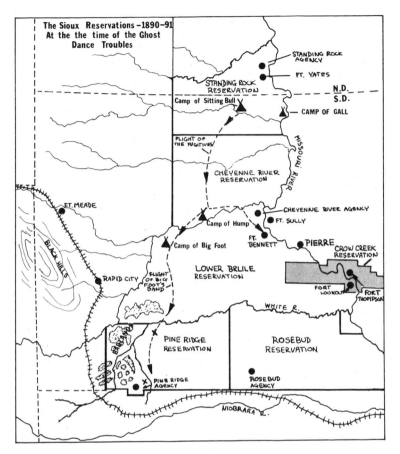

The Sioux Reservations –1890–91
At the the time of the Ghost
Dance Troubles

By official request, Buffalo Bill Cody arrived at Standing Rock to negotiate with Sitting Bull. The agent, James McLaughlin, argued that using a white man in such a role would be the most certain way to provoke the old chief. McLaughlin, a former army officer, did not admire Sitting Bull; he considered him treacherous, deceitful, and cowardly. But he thought he understood Indian psychology. His counterproposal was that the arrest should be made instead by the Reservations' Indian police, a loyal and well-trained group of officers commanded by Lieutenant Bull Head. While they closed in on Sitting Bull, two troops of cavalry would be standing off within covering distance, with a Hotchkiss rapid-fire gun as extra insurance.

Though ex-major McLaughlin's judgment couldn't have been more wrong, that's how the decision went. At dawn on December 15, Bull Head appeared outside of Sitting Bull's log cabin, backed by forty-three policemen, with the cavalry force at too great a distance. Bull Head had welcomed the job. He hated Sitting Bull and hated also his chief bodyguard, Catch the Bear.

The medicine man was found sleeping on the floor when Bull Head burst into his log cabin, struck a light, and read to him the arrest order. Sitting Bull was ready enough to go along and sent one of his wives to saddle his favorite mount, a trick circus horse that he had bought while with Buffalo Bill.

The police tried to hurry him into his clothes, and meanwhile the word was racing around the camp that the police had arrived to take him. The medicine man's followers rushed to assemble outside the cabin and block the way. The police, scenting the impending danger, took hold of Sitting Bull while he was but half-dressed and dragged him outside. Outraged at being manhandled, he bellowed in protest.

Then to compound his humiliation, the wife who had brought up the horse started to gibe him, and his teen-age son, Crow Foot, taunted him as a coward for submitting so weakly. The ridicule from the boy was the last straw. Digging in his heels, Sitting Bull called on the circle of warriors to rescue him from the police.

Bull Head and Sergeant Shave Head each held Sitting Bull by one arm. Sergeant Red Tomahawk was covering from the rear. The rest of the police—"Metal Breasts," the Sioux called them—formed as a wedge to break a path through the menacing warriors.

They might have made it but for the sudden appearance of Sitting Bull's personal bodyguard, Catch the Bear, who came on cursing Bull Head, lofting a rifle and threatening to use it.

Sitting Bull cried out, "I am not going! I am not going!"

Catch the Bear aimed his rifle and pulled trigger.

Bull Head dropped, one bullet in his leg.

As Bull Head hit earth, he turned and fired one round into the side of Sitting Bull, who was shot from behind at the same time by Red Tomahawk.

Simultaneously, Shave Head was hit by a bullet and the three went down almost together.

So began the fight between about 150 of Sitting Bull's frenzied supporters and the remaining forty active policemen. It was an unprecedented Indian death grapple, Hunkpapa against Hunkpapa, fellow tribesmen clubbing, stabbing, and choking one another. Some few of the Indians were Blackfeet. Most were Sitting Bull's people.

The policemen, performing in surprisingly good order, fell back to the cover of Sitting Bull's cabin. The old chief was already dead from a bullet through the head. Crow Foot had been killed within a few seconds of his father. Another bullet had finished off Bull Head.

After about two hours, the cavalry force, which had been reluctant to run any risks, advanced and relieved the beleaguered police. Six of them were dead. Three had been wounded. Outside the cabin lay the bodies of eight of Sitting Bull's Hunkpapa followers.

One of the legends descended from this exchange of violence is that the saddled circus steed performed a routine of tricks and capers between the fire lines wholly on its own, and later came through unhurt. It is the one light note in the story.

Among the tribesmen there was no spontaneous and violent reaction to the news of Sitting Bull's death. The Indians remained sullen and restive, but the old medicine man had so far lost favor with his people that they seemed hardly to mourn him. The dead lay unburied for two weeks. Still, the rumor went round that the army and police together had coldly plotted the murder of Sitting Bull, which accusation is repeated in some of today's literature.

Chief Hump was the second name on the most-wanted list. The army heard that the Oglala chief was ready to break out from the Cheyenne River Reservation with about five hundred warriors. At Hump's camp, ghost dancing had continued unabated. An army officer stationed in Texas, Captain E. P. Ewers, was known to have won Hump's confidence in times past. He was rushed to the scene. Brushing off warnings that he might be scalped, Ewers rode alone to deal with Hump. That piece of the scare evaporated when Hump greeted his old friend with enthusiasm and agreed to do whatever Ewers wished.

The third prime suspect was sixty-year-old Chief Big Foot, who was generally regarded as a peace-loving Indian. Big Foot's village on the Cheyenne River was under watch by a squadron of the Eighth Cavalry commanded by Lieutenant Colonel E. V. Sumner. After several meetings in which Sumner found Big Foot to be quite friendly, Sumner disregarded an order coming directly from General Nelson Miles that he should arrest the chief forthwith.

But then, after Sitting Bull was killed, Big Foot and his people moved out, saying that they were going to the agency to collect their annuities. Soon after, the information came to Sumner that Big Foot had set up camp near the Cheyenne River, where he had taken in several score of Sitting Bull's followers who had fled south after the killings.

Sumner at once went after him. When overtaken, Big Foot swore that he was as friendly as ever and that he had harbored the fugitives because they were his brothers, were near exhaustion, near freezing, and near starved. Every word of it could have been true. Yet what Big Foot had done had fully compromised the position of Sumner, who had risked a reprimand rather than arrest him.

Sumner told Big Foot that he now had no choice but to

take him and his band into the agency next day; then he dispatched a courier to bring up more units from the regiment.

That night Big Foot and his people fled the location and headed for the Badlands. The notch where these fugitives "went over the wall," as Dakotans say, bears the name of Big Foot Pass.

Most of the army force that had been fielded to Dakota —approximately three thousand men—had deployed to the fringes of the Badlands and were moving as a screen, trying to flush the Indians eastward and north without killing anyone.

The sweeping maneuver was already promising a final success. By the time Big Foot and his band fled south, the great body of fugitives was already pushed from the Badlands and was moving in the opposite direction, back to the agencies. The army had met no resistance and there had been no killings.

As Big Foot's advance worked into the fringes of the nightmarish terrain looking for company while failing to find any Indians, it bumped into a squadron of the Seventh Cavalry commanded by Major S. M. Whitside, who in the pro-Sioux accounts of Wounded Knee is cast as a deep-dyed villain for no sensible reason.

Big Foot, who four days earlier had caught a bad cold, was down with pneumonia by this time and riding on a travois. Someone raised a white flag for him and asked for a parley. Whitside replied that there was no alternative for the Indians other than unconditional surrender, which demand, in the circumstances, was hardly arbitrary. Either Big Foot's band was a war party or it was not, and there was no speedier way to find out.

Big Foot agreed to the terms. The captives were conducted to a wide spot in the trail named Wounded Knee, hardly more than a post office that took its cachet from a nearby creek. Among the soldiers who had assisted in maneuvering

Big Foot into this position was a young captain, John J. Pershing, making his first appearance in anything of historical consequence.

Getting the news of the capture, Colonel George A. Forsyth came riding with more troops of the Seventh Cavalry to take over the command from Whitside, who was more than happy to yield. Forsyth already had a claim on fame and not only as a successful Indian-fighter. As a junior aide in the Civil War, he had accompanied General Phil Sheridan on his celebrated ride to Winchester, which feat, like The Charge of the Light Brigade and the play about to unfold at Wounded Knee, was made ever memorable once a poet took it to heart.

Forsyth got started right. Not only did he provide the suffering Big Foot with a warming tent and stove; the regimental surgeon was directed to give the chief his personal attention. Today this would be considered the faultless public relations approach.

The fugitives' camp was strongly outposted by Forsyth's soldiers. Within easy range of it, four Hotchkiss guns were emplaced on a commanding hill, so sighted that they bore directly on the tepees.

The situation seemed snug enough. Under Forsyth were 470 cavalrymen and a platoon of Indian scouts. Of the 340 Sioux who had come along with Big Foot, only 106 were warriors and they appeared to be responding passively. Total surrender having followed their prolonged ordeal of hunger and exposure, the Sioux were apparently in no condition to make further trouble.

There is a description of the Seventh Cavalry's posture of that night that is to be found in the book *The Wounded Knee Massacre From the Viewpoint of the Sioux* by James H. McGregor.

It reads,

> The soldiers' tents were lined up in military order, the cavalry horses sleek and blanketed, munched their hay and oats in contentment while

the big rugged Government mules, staked out with West Point precision, bit and kicked each other in a playful mood. Supper had been served on time, cooking utensils and dishes had been disposed of in the usual military fashion. The officers' tents were pitched a short distance from and back of the enlisted men, the tent ropes were taut, and canvas showed not a wrinkle while inside the heat from the small stove radiated comfort. All wool Government blankets piled high added to the prospect of a comfortable night by men who held the fate of the other camp in their hands. No doubt the officers as well as the soldiers were discussing the Indian situation and perhaps enlarged upon the imaginary danger they were in from the prostrate Big Foot and his woebegone and disheveled followers. "Remember Custer's Massacre" and "Revenge for the Annihilation of the old Seventh Cavalry" and other expressions were in common use and designed to instill hatred of the Sioux in the breast of the new recruits.

Provided there is any realism in those lines, and if it can be said that the descriptive passages have even a faint resemblance to the conditions of a cavalry scratch bivouac after a hard march, then possibly the closing lines about the bloodthirstiness of the Garry Owens are to be taken seriously, also. Oddly enough, however, this book is vended by the National Park Service.

Forsyth might have waited a little longer for a cooling. He could have given more attention to the physical needs of the Indians while keeping the main body of troops away from close contact with them. But the weather had turned bitter cold; there was no fuel at hand and his food supply was running short. Being under these and other pressures to return the band to the agency as quickly as possible, he set about getting the warriors disarmed prior to starting the march back. The main point to be noted is that all of the critical decisions about procedure were *his* to make, and there were no signs of extraordinary tension in Big Foot's people.

In the early morning of December 29 the warriors were mustered as a body, while the armed cavalrymen on guard duty formed within a few feet of them, their weapons in hand. In the circumstances, it was pretty much a routine show of force and Forsyth could hardly have risked anything less. In groups of twenty or so, the warriors were sent off to the tepees to get their weapons and then yield them.

Because the order put too much trust in Indian nature and brought braves and soldiers within jostling distance of one another, the attempt was not more awkward than dangerous. When after an hour the shuttle back and forth was completed, less than a half-dozen nonfunctioning rifles had come of it.

Thereupon, following orders, some of the soldiers began searching the tepees for arms, which task required rooting around through the furnishings, a task that can never be done gently by men acting in a hurry.

The squaws started screaming and making a great clamor of protest and the seated warriors glowered and growled.

Yet the white flag still fluttered above Big Foot's tent.

By the end of their hour of search, the soldiers had found only about forty weapons, most of them old and not a few in disrepair. Here was a first but belated warning that a prearranged plan of deception was underway, though it was not taken seriously. Yet far more than that had been missed.

While the search detail of cavalrymen had been poking about in the tepees, a Sioux medicine man, Yellow Bird, had been walking among the sitting braves exhorting them to strike.

"You wear ghost shirts," he told them, "and no white man's bullet may hurt you."

No interpreter being present to hear Yellow Bird, the significance of his patter was missed altogether by the cavalry-men who were guarding the prisoners, and no attempt was made to stop him.

The search completed, the body of cavalrymen formed up again, directly confronting the warriors. Then on impulse, or because he saw something suspicious, one soldier dropped to his knees to look under the blanket of a squatting Sioux named Black Fox.

Black Fox jumped to his feet, whipped out a rifle from under his blanket, and fired into the search party.

Ever since, Black Fox has been identified as the unspeak-able and prime-moving villain of the drama, but for whose action it might have gone off quietly.

Nothing could be more erroneous than that; it leads to a false interpretation of all that thereafter happened.

Instantly, as though they had been awaiting a signal, the other warriors did the same, volley-firing into the massed sol-diers with rifles theretofore carefully concealed under their blankets.

There is no doubt who started that day's fight, though it is often called a massacre. Forsyth may have been clumsy and his soldiers could have been rude and provocative, but delib-erate Sioux action, so timed as to indicate that it had been well plotted, initiated the slaughter. Bury My Heart at Wounded Knee may be a lovely phrase. It is still a false and misleading sentiment, dignifying conspiracy and honoring treachery.

"In such a crisis the Sioux were always likely to give way to panic or blind rage and in either case to begin shooting," writes an apologist in one explanation that fails to explain. What he says could be true enough. It applies to many primi-tive peoples. Captain Cook wrote the same thing about the Tahitians two centuries ago. An Ethiopian, General Yassu, said it of the Congolese in 1961.

Does such an elementary idea excuse treachery? Big Foot's

band had been surrendered unconditionally. That meant that all arms should be yielded peacefully upon request. This is not the mere symbolic gesture of surrender; it is the essence thereof. Quite possibly, according to the Sioux code, that may not have enjoined the warrior to comply absolutely. But any soldier, by his code, was not wrong in believing that the surrender of arms was the heart of the contract. No man doing military guard duty should be required to move out knowing that a loaded, hostile rifle is within a few feet of his head. To insist that the Sioux who trailed along with Big Foot did not understand this stretches credulity beyond normal limits.

The prime movers in the band were older men. They were not innocents; they had been through like dealings with the army for more than a decade. They knew the routines. Granted that the ghost-dance craze had brought about an emotional imbalance in many of them, the takeover of the reservation by the army—its consequence—could hardly be blamed for the mass hysteria. The army had taken to an unwelcome task with commendable restraint. Of its performance as intervenor, the Sioux had still been given no legitimate cause to complain. To brush off the fact is to bury more hearts at Wounded Knee than rightly belong there. Yet it is done right along. For no good reason in common sense, Wounded Knee has been chosen as the field whereby to prove forevermore the soldier's guilt and the warrior's victimization.

Once such a tragedy of violence and horror is unloosed, there is no telling where it may end. Armed men massed and suddenly panicked may not be held to account. Nigh mindless, they are wholly irrational in action.

So it is wholly vain that afterwards from their easy chairs historians and tacticians lament that all control became lost, that no one intervened to block the almost inevitable reaction, and having thus deplored, from that point move to apportion the blame between the sides. While as a human creature, man is rational and emotional, at the cutting edge he is animal, framed in the struggle for existence. In that unfathomable and terrible instant of unexpected change when his life is put at stake, he responds to his most primitive instincts and becomes unaccountable. A platoon, a company, may be that quickly shocked beyond the bounds of reason and the hiatus may continue until the completion of the action. Described in two of my books, Milsap's Patrol in the Normandy invasion and Millett's Bayonet Charge in Korea, are instances of this kind of thing happening. There are still more recent examples that should enable us better to understand what went wrong at Wounded Knee.

Without any order being called, the cavalrymen under direct attack either took to their heels or fired back. No officer was in position to stop them. None could have put himself there had he so chosen, so close were the sides joined, so deafening was the tumult. Rifles were exploding right in the faces of soldier and brave. This hand-to-hand trading of fire could hardly have lasted more than a minute. The point-blank carnage was grim and great.

Their magazines emptied, the Sioux came on with clubs and knives for the final death grapple. These weapons, too, had been concealed under the blankets. Should any further item in proof be needed that they had prepared not simply to defend themselves but to attack?

Under the agreement made with Big Foot in the hour of surrender, all weapons were to be peacefully yielded.

The crews manning the Hotchkiss guns on the nearby hill had been alerted by the first sounds of fire from the low ground. Then stray bullets began kicking up the dirt around them and they sprang to action. Even so, such was the distance that they had no clear idea about what was happening. In lieu of orders, they did what comes naturally to soldiers when their senses tell them that the force as a whole is under attack. From the heights, the four guns opened fire on the camp, setting the tepees ablaze and killing indiscriminately the noncombatants and warriors trying to flee the fight. The shells raked and exploded the village at the rate of one round per second, intensifying the excitement while extending the killing zone. An impersonal fire, it can neither be called wrong nor termed accurate. Not a few soldiers died from the Hotchkiss barraging.

Stampeded by the Hotchkisses, women, children, and the few surviving braves quit the tepees and fled for the hills. The frenzied cavalrymen and Indian scouts, once the heavy fire lifted, pursued to cut down many of these pitiful fugitives, showing them little or no mercy. Here is the sequence in Wounded Knee that is most generally condemned and really nothing sensible may be said in mitigation of it. Rarely in such episodes does the heart take over when the brain is less than half functioning. A scant minority of the Sioux dependents and six or seven of the braves got away by hiding in caves or potholes and under ledges, in which the region abounds. There is not one other note of uplift in the story. The grisly chase and killing went on for more than three hours and the trail of bodies extended outward from the camp for more than three miles.

By the end of it, upwards of 170 of the Sioux had been killed, or sixty more than the total number of warriors. Some non-combatants had been slain by the rain of Hotchkiss fire on the camp. Sixty of the cavalrymen lay either dead or wounded, which loss is too commonly disregarded or treated as insignificant by Americans bent on making of Wounded Knee something that it definitely was not. No such blood toll could have been taken of the Seventh Cavalry had the Sioux attack on the soldiers been accidentally triggered rather than a well-planned coup. The cold figures say that there were many rifles under the blankets, and that when they were fired, the Indians shot to kill. That much must be clear to anyone familiar with close-joined combat. The mute statistical evidence is sufficient proof that the surprise, like its shock impact, was nigh total, though the figures also say that about half of the Indians survived. All of this is brushed aside by the bleeding hearts who make of this mournful affair an unmitigated military atrocity, a massacre that need not have been.

Wounded Knee was a battle—the last battle—a battle without victory, there being nothing winnable for either side—a battle, true enough, of which there is nothing to be proud—a battle over which many tears have been shed, usually about the wrong things—but still, a battle.

People in the burial party who moved out with wagons on New Year's Day to remove the Indian dead found several live Indian babies wrapped in shawls and blankets next to the cold bodies of their dead mothers, although the temperatures of that fell week hovered around zero.

The fallen Sioux were put away in a common grave. There was no religious service. The missionaries thought it inappropriate to appear.

Forsyth's soldiers rounded up the far-scattered survivors of Big Foot's band and shooed them back to the reservation. A few more cavalrymen met death before resistance died. General Miles arrived at Pine Ridge to oversee such measures as had to be taken to bring about tranquilization. By mid-January tribesmen were again feeding more or less regularly and the Dakota scene soon thereafter quieted.

The army, as per regulations, conducted its own investigation before returning authority to the Interior Department. General E. D. Scott's report had this as its essence, "There is nothing to conceal or to apologize for in the Wounded Knee Battle . . . The firing was begun by the Indians and continued until they stopped."

In that verdict there was some whitewash and some truth, though certainly not the whole truth. It was in any case less mistaken than the oft-repeated charge that the soldiers of the Seventh Cavalry killed out of sheer blood-lust to avenge, fourteen years later, the death of Custer. Regiments do not think upon vengeance. Besides, the Garry Owen Regiment had no such adoration for its dead chief and in other brushes with the Sioux, in the time between, as happened when Crook spared American Horse's people, the cavalrymen had given the Sioux quarter.

At Wounded Knee, that tragic field with the doubly melancholic name, there died together with Big Foot and too many of his band the last spark of organized and lethal resistance in the Plains Indians, just as there died also the Ghost Dance religion. Faith failed with the shirts that would not turn back bullets.

The high priest of the religion, so soon shorn of reverence, professed shock at the terrible news from the blood-drenched corner of Dakota. But he did not fade away quietly and with dignity. From one Indian base camp to another, Wovoka moved about protesting to anyone who would listen that the tribes had twisted the meaning of his words.

This second time around, no Indians flocked to him that they might again sit at his feet to hear final truth untwisted, then start anew on an old path. The tribes gave him no attention. He had become a bore. And with that, he was almost as dead as Sitting Bull, Big Foot, Crazy Horse, and other braves who had departed this life for the happy hunting ground.

Such was the last and probably the only genuine miracle performed by Wovoka, the achievement of an almost instant unimportance.

Chief Red Cloud lived on for another fifteen years following Wounded Knee. An ancient, wrinkled as a dried apple, stooped and almost blind, he found little honor and less ease in his dotage, though he had talked with Presidents and his profile had become a national property.

Once he was arrested for killing a few birds out of season. Although he pleaded not guilty, this Oglala who had once thought of all of the game on the Plains as his own to take was fined $65 and only got release by giving up two of his horses.

Listen to his lament as recorded by a white friend at the Pine Ridge Agency, "You see this barren waste. Think of it! I who used to own rich soil in a well-watered country so extensive that I could not ride through it in a week on my fastest pony am put down here! Why I have to go five miles to get wood for my fire! I must beg for that which I own. If I beg hard they put me in the guardhouse. We have trouble. My heart is heavy. I am old. I cannot do much more."

Life had been long, but it had not been good to Red Cloud. Long or short, it is rarely good to Indians. "As they see themselves," a wise man said, "they seem to be fenced in with no future and nothing to do but draw and eat their rations and then die."

Though harsh be that prospect, it is not peculiarly Indian.

Index

Index

Index

Index

Index

Index